STRIKE UP THE BAND

STRIKE
UP THE BAND

NEW YORK CITY
in the Roaring Twenties

HELEN CRISP
and
JULES STEWART

REAKTION BOOKS

To Dudley and Laura, New Yorkers to their marrow

Published by
Reaktion Books Ltd
Unit 32, Waterside
44–48 Wharf Road
London N1 7UX, UK
www.reaktionbooks.co.uk

First published 2024
Copyright © Helen Crisp and Jules Stewart 2024

Printed and bound in Great Britain by
TJ Books Ltd, Padstow, Cornwall

A catalogue record for this book is available from the British Library

ISBN 978 1 78914 856 5

CONTENTS

Foreword
by Gregory J. Peterson

In this book we'll take a walk through time in the city as well as its places. Helen Crisp and Jules Stewart talk us through what New York City was: a city of burgeoning creativity; a city of clubs, theaters, speakeasies; jazz bands, Broadway hits; new women, new garments, new dances. And a city in a new shape. That was 1920s New York, but there's no place like New York City in the present. As a native New Yorker, and one who has lived his entire life within the five boroughs, I can testify to that. But whether you consider it "the greatest city in the world," as the Schuyler Sisters claim it to be in the musical *Hamilton*, referring to New York in the 1700s, or any time since then, there can be no doubt that the 1920s in New York was a pivotal era that changed the face of the city in ways that are still palpable today.

On a typical walk through the city, one is constantly reminded of and buoyed by that stylish, seminal era. Starting with the most obvious emblems, we look to those energizing artifacts of 1920s architectural design, the masculine, majestic, and elegant Empire State Building, and its more feminine, jazzy sidekick the Chrysler Building. Although they were not completed until the 1930s, those skyscrapers are both products of 1920s Art Deco design esthetics. Epitomizing the new skyscraper construction techniques of steel frames, reinforced concrete, and curtain walls, they both vied for the title of the world's tallest building. The Empire State Building won, and maintained that title for 39 years, until it was superseded by the World Trade Center, downtown, in 1970. The Empire State Building and the Chrysler Building now serve as friendly midtown landmarks, the papa and mama skyscrapers visible all around the city, reassuringly reminding you that yes, you are home.

Architectural design of the 1920s also transformed the shape of the city with the arrival of the streamlined features of the McGraw-Hill Building, and the five stunning towered apartment buildings that define the skyline of Central Park West. Those landmarks were all designed in the frothy 1920s, when people thought there was plenty of money, and built largely in the dank early 1930s, during the Great Depression, when labor was cheap. Walking north from Columbus Circle, you see the Century, the Majestic, the San Remo, the Beresford, and the El Dorado. They forever changed the view west from Central Park, just as the new, spindly buildings soaring above Billionaires' Row now are transforming the view toward Central Park South. One can only wonder whether the rise of the towers over Central Park West were as unwelcome then as the Billionaires' Row buildings are today.

The 1920s was a great period for "pre-war" domestic architecture, when rooms were large, walls were solid, and ceilings were high, although not without cost. Almost all the gracious nineteenth-century Gilded Age mansions that lined Fifth Avenue opposite Central Park, as well as Park Avenue, were demolished to make way for the stately, spacious, white-glove apartment buildings currently lining those avenues. The same may be said of Riverside Drive and, as it appears, the lion's share of the Upper West Side, a gallant and serene neighborhood that has been landmarked in its entirety. The apartments in these buildings are still highly prized for their elegant proportions and gracious layouts; the most acclaimed architects of the day, Rosario Candela and Emery Roth, are unequaled in their historical legacies. Step inside their lobbies and Fred and Ginger melodies will dance through your mind. But good luck trying to land an apartment in one of those cherished buildings today.

Radio City, now more commonly referred to by its formal name, Rockefeller Center, was built as an urban-renewal project between 1929 and 1940, adding another radiant example of 1920s Art Deco design to the cityscape. There, a true New Yorker's pulse will race when enjoying a performance by the Radio City Music Hall Rockettes. This all-female dance troupe is the virtual embodiment of 1920s zeitgeist, with its assembly line of 48 (now 36) identical dancers, all industriously tap dancing and kicking with wholesome elegance, reflecting the era's fascination with precision and mechanization. First seen in Minnesota in 1925 as the Missouri Rockets, they were imported to Manhattan and ultimately renamed the Rockettes and have dazzled audiences ever since. Most New Yorkers I know have been enjoying their performances at the Radio City Music Hall Christmas Spectacular since childhood.

The dance and liberal arts of the era still have a tight grasp on New Yorkers' imaginations. The city was the country's undisputed music capital, and Duke Ellington, Cole Porter, and (probably more than anyone) Brooklyn-born George Gershwin produced indelible aural images of the town. While "Strike Up the Band," the upbeat, quasi-martial showstopper he penned with his brother Ira, conjures generic Americana, Gershwin's *Rhapsody in Blue* musically encapsulates the new vibrancy of a city with its ultra-American, really ultra-New York blend of classical and jazz rhythms, both brooding and exhilarating. Broadway shows brought American musical theater from the pervasive frivolity of the Ziegfeld *Follies* to new levels of social relevance and profundity with the opening of Jerome Kern and Oscar Hammerstein II's classic musical *Show Boat*. It tackled themes of racial prejudice and changed the direction of American musical theater. Some consider it the original American musical. Its most famous tune, "Ol' Man River," conjures images of the South, but a New Yorker will think of it first of all as a great Broadway show tune. American songbook standards from this era on Broadway include "Tea for Two," "I Want to Be Happy," "Anything Goes," and

"I Get a Kick Out of You." Undoubtedly such tunes were performed in Central Park's Naumburg Bandshell, a 1923 delight where free outdoor concerts are held to this day.

Duke Ellington, the composing and conducting giant of the Big Band Era, formed his eponymous Orchestra in 1923. Hearing his music today conjures thoughts of the famous Cotton Club and the Harlem Renaissance. The musical and literary legacies of the bandleader and film star Cab Calloway, the author and filmmaker Zora Neale Hurston, and the writer Langston Hughes are still compelling. Hughes, a prominent African American poet and social activist, was a central figure of the Harlem Renaissance, an explosive cultural and intellectual movement centered on Harlem during the 1920s that captured the mood and aspirations of black Americans at that time and broke through cultural barriers.

Other literary landmarks are the works of F. Scott Fitzgerald, whose *The Great Gatsby* describes a culture consummately American, consummately New York: that of a man who comes to the city from nothing to seek his fortune, then, having done so, pays a heavy price. The leaves of that great novel might easily have been clipped from the pages of any edition of the *Wall Street Journal* today.

The societal mood of the era was not all dazzle. The Ash Can School of realist painters flourished at this time, documenting the hardships of New York life endured by many, and Edward Hopper, too, distilled his bleakly beautiful views of the city. The Museum of Modern Art, now arguably the most important world museum venue for modern and contemporary art, opened in Manhattan in 1929. The Precisionist movement manifested itself in the 1920s through the works of Charles Sheeler and Charles Demuth, whose art reflects the sharp, clean, geometric lines of urban factories and machines, echoing the Rockettes' precise kinetic dance movements.

But it's not only architecture, music, and art that were indelibly etched on a New Yorker's daily experience. Scientific inventions of seismic effect also shape our daily lives. Sound on film, for example, was invented in the Bell Telephone Laboratories in Greenwich Village in the early to mid-1920s, and the first theatrical film with a synchronized sound dialogue, *The Jazz Singer* starring Al Jolson, premiered at Warner's Theater, 1664 Broadway, on October 6, 1927.

Here's another technical advance I'm certain almost no one thinks of (although maybe you will now). A walk through the city would not be the same without the invention of green, yellow, and red electric traffic lights, which were introduced to the New York public in 1920. This system has proved a popular and effective way of promoting safety, decorum, and courtesy (such as there is) on city streets.

Anyone walking down the streets of New York will not be surprised that the practice of speaking up for oneself is passionately exercised here, so it should be no surprise that in 1920 the American Civil Liberties Union was formed in New York City to protect everyone's right to do so. The Town Hall, a National Historic Landmark opened by Suffragists on January 12, 1921, has been the site of countless political debates. It has the unmistakable look and feel of a grand 1920s public venue and was the site of the musical debuts in the United States of the composer Richard Strauss, the violinist Isaac Stern, and the great contralto Marian Anderson gave her first New York recital. It also sends a shiver down my spine, personally, in that it is where I studied for my New York State Bar Exam.

But walk just a few blocks from the Town Hall and you'll find yourself enveloped in a cluster of classic New York theaters. Any regular theatergoer will instantly recognize the look, the feel, the pre-Art Deco comfort and grace of 1920s Broadway theater design, from the crystal chandeliers to the filigree plasterwork, gold-leaf proscenium arches, painted murals and plush, carpeted aisles. The 1920s may have left its most indelible mark on the Theater District. Still vibrant, still packing in tourists, you may visit the Ambassador (1921), Broadway (1921), Cort (1922), Imperial (1923), August Wilson (1925), Eugene O'Neill (1925), Biltmore (1925), Lena Horne (1926), Music Box (1926), Ed Sullivan (1927), Golden (1927), Majestic (1927), Neil

Simon (1927), St. James (1927), and Barrymore (1928)—and those are just the ones that easily come to mind. You can imagine Fred and Adele Astaire tap dancing in white tie and ballgown on those boards, and in fact, they did!

In sports, baseball fans will be sorry to realize that Yankee Stadium, opened in the Bronx in 1923 and known as "The House that Ruth Built," is no longer with us, having been demolished and replaced in 2010. A trip to the new Yankee Stadium is designed in homage to the original and does recall its stately grandeur. "Ruth" was the incomparable slugger "Babe" Ruth, whose stellar career spanned the entire decade and more. But New Yorkers still celebrate his fame whenever they eat a "Baby Ruth" candy bar. The caramelly, nutty, chocolatey candy bar was introduced in 1938, and its marketers insist it was named after an actual baby called Ruth, but fans know exactly whom they're cheering when they bite into one.

Hamilton's Schuyler Sisters sing of their love of the city on the stage of the Richard Rodgers Theatre, formerly Chanin's 46th Street Theatre in 1925. I won't argue that New York was the greatest city in the world of the 1770s, but it's a shame they were not here to experience it in the 1920s, or now, as the 1920s left it so much richer. *Strike Up the Band* tells its story.

Liner entering New York Harbor at the outbreak of the Spanish flu.

1

Down Hearted Blues

When the Norwegian ocean liner *Bergensfjord* steamed into New York Harbor on the afternoon of 14 August 1918, the ship carried with it more than just crew and passengers. A killer stowaway was lurking on board, a new and aggressive form of disease that was soon to spread death on a global scale not known since the bubonic plague in the fourteenth century. As the ship made its approach to the Brooklyn dockyard, an onshore radio operator received an alarming telegraph message from the skipper. Captain Kjeld Stub Irgens of the Norwegian-America Line vessel reported that some twenty passengers and crew members had gone down with a mysterious illness. Four had died on the voyage, and the rest showed signs of what was initially believed to be bronchial pneumonia. They were suffering from high fever, sore throat and severe headache, symptoms that brought to New York the first cases of the worst pandemic in modern history, the misnamed Spanish flu.[1]

A few weeks later New York recorded its first fatality from the influenza virus. By 28 September the number of deaths had doubled to 324 in a matter of 24 hours. This prompted Health Commissioner Royal Samuel Copeland to issue what would in a few months be remembered as a tragic understatement: 'I realize the possible seriousness of the disease and the danger of an epidemic.'[2] Copeland, a steely-eyed academic and homeopath, held to the belief that the bug was merely a variant of the grippe that had ravaged New York in 1888. To compound the miseries, that year also unleashed the city's fiercest snowstorm on record, known as the Great Blizzard of 1888, which claimed the lives of more than two hundred New Yorkers. The health commissioner reassured people that no effort was being spared to isolate and treat the victims of this new and enigmatic infection. However, he warned, this was proving difficult owing to the number of doctors and nurses who were absent, treating the wounded on the battlefields of Europe. On 4 October, a week after Copeland's remarks, the number of reported new cases had risen to nearly 1,700, more than a fivefold increase in a single day.[3] Copeland and the city's medical authorities were now obliged to face up to the fact that they were confronted with something far more ominous than a recurrence of the grippe that had struck some thirty years previously. After reviewing the fatality statistics for that October day, Copeland decided to order by proclamation a number of steps to combat the contagion and spread of the influenza pandemic.

The measures Copeland put in place were far less stringent than during the several lockdowns imposed in New York and around the world when, in March 2020, the World Health Organization declared COVID-19 a pandemic. In order to prevent a complete shutdown of economic life, Copeland limited retail opening hours to between 8 a.m. and 4 p.m. Only food shops and chemists were allowed to operate to normal working hours. The city's health department feared that the greatest cause of contagion were crowded subway carriages, so it ordered a dispersal of commuters by maximum numbers at stations in the morning and evening rush hours. This was inexplicably at odds with the 'business as usual' policy that permitted factories and offices to carry on operating, albeit at shortened eight-hour shifts.

Even more bewildering, given today's knowledge of the disease and how it is contracted, was the ruling that allowed theatres and cinemas to remain open. They were considered 'community houses' serving those living within walking distance and, moreover, venues where audiences could be given instruction on how to deal with the disease. Schools and churches carried on as normal, in contradiction to the logic that placed restrictions on travel by public transport.

As for household gatherings, Copeland's rationale stood significantly at variance with what are today held to be common-sense preventive measures. He stated in a report,

> The Health Department has not deemed it necessary to quarantine families in which there are cases of influenza because this disease is held not to be communicable by one who has not himself got influenza. It matters not that a person is exposed to the malady unless he himself is stricken with it.[4]

On the more enlightened side, limitations were placed on smoking in public places, a move truly ahead of its time. Likewise, New Yorkers caught spitting were routinely rounded up and brought before courts. Records suggest that few escaped without fines. On

New York traffic policeman during influenza outbreak.

STRIKE UP THE BAND

4 October 1918, for instance, 134 men were handed $1 fines at Jefferson Market Court and another three at the Yorkville Court for spitting on subways, subway platforms and elevated trains.

It speaks volumes about the health authorities' misguided confidence that they had eradicated the disease that on 5 November city officials boldly pronounced New York safe. The folly of their action was revealed less than a week later. The seeds of disaster were sown on 11 November, when tens of thousands of jubilant New Yorkers poured into the streets to celebrate the end of the First World War. Social distancing was an alien concept to this crowd, making a terrible spread of the influenza all but inescapable. There inevitably followed second, third and fourth waves, bringing a general state of confusion, along with a disintegration of trust in the city authorities. For the next year and a half, New York was a city paralysed by fear. By the early spring of 1920, when the pandemic was well and truly over, more than 30,000 people had succumbed to the virus, nearly five times the number of soldiers from New York City killed in the First World War.

Happy Days Are Here Again

With the horrors of the war and the influenza pandemic slowly fading from memory, New York set out to hit the party trail. The city lost no time in becoming a frolicsome world of capering and high jinks. The day the first report of peace on the Western Front was announced, 11 November 1918, couples began one-stepping and foxtrotting along a flag-decked Fifth Avenue. That night the leading ballrooms looked as they had done in the days when grandees of such notable families as the Castles and the Waltons dominated Manhattan's social life. Hotspots such as the Biltmore, the ballrooms of the Hotel Astor and the Waldorf-Astoria grill were hosting the new craze for letting loose on the dance floor. Dance pavilions began to spring up not only in Manhattan, but also in the outlying boroughs. The Bronx inaugurated the Crystal Palace and Hunt's Point Palace.

The upper regions of Manhattan had the Audubon, while Brooklynites found several new dancing halls at their service. The rejuvenation of ballroom dancing even aroused interest among physicians and psychologists, who saw this fresh interest in the poetry of motion as a remedy for overwrought nerves and shell shock.

January 1920 was the height of one of the coldest winters on record in New York, with one 72-hour period of relentless snow and sleet that brought the city to its knees. Yet, encouraged by a steady fall in infection rates and the end of the pandemic within sight, people were determined to turn their backs on the anguished years of war and pestilence. As the spring thaw set in, New Yorkers were treated to a magical appetizer to stimulate their taste for good times ahead. The Wonder Wheel opened in Coney Island, the funfair in southwestern Brooklyn.[5] Since its construction, this 150-foot-tall Ferris wheel has continued to bring shrieks of amusement from thrill-seekers, and today enjoys official New York City landmark status. The 200-ton wheel has been a source of colourful anecdotes since the first of its average 200,000 riders a year set foot in its 24 sliding and fixed cabins: from the Greek immigrant hot-dog vendor-turned-impresario Denos Vourderis, who promised atop the wheel one day to buy the contraption for his girlfriend if she accepted his proposal (he later did so), to the celebrated psychoanalyst Sigmund Freud, who was reputed to have claimed that it was the only place of interest he could find in America.

To accommodate the multitude of pleasure-seekers heading off for a weekend at this seafront amusement park, the first subway line to Coney Island was put into service shortly after the opening of the Wonder Wheel. It was now possible for the frolicsome set to reach the fairground by subway from as far away as the Bronx, travelling on what was at that time the world's largest mass-transit railway, whose more than 200 miles of track even surpassed the length of the London Underground system by more than 50 miles.

Take Me Out to the Ball Game

The moment had arrived: it was now time to set in motion a life of much-yearned-for fun. This took on a variety of guises, of a rather more demure nature than chomping on a Nathan's hot dog in a cabin dangling 150 feet above the Coney Island boardwalk. The sheer delight of movement, unencumbered by the strictures of war and pestilence, embodied to the core this new-found sense of liberation. The debut of the Coney Island Wonder Wheel in 1920 had become one of its first manifestations. The next step was an awakening of a thirst for sports. These were the halcyon years of tennis stars Bill Tilden and Helen Wills, baseball immortal Babe Ruth, golfer Bobby Jones, prizefighter Jack Dempsey and football halfback Red Grange, when the popularity of sports reached fantastic heights, as millions of New Yorkers found they could buy seats to watch their favourite players.

In February 1921 the New York American League Baseball Club announced an investment of nearly $3.2 million in a new home ballpark for their team, the Yankees, to be built on a 4-hectare (10-ac.) plot in the Bronx, on the east bank of the Harlem River. Until that time, the Yankees had rented the Polo Grounds in Upper Manhattan from their rivals the New York Giants. This was the future home of the 67,000-seat Yankee Stadium. 'On this terrain there will be erected a huge stadium,' pronounced the club's co-owner Colonel Jacob Ruppert, 'which will surpass in seating capacity any structure hitherto built for the accommodation of lovers of baseball.'[6] The playing area was so vast that it was not until the 1990s that a batter managed to slam a baseball beyond the stadium walls.

The inaugural game, in April 1923, drew a crowd of more than 74,000, with nearly 10,000 fans standing in the aisles to applaud Governor Al Smith when he threw out the first ball. The cheering soared to ear-splitting level when the Yankees beat the Boston Red Sox 4–1 in that game. The first home run was hit by none other than

The first New York Yankees baseball team.

Babe Ruth, the legendary grand slammer who had signed on with the Yankees in 1920.

The year that Yankee Stadium, nicknamed 'The House that Ruth Built', opened its doors also brought the revival of another mass spectator sport that for several years had been denied to New Yorkers. Boxing had been used to train troops during the First World War, but was banned owing to safety concerns in 1917. The passage of a law enacted by Speaker of the State Senate James 'Jimmy' Walker in 1920 brought prizefighting back to the public arena, albeit with tougher rules to contain the brutality of the sport, such as limiting matches to fifteen rounds and creating a regulatory body, the New York State Athletic Commission. As Kenneth Jackson explains in *The Encyclopedia of New York City* (1995),

> Although boxing remained centred in ethnic and working-class neighbourhoods and clubs, it now attracted the interest of the middle and upper classes as well. Championship fights took place sometimes in large ballparks but more often in indoor arenas, such as St Nicholas Garden and especially Madison Square Garden.[7]

As New York's landmark sports arena, the Garden soon became the setting for a variety of sporting events. One of the greatest matches in boxing history took place there in December 1920, when the heavyweight champion Jack Dempsey thrilled a packed stadium with a twelfth-round knockout punch to his long-standing adversary Bill Brennan. From the Dempsey era to that of Joe Louis (roughly 1925–45), the arena hosted 32 world championship bouts. So closely linked were prizefighting and Madison Square Garden that in 1924 the pugilist sport inspired Goldwyn Pictures to produce the film *The Great White Way*, a silent comedy centred on boxing, directed by E. Mason Hopper and starring Anita Stewart.

In fact, these hugely fashionable spectator sports took place in an earlier incarnation of Madison Square Garden, which was demolished in 1924 to be rebuilt on Eighth Avenue between 49th and 50th streets. New York's new temple of sport was designed by the noted theatre architect Thomas W. Lamb and built at a cost of $4.75 million in 249 breathtaking days by the colourful boxing promoter George 'Tex' Rickard. Like Babe Ruth's Yankee Stadium, it was appropriately dubbed 'The House that Tex Built'. The year after Madison Square Garden opened its doors in 1925, the indefatigable Rickard founded the professional ice hockey team known as the New York Rangers. Madison Square Garden has been their home since the Rangers' opening game in 1926. When Rickard died three years later, tributes poured in from all quarters, including Jimmy Walker and former Governor Smith, who hailed him as 'the greatest promoter, who did more than anyone to elevate boxing'.

SINCE TIME IMMEMORIAL, New Yorkers have delighted in proclaiming the grandeur of their city to the world at large. The indomitable quest to break loose that characterized the 1920s transcended the city's frontiers, when New York became the launch pad for two record-breaking milestones. In August 1926 the New Yorker Gertrude Ederle, known as 'Queen of the Waves', took her athletic prowess to England to become the first woman to swim the English Channel. Ederle's 14-hour and 34-minute crossing beat by two hours the previous record, set by the Argentinian marathon swimmer Enrique Tiraboschi. After returning to New York, Ederle played herself in the silent romantic comedy *Swim Girl Swim* (1927), and even had a song-and-dance routine named after her. Nine months after her feat, in the early morning of 20 May 1927, the celebrated aviator Charles Lindbergh took off from Roosevelt Field on Long Island to attempt the first non-stop Atlantic crossing. His single-engine monoplane, *The Spirit of St Louis*, flew bravely for more than 33 hours through storm clouds, perilous ice and blinding fog, to land at Le Bourget Aerodrome in Paris on the night of 21 May. On his return journey by sea to New York, Lindbergh was feted with a ticker-tape parade up Broadway to Central Park Mall, accompanied in an open limousine by Mayor Walker and cheered on by more than 200,000 onlookers.

The Sheik of Araby

New Yorkers flocked in their tens of thousands to Yankee Stadium, Madison Square Garden and the Polo Grounds to satiate their craving for spectator sports. The next step was to address the war generation's pent-up appetite for outdoor recreation. On to centre stage steps the towering figure of Robert Moses, all 6 feet or more of him, to take on the protagonist role in opening and revitalizing New York's parks and sea resorts and also to provide the infrastructure for people to access these amenities.

Before 1924, New York had no unified park system, not for the state or for the city. Scattered throughout the wooded and mountainous natural beauty spots of upstate New York were some forty parks and places of historic or scientific interest, each managed by its own autonomous administrative body. In that year, Governor Smith set up eleven regional commissions under a Council of Parks, to be financed by a $15 million bond issue. The idea was inspired by a State

Park Plan of 1922 proposing a more closely unified system, a scheme that had been drawn up by Moses, who in 1924 was appointed Council chairman. The following year, the governor approved the creation of the Long Island State Parks Commission, a body that Moses was similarly appointed to oversee. The organization's annual budget was set at $225,000, a sum that Moses employed to put into action his ambitious programme of parks and road systems.

Moses – by all accounts a highly controversial, cantankerous individual – left an indelible mark on New York on a scale unrivalled by any urban planner before or since. During his career, he came to hold the chairmanship of a dozen New York urban development bodies, and today numerous locations and roadways bear his name: Robert Moses State Park, Robert Moses Causeway, Robert Moses Hydroelectric Dam and even a Robert Moses playground in Manhattan's Murray Hill neighbourhood. During his tenure as chief of the New York State park system, the state's inventory of parks grew to more than 1 million hectares (nearly 2.6 million ac.). By the time he left office, he had built 658 playgrounds in New York City alone, plus 416 miles of parkways and 13 bridges.

Moses was born into a German Jewish family that had little in common socially with their compatriots of the Lower East Side. He grew up off Fifth Avenue in fashionable Uptown Manhattan and took degrees from Yale and Oxford universities. When not indulging his fervour for swimming, he worked on a thesis in political science that was to earn him a doctorate from Columbia University. In short, he was a patrician who, to the chagrin of his many critics, imposed his unyielding dogma on the landscape of New York City. When once accused of being responsible for the heavy automobile congestion on the city's roads because of a lack of investment in mass transit, Moses responded that mass transit was other people's affair, not his.

The man the press dubbed the 'Master Builder' provided an escape valve for Manhattanites fleeing the congested city in search of recreation in green areas. Long Island was the favoured destination, today reached by a cat's cradle of superhighways moving traffic in and out of New York. Millions longed to escape the city's sweltering summer streets, and Moses identified Long Island as a holiday haven, a dream that materialized as Jones Beach and the Southern State Parkway. If this meant the empowerment of the motor car, so be it. Moses himself never learned to drive but had at his disposal a staff of chauffeurs on call 24 hours a day. Many of his business meetings were conducted in one of his limousines. The Long Island newspaper *Newsday* recounts one of these planning excursions:

> One day in 1926, Moses took several architects and engineers across the bay and on to a deserted sandbar called Jones Beach. One of the architects later remarked that there was no way to reach the sandbar except by boat, while Moses was talking about bathhouses like palaces and parking lots that held ten thousand cars.[8]

Huge floating dredges were brought into the bay, and over a period of several months they pumped more than 40 million cubic yards of sand out of the bay bottom and onto the beach. In August 1929 Jones Beach, in all the magnificence Moses had envisaged, was inaugurated as 25,000 cars filled with sun-seekers rolled across the Wantagh Causeway.

Moses made New York – once heralded as the pioneer of mass transit – the nation's first city of the automobile age. Those who opposed his enthusiasm for road building, as well as the alleged attempt to restrict his seaside playgrounds to the middle classes, went so far as to accuse him of building the parkway bridge crossings too low to accommodate buses, a claim he vehemently denied. The bare fact is that before Moses, there was no Triborough Bridge, Jones Beach State Park, West Side Highway or Long Island parkway system. There can be no doubt that he played a larger role in shaping the physical environment of New York than any figure in the twentieth century.

Strutting the Airwaves

In the *Readers' Guide to Periodical Literature* for 1919–21, which registered all the magazine articles for those years, less than a quarter of a column of references is devoted to commentary on radio. The list of radio articles for 1922–4, on the other hand, takes up nineteen columns.[9]

The initial broadcasts of the early 1920s sparked widespread enthusiasm for this new form of entertainment. Instead of having to travel to Times Square theatres or Midtown music halls to purchase tickets for a show, entertainment was now accessible – to those with deep pockets – from the comfort of their homes. As with the automobile, another consumer novelty targeted at the mass market, the radio in its embryonic stage was a rich person's plaything. At the beginning of the 1920s a radio carried a price tag of more than $200, nearly equivalent to the average New York household's monthly income. But a steady drop in prices became commensurate with a fast-growing enthusiasm for this new gadget, as it did with the motor car. By the end of the decade, New Yorkers in almost all earning brackets were happy to rush out and pick up a radio of the latest model for as little as $35. An unwieldy contraption known as the Audion amplifying vacuum tube had been around since the early years of the century. This device served as the grid for what was to become the first radio receiver put on the market for general consumer use. The next stage materialized as a breakthrough by Edwin H. Armstrong, a young New York engineer who incorporated the Audion tube into the radio. Years later, the addition of the transistor created a new type of radio that was smaller and more portable than the hefty, polished-wood consoles of earlier days. New Yorkers now had an entertainment apparatus that allowed them to tune in to the entertainers of the day over cocktails or even foxtrot across the living-room carpet, freed from the encumbrance of headphones.[10]

Armstrong was an individual as anomalous as the decade during which his invention hit the mass market. In 1923 the 33-year-old FM

inventor scampered up the WJZ radio antenna (now station WABC) atop a twenty-storey building in Manhattan, where he reportedly performed a handstand. When asked by an astonished witness what had motivated him to do it, Armstrong replied, 'I do it because the spirit moves me.' It was a darker spirit that 31 years later prompted Armstrong to fling himself from a window of his luxurious Upper East Side home. His body was found fully clothed, even to hat, over-coat and gloves, along with a pencilled farewell to his estranged wife.

Armstrong's invention took hold of a city, indeed an entire nation. By the winter of 1921, radio addicts were overwhelming their friends with chatter about regenerative circuits, Sodion tubes and crystal detectors. A popular song in the Ziegfeld *Follies* revue of 1922 told of a man who hoped his love might hear him as she was 'listening on the radio'.

Before long, a warehouse district in Manhattan's Lower West Side was transformed into the home of up to fifty electronics shops specializing in radio sales. New Yorkers have a penchant for attaching nicknames to the city's commercial districts, according to the business carried on in each neighbourhood: Meatpacking District, Garment District, Diamond (jewellery) District and so on. In 1921 Cortlandt Street was the focal point of 'Radio Row'. The first of many radio-related stores along the street was City Radio, a humble, homespun shop founded in 1921 by the retail entrepreneur Harry L. Schneck. It was a bold enterprise at a time when the radio was still in its embryonic stage and there was some scepticism about how popular it would turn out to be. 'Radio was a novelty,' says Harry's son Bill Schneck. 'Most people were intimidated by it. The idea of information coming across the air through the ether was something that was one step away from black magic.' Following Schneck's success, the area quickly became the commercial nerve centre for other well-known retail names, among them Arrow Electronics, Avnet and Schweber Electronics.[11]

Six years after the first radio shop opened its doors, Cortlandt Street retailers held a 'Radio Jubilee' in celebration of this ground-breaking advance in the entertainment world. Perhaps with an excess of hyperbole, one newspaper reported that 'Cortlandt Street was Radio Row, while Broadway was just a thoroughfare.' On that day in 1927, the street was closed to traffic and decorated with flags and bunting. Joseph V. McKee, President of the New York City Board of Aldermen, put in an appearance to present a 'key to Cortland Street' to the reigning Miss New York, Frieda Louise Mierse, while a contest was held to name a 'Miss Downtown Radio'.

For nearly forty years until 1966, when the road and its commercial premises were demolished to make way for the World Trade Center construction site, Cortlandt Street remained the central axis of the city's radio trade. 'To one visiting it for the first time the phenomenon is particularly bewildering,' the *New York Times* reported.

The clamour is heard even as one walks through the subway tunnel to the street exit and one emerges into an unreal world. Alice's Wonderland had nothing on this. The first impression and, in fact, the only one, is auditory – a reverberating bedlam, a profusion of sounds which only an army of loudspeakers could produce.[12]

Of course, the cost of a radio might have seemed exorbitant compared with that of a 20-cent cinema ticket. On the other hand, the proud owner of an elegant Crosley Regular 51 or Spirit of St Louis model could tune in to a hitherto unimaginable selection of entertainment at the flick of a switch. By the mid-1920s, nearly fifty daily and weekly programmes dominated the airwaves, in New York City as well as across the country. There were shows to satisfy every

Atwater
Kent radio.

listener's taste. *Old Gold on Broadway*, sponsored by the cigarette brand Old Gold, broadcast live from inside New York theatres. Its programmes included an excerpt from the Ziegfeld *Follies*, featuring on stage top celebrities from the New Amsterdam Theatre. *The Palmolive Hour*, put on by Palmolive Soap, offered a repertoire of jazz, show tunes and opera selections on New York's station NBC Radio. *Amos 'n' Andy* was an enormously popular slapstick sitcom set in Harlem. *The Voice of Firestone*, also broadcast on NBC, featured leading singers of the day in selections of classical music, opera and operetta. The duo of tenor Billy Jones and baritone Ernie Hare brought gladness to millions in the early 1920s with their NBC Radio musical programme *The Happiness Boys*. By 1928 they had become the highest-paid singers in radio.

By this time, New York had succumbed to the fad for mah-jong, a game introduced to America by Joseph P. Babcock, Standard Oil Company's representative in China. As Frederick Lewis Allen explains in his 'informal history' of the 1920s, *Only Yesterday* (1931), 'People

People became obsessed with mah-jong in the 1920s. Joseph P. Babcock began importing sets of the medieval Chinese tile game in 1922.

who were beginning to take their radio sets for granted now simply left them turned on while they "broke the wall" and called "pung" or "chow" and wielded the Ming box.' It became common to find people bobbing up and down in swimming pools around a floating mah-jong board, a radio blaring away on the poolside.[13]

Ain't Nobody's Business

There was a darker side to 1920s New York, an unsavoury development that had little to do with sipping highballs or tripping the Charleston. The city was locked in the grip of a sinister political machine known as Tammany Hall. Tammany's power was almost limitless throughout the 1920s and in the years leading up to that decade, thanks mostly to the support it enjoyed from hundreds of thousands of Irish immigrants who had begun to arrive after the Great Famine of 1845. Within a decade of that catastrophe, more than 900,000 impoverished Irish had passed through the Ellis Island processing centre in New York Harbor, facing the Statue of Liberty. A large number of these destitute newcomers remained in the city, altering its social profile forever. Any attempt to integrate into the fabric of New York society was thwarted by those of ethnicities who had come before. The Irish were held in contempt by the Protestant establishment, as well as by other ethnic groups, who saw them as a threat to their livelihoods. What these Irish sought from politics was not so much power as protection. Tammany, an arm of the Democratic Party, was eager to provide that security. All the bosses demanded was a promise to vote for their candidates in city elections.

> Tammany helped Irishmen get their naturalization papers before the end of the waiting period. Whenever a gang leader got into trouble, a Tammany lawyer appeared for him in court, and a Tammany bondsman put up his bail. Tammany pulled strings to obtain licences for the many Irishmen seeking to

open saloons . . . All Tammany asked in return was that the Irish prove their gratitude by voting Democratic [the Tammany party] regularly and even repeatedly.[14]

This breeding ground of sleaze did not come about as an upshot of a post-war relaxation of morals. The clique of crooked officials who were to ride roughshod over accepted standards of political behaviour and spread their patronage across New York for more than two centuries was founded in 1789 as a Democratic Party club. Tammany Hall's guiding spirit was William Mooney, an Irish-American veteran of the War of Independence who became the society's first boss or *Sachem*, the North American Indian name for a paramount leader. Mooney had at the outset endeavoured to set up a beneficent organization to support the common citizen.[15] Although its activities were at first mostly social and ceremonial, Tammany gradually became City Hall's all-powerful machine. It came to exercise iron-fisted control over Democratic Party nominations and patronage in Manhattan as well as the outer boroughs.

Mooney and the *Sachems* who followed in his footsteps introduced community aid programmes, such as the appointment of precinct captains charged with helping people in their neighbourhood in times of emergency. They found jobs for Irish Americans and provided assistance with legal problems, and, in return, were guaranteed their beneficiaries' votes in local elections. Ballot-box fraud was standard, but almost all Tammany Hall candidates achieved an outright win thanks to this attention to their well-being. The Irish dominated the machine and key posts, regardless of the changing ethnic make-up of their neighbourhoods. In due course, German and Jewish people also came to ally themselves with the Tammany Hall apparatus and secured positions for themselves in local and state assembly bodies.

This was the face of compassion that Tammany Hall took pains to present to the community at large. The organization cut across

Tammany Hall tiger following an enemy Democratic
Party candidate into a wooded area.

all economic, social and political aspects of city life. Bossism provided jobs, food, friendship and advice for its adherents, who in return remained loyal to the machine, which proved itself adept at cutting through the red tape of bureaucratic administration. The bosses invariably claimed to speak and act on behalf of the common people. But lurking beneath the surface was something much less wholesome. The name of the game was kickbacks, institutionalized graft involving payments from almost anyone seeking a green light from City Hall for construction and supplier contracts, local government appointments and virtually anything for a friend.

I'll Build a Stairway to Paradise

The man who personified this scourge of corruption and, moreover, cheerfully got away with it for years, was Mayor James J. Walker. Known variously as 'Gentleman' Jimmy Walker, 'Beau James' and the 'Nightclub Mayor', Walker cultivated the image of a fun-loving friend of the people and, as such, did not fail to endear himself to New Yorkers of his generation:

> He was a dilettante with style and it seems somehow fitting that he was the first whose inauguration was broadcast live on radio. Voters greeted his appointees for the police and health commissioners with universal approval. Few complained

that Tammany retained twenty of the twenty-five commis-
sionerships. Walker made his administrative responsibilities
secondary to enjoying the wonders of his hometown.[16]

Walker, the son of an Irish alderman from Greenwich Village, clawed
his way up the ladder of New York politics using a set of impeccably
manicured fingernails. His initial love, however, was the music business, specifically vaudeville and songwriting, in which he enjoyed
impressive success. His first and only hit was the romantic ballad
'Will You Love Me in December as You Do in May?' (1905), which
netted him a hefty $500 advance: 'Walker, always a dandy, used the
advance to buy three custom-made suits . . . a dozen silk shirts, four
pairs of shoes with sharply pointed toes, three fedora hats, a new
walking stick and gifts for his mother and girlfriend.'[17]

That tune marked Walker's hail and farewell to the world of entertainment, although it did not turn down the lights on his career as
an entertainer in public office. Tammany Hall was instrumental in
catapulting him from the New York State Assembly to the Senate. In
1925 the Democratic bosses selected their debonair protégé to stand
in the mayoral race. Walker effortlessly swept aside his Republican
Party rival Frank D. Waterman, of Waterman Pen Company fame,
to gain a landslide victory.

In the six years, from 1926 to 1932, that he ruled City Hall, New
Yorkers turned a blind eye to Walker's corrupt shenanigans, not to
mention his incorrigible boozing and notorious philandering. Such
was the spell that Beau James cast over his constituents that in the
mayoral race of 1929, the dapper, much-admired dandy in spats and
waistcoat once again saw off the Republican contender – none other
than Fiorello La Guardia, his firebrand, Italian-Jewish Greenwich
Village neighbour.

Walker became a familiar fixture in New York cabarets. His favourite was the Casino in Central Park, where he would pull up in his
expensive Duesenberg, accompanied by his mistress (and later wife)

the Ziegfeld girl Betty Compton. As he stepped out of the racy saloon car, the mayor would be greeted with rapturous applause as the man whose lifestyle perfectly fit the mood of the city. To his fans, Walker was the champion of entertainment and the protector of the working class, the man who brought back baseball games and prizefighting on Sundays, opposed subway fare hikes, and stood as a fierce opponent of Prohibition.

One of the most colourful incidents in Walker's many nights of carousing took place during a habitual clandestine visit to the 21 Club speakeasy. One night, when Beau James was entertaining one of his girlfriends at a table in the secret basement saloon, the Feds staged a raid on the club. They never suspected that the mayor was wining and dining in the secret snug beneath their feet. Walker, stuck for five hours in the basement, was so outraged that he telephoned the police and instructed them to come at once to ticket the Feds' cars.

The nemesis that awaits the holder of high office who interprets 'high' as signifying above the law lurks only one wrong step away. In Walker's case, questions began to arise about how he had managed to pay for five months' holiday time in the first two-and-a-half years of his tenure. The scandal that erupted over his extravagant spending prompted him to resign and flee to Europe with his mistress, to escape the threat of prosecution. He eventually returned to New York, where in 1946 he died of a stroke at the age of 65. Walker's misdeeds and transgressions failed to detract from his enormous popularity. His funeral cortege was escorted up Fifth Avenue to St Patrick's Cathedral by a squad of motorcycle patrolmen. Thousands of admirers from all walks of life queued to leave floral wreaths and messages at the bier, including Jack Dempsey, the actor George Jessel, the singer Sophie Tucker, Eleanor Roosevelt and leaders of the Patrolmen's Benevolent Association. Walker's wrongdoing, whatever burden it may have inflicted on the taxpayer, was in a perverse way accepted by his devotees as the entry charge to a performance of panache and merriment by New York's roguish and most scandalous mayor.

Interior of a crowded bar in New York City moments
before Prohibition came into effect.

2

Ain't (Much) Misbehavin'

Volstead was a name that aroused passions ranging from resent-ment to outright rage among New York's drinking class in the 1920s. In January 1920, at the stroke of a pen, stepping into a bar to have a beer or a whisky, buying alcoholic drinks from a store to take home, and ordering wine with a meal – all of which had been part of everyday life – became illegal. The bill enforcing this was conceived and drafted by the Anti-Saloon League's leader, the attorney Wayne Wheeler. But the name that people associated with the legislation was that of Andrew Volstead, chairman of the House Judiciary Committee, who managed the bill. Throughout the 1920s New York and the rest of the country was subject to the prohibition of the production and sale of alcoholic beverages. The National Prohibition Act, to give it its official name at the time, was the piece of legislation that brought into being the Eighteenth Amendment to the Constitution, prohibiting the production, sale or transport of 'intoxicating liquor' to the public. When the Act took effect, it brought about a social change with regard to the relationship of a huge swathe of the general public to the rule of law and the notion of being 'law-abiding'.

Campaigning for Prohibition had been running for many years, with the arguments for and against put forward by various groups representing citizens (especially women's groups), churches, and the alcohol and hospitality industries on different sides of the debate. Alcoholic drinks had been commonplace in America from the earliest days of colonization, and in the nineteenth century there were so many distilleries that spirits were often cheaper to drink than tea.[1] The temperance movement came to prominence at mid-century as the consumption of liquor increased, leading to antisocial behaviour, families not being supported as wages were spent on liquor, and domestic violence. Liquor in all its forms was therefore seen as a threat to ordered society, and something that must be prohibited by law. The first such legislation came into place in Maine in 1851, setting out fines and imprisonment for those convicted of producing and selling liquor. Other areas followed suit, but this resulted in a backlash by citizens who found it an interference by government in their everyday lives. By the end of the decade all such laws at state level had been repealed.

However, the temperance movement experienced a resurgence from the 1870s onwards, led by churches and coinciding with the growth of the women's suffrage movement. The two causes became intertwined, and many women were supportive of temperance owing to the harm wreaked on family life through drink. There was a sense that women needed the vote if they were to be protected within marriage from abusive husbands addicted to liquor, and to play a full part in an ordered and temperate society. This was before widespread support for general suffrage for women. The Women's Christian Temperance Union (WCTU), founded in 1874, was one of the most influential groups, and quickly gained a membership of over 250,000. At a rally in 1876 Frances Willard, at that point head of the WCTU Publications Department, said that women should have the right to vote on issues regarding liquor, so as to be able to protect family life and children.

One route to this aim was education for children on the evils of alcohol. This argument proved effective, and in 1882 Vermont passed a state law to make temperance education compulsory for children. This example was followed by the states of New York and Pennsylvania. Four years later the WCTU had persuaded Congress to make scientific temperance instruction mandatory in public schools and military academies. By 1901 every state had passed this law and the course was taught to every child attending school.[2]

The liquor industry did not stand still during this period, and also marshalled its arguments and political support. The growth in immigration from Europe at the end of the nineteenth century and beginning of the twentieth meant that a larger part of the population was used to consuming alcoholic drinks as part of daily life. Consumption grew, particularly that of beer, which was intrinsic to many European societies. Brewers made enormous fortunes during this period. The liquor industry lobbied state and national legislators in an effort to block laws affecting the trade, but it did itself no favours with some of its advertising, which suggested that beer was a healthy drink for children. A poster advertisement, for example, showed a picture of a toddler in a high chair, with copy reading: 'The Youngster ruddy with good cheer, Serenely sips his Lager Beer.'[3]

Following on from the WCTU, the Anti-Saloon League (ASL) came to the fore in the early years of the twentieth century, pushing for a ban at constitutional level on the manufacture and sale of alcoholic drinks. The ASL saw New York as a key target, having one of the highest levels of alcohol consumption in the country. It was estimated that New Yorkers spent $365 million a year on beer and strong liquor, with per capita consumption three-and-a-half times the national average.[4] In particular the ASL targeted Tammany Hall, since grass-roots political deals were often hammered out in saloons, and the institution was known to be corrupt. The ASL adopted a strategy of targeting local districts to go dry, one at a time, by passing 'local option' laws. The campaign was spearheaded by William H. Anderson, who arrived in New York from Maryland in January 1914 and presented his methodical plan in a news conference, claiming that he would succeed in getting alcohol abolished in the city and the state.

This seemed preposterous to many who read it in the next day's papers, yet the ASL had a record of success and became a powerful force in New York state politics, achieving its goal in five years from setting out the aim.[5] Prohibition thus did not 'come out of nowhere', but was the result of more than forty years' skilled campaigning by people dedicated to the cause.

The Volstead Act set out the intention to ensure that the use of intoxicating liquor as any sort of beverage was prevented. The definition of an intoxicating liquor was set at 0.5 per cent alcohol, an extremely low limit that covered all wines and beers and took many by surprise, even Prohibition supporters, many of whom were looking to ban the sale and consumption of 'strong spirits' through legislation. The campaigners celebrated as the Eighteenth Amendment was voted through the House of Representatives in December 1917, passing by 272 votes for to 128 against. This was followed by the ratification process as each state voted on the amendment, a process that was complete by January 1919. The legislation came into effect a year later. Its supporters imagined that it would reform America into a law-abiding, orderly and productive society. Instead, however, the effect of Prohibition was to open the floodgates to organized crime, corruption and an ambivalence to the law among many, starting with Prohibition and soon leaching into other areas.

My Blue Heaven

New Yorkers were not about to let a piece of legislation deprive them of a drink. Rather than change their habits, people found ways of obtaining alcoholic drinks, and a flourishing criminal market grew up to meet the customers' requirements. The law itself was a legalistic mix of restrictions and permissions, which opened up various loopholes that were furiously exploited. The Act was weakened by a lack of resources for enforcing the law. The funding made available was $4.75 million (equivalent to roughly $85 million today), and dedicated enforcement infrastructure was also lacking, with responsibility split between local, state and federal agencies.[6]

It is estimated that in the 1920s the city had 32,000 speakeasies, twice the number of legal saloons before Prohibition. Throughout the entire Prohibition period, although overall alcohol consumption went down, most people who wanted to buy liquor would find some way to get it, and in New York there were countless suppliers. Because the Eighteenth Amendment and the Volstead Act did not make it illegal to drink alcohol, but only to manufacture and sell it, many organizations and individuals stockpiled liquor before the ban went into effect. Restaurants, bars and liquor shops were desperate to sell their stock while they legally could, so many started the Prohibition period with a domestic supply that might last months or even years, while others bought up supplies with the idea of starting an illegal bar in their home or other premises. Rumour had it that the Yale Club in New York City had a fourteen-year supply of booze in its basement. Many criminal gangs had also used the period of drafting and ratification of the legislation – well over a year – to purchase and store enormous quantities of whisky, rum, gin, wine and other alcoholic drinks, knowing that they would soon have a captive market.

The slang terms 'rumrunners' and 'bootleggers' are sometimes used interchangeably, but each had their own beat. Rumrunners were those who were illegally bringing into the country large amounts of branded foreign spirits – rum from the Caribbean, as well as gin, whisky, wine and liqueurs – usually in boats but also over the land borders. Producers of premium spirits in Canada simply needed to get their product to the port of Windsor, Ontario, and it could be shipped in a 1-mile voyage to Detroit. The entire border with Canada was riddled with convenient spots to transfer consignments into the northern U.S. states, and it was impossible for enforcement officers to patrol the complete length. It was a similar story to the south, as wine, beer and spirits were smuggled over the Mexican border at a myriad of places, to enter California, New Mexico, Arizona and Texas.

The eastern seaboard became another major route of entry for smuggled liquor. The Prohibition Act demarcated a 3-mile limit from the shore, and beyond this ships were moored, loaded with cargoes of booze. The importation routes that had previously been direct to the United States were diverted to Cuba and other Caribbean islands, including Jamaica, the Bahamas and the Dominican Republic, where the imported booze was augmented with locally produced rum. The large boats would make runs from the islands to moor up in the demarcation zone. The rumrunners would motor out in smaller boats, load up and land the crates on the mainland, aiming to avoid the agents of the Prohibition Bureau and a strengthened body of coastguards, who had miles and miles of shoreline to patrol. There were inevitably chases, and some rumrunners were caught, but the throwing overboard of one load of illegal liquor from time to time was factored in as part of their business model.

Some ships were anchored semi-permanently just outside the limit and replenished by supply ships, which were quite legally going to and from the Caribbean islands with cargoes of alcoholic drinks. The moored ships also operated as floating restaurants and hotels. Customers could be ferried, hire a boat, or sail their own yacht to moor alongside, and come on board to drink and gamble legally outside the U.S. national jurisdiction, eat a meal and possibly spend the night, before returning to shore. These anchored ships stretched for miles and were nicknamed 'Rum Row'.[7]

The bootleggers were those selling alcohol to speakeasies and to individual customers for home consumption. They would sell both smuggled booze and large amounts of beer (which was nearly all produced domestically, rather than being smuggled in), together with illegally distilled moonshine whisky and 'bathtub gin'. This clear spirit, distilled from grain alcohol, with added water and juniper berries, was not actually fermented in a bathtub. The term was used because the bottles tended to be too tall to fit under a sink tap and had to be topped up with water from the bath taps.

Prohibition agents examining barrels on captured rumrunner boat, 1924.

Some of the spirits brewed in outhouses and cellars were truly lethal, using unconventional sources for the alcohol, such as rubbing alcohol, and distillation techniques that were not well controlled, leading to very high alcohol content of up to 75 per cent. Applejack was a traditional apple brandy distilled by freezing cider and removing the ice, resulting in a liquid with a higher alcohol content. Unfortunately, as well as ethanol, the liquid also contains harmful methanol, esters, aldehydes and fusel alcohols that would be removed by more conventional distilling methods.[8]

Such unregulated and unreliable distilling led to the sale of some dangerous spirits, but this was minor compared to the catastrophes that came about through the use of stolen industrial alcohol, used to produce fake gin and whisky. Industrial alcohol was still being produced on a large scale, since it was used as a solvent in many industrial processes and as a constituent of some cleaning products. By about 1922 the organized gangs' pre-Prohibition stockpiles of alcohol were long gone. Gang members took to hijacking lorries from the industrial plants, aiming to redistill the alcohol and sell it as a drinkable product. The government had been aware of the problem of these supplies, and the Treasury Department's Prohibition Bureau instructed industrial alcohol producers to add 4 per cent wood alcohol, a substance known to be poisonous even in small amounts.

Bootleggers stole some 10 million gallons of the poisoned alcohol. They aimed to 'purify' it by redistilling it, taking advantage of the fact that the wood alcohol evaporates at a lower temperature, so it would be the first vapour off the heated liquid. Unfortunately, this could only be partly successful in removing the wood alcohol. Many batches of the cheap alcohol that resulted caused blindness or paralysis, mostly among the poor, who could not afford branded, smuggled spirits. On New Year's Day 1927 Bellevue Hospital in Manhattan was full of people suffering from alcohol poisoning after the previous evening's celebrations, and 41 people died on that day alone. Throughout 1927, of the 480,000 gallons of liquor seized by the Treasury's Prohibition agents in New York, 98 per cent contained poisonous additives, and liquor seized from 55 of the city's speakeasies proved to have traces of wood alcohol.[9]

The rise in popularity of cocktails was to a large extent because of the need to smother the raw taste of illegally distilled spirits with fruit juice, Coca-Cola, cream or soda water and small amounts of genuine, strongly flavoured liqueurs. The cocktails swiftly took on a mantle of gaudy glamour. Those that were popular in the 1920s include the 'Bee's Knees', the name being a reference to the honey content and also the popular slang of the period, in which the 'the bee's knees' was 'the best'. The mix included three measures of dry gin, with one measure each of lemon juice and honey syrup. Another relatively simple cocktail was the 'Orange Blossom', a favourite of Zelda Fitzgerald, comprising two measures of gin and one measure of orange juice, with a teaspoon of sugar and a slice of orange. The 'Sidecar' was the epitome of a modern drink, a brandy-based cocktail containing triple sec, lemon juice and sugar that captured the daring of riding motorcycles. At the core of the 'Pink Lady' was traditionally distilled American applejack brandy, mixed with gin, lemon juice, egg white and two dashes of grenadine syrup, while the 'Corpse Reviver' was a terrifying-sounding mix of dry gin, Cointreau, Cocchi Americano and absinthe.[10]

Walk Right In

Prohibition meant that drinking alcohol took on the new glamour of an illicit pleasure, encompassing the thrill of being 'in the know' about where the speakeasy bars had opened up or having a contact to get in. Previously legal saloons, which were open to men only, had closed in January 1920. People who wanted to buy alcoholic drinks could go to a chemist to get a limited supply for 'medicinal reasons' or to a clergyman to obtain altar wine for 'religious reasons', make contact with a bootlegger, or knock on the door of an illegal bar, where the doorman would open a spyhole to check out the customer, who had to give a password in a low voice to avoid being overheard – hence 'speakeasy'. These new arrangements changed New York social life completely, with men and women drinking together in bars for the first time. The venues ranged from fancy nightclubs, with bands playing the defining jazz music of the era, to dingy basements and back rooms, with minimal furnishings and the rawest of liquor. Another ruse was the 'house party', where people were not explicitly paying for the drinks – hence not illegal – although it was understood that there was an entry fee, but this was 'informal'. There was also a rise in restaurants, many run by Italian Americans, some, but not all, of whom had direct links to the Italian Mafia. The restaurants were popular with women because they offered table service and served wine with Italian food, which came to prominence as the cuisine for a night out during the 1920s.

The bars, restaurants and clubs were paying their bootleggers to supply the illegal drink at hugely inflated prices, and also paying protection money to organized crime gangs – and sometimes to the police as well, to look the other way. Many of the speakeasies were directly run by criminal groups, which seized the opportunity to be involved with these lucrative bars, supplying the alcohol and getting all the profits, rather than just a rake-off. Throughout Prohibition illegal bars sprang up throughout the country, nowhere more so than in New York, which also became the centre for organized crime. Mafia leaders Joe 'The Boss' Masseria, Frank Costello, Charles 'Lucky' Luciano and Salvatore Maranzano were all competing, as were the Polish-Jewish gang leader Meyer Lansky, the Irish-born Owney Madden and the German-Jewish Dutch Schultz, to name just the most prominent operators. The gangs were involved in bootlegging, running speakeasies, protection rackets, gambling and a host of other criminal activities. In certain Midtown areas of Manhattan there were reckoned to be two hundred speakeasies per street. With so many venues around, competition grew to get the punters in, resulting in a range of live entertainment on offer, from jazz bands to dancing and floor shows with chorus girls.

Established venues, such as the Colony Club, were the haunt of the true socialites, the 'Four Hundred' members of New York's social register of upper-echelon families, rather than the masses who were newly trying to emulate them. The upmarket places stayed open ostensibly as restaurants, but at many of them customers in the know were able to drink in the private dining rooms. One place that did not violate the Volstead Act throughout Prohibition was the Waldorf-Astoria hotel, on its original site on Fifth Avenue from 33rd to 34th streets. It remained 'dry' throughout the period, until it closed in 1929 for demolition, to make way for the Empire State Building. Some of the more elaborate speakeasies became theme bars, such as the Pirate's Den, its decor imitating the interior of a ship with barrel tables, battered copper mugs and draped nets, hung with maps, toy ships and lanterns, while the waiters dressed as eighteenth-century pirates and also entertained with mock sword fights. There was also the Country Club on 58th Street, operated by Belle Livingstone, an actor famous in the 1890s for her 'Gibson Girl' curvy figure. Running out of money after a long sojourn in Europe, she returned to New York and found that the way to make a living was to open a speakeasy. The Country Club had vaulted Florentine ceilings, Italian marble floors, an indoor miniature golf course, a brook stocked with goldfish, a games room with ping-pong tables and backgammon, and a lounge with a long wooden bar.[11]

Speakeasies were some of the worst-kept secrets, as some venues became well known for a classy night out and others just notorious. Prohibition made it challenging to live the life of an urban sophisticate in the 1920s, but also provided opportunities for thrilling, risky behaviour through the flaunting of the Volstead Act.

Sought-after venues included the Back of Ratner's on Norfolk and Delancey streets, which is still operating as the Back Room, serving beer in paper bags and cocktails in teacups to pay homage to its speakeasy roots. During Prohibition, it was simply known as the Back of Ratner's, a kosher restaurant in Delancey Street. The restaurant had a number of exits and entrances on the two streets, which made it the perfect gathering place for underworld bosses. Bugsy Siegel, Luciano and Lansky were known to hold meetings there, and the location was conveniently close to a garage under the Williamsburg Bridge, where Lansky would rent cars and trucks to bootleggers. Film stars and Broadway actors would also hang out at this speakeasy, which added to its attraction, with a unique mix of famous and infamous patrons.

Two famous speakeasys were old-time bars that closed, then reopened in different guise. The Landmark Tavern on 11th Avenue had

Drinkers enjoying the illicit glamour of the Prohibition speakeasy.

been open as a saloon since 1868. In response to Prohibition, the family running it closed the ground-floor bar and opened a speakeasy in their apartment on the third floor. The Ear Inn at 326 Spring Street was built as a town house which then became a tobacco store in 1817. In a change of business, by the 1850s, a brewery had been established on the premises, selling mostly to sailors arriving in port. At the turn of the century, becoming more sophisticated, a restaurant and a dining room was constructed where the backyard and outhouse once stood. With Prohibition the establishment became a speakeasy, brothel, boarding house and smugglers' headquarters. The Ear Inn is still at Spring Street, gaining its current name from an alteration to the illuminated neon 'Bar' sign that had been in place since the 1940s. It claims to be the oldest establishment in New York continuously serving alcoholic drinks.

In 1922 the eponymous Chumley's was started up as a speakeasy by the socialist activist Leland Stanford Chumley, at 86 Bedford Street in Greenwich Village, converting what had been a blacksmith's shop, near the corner of Barrow Street. The speakeasy had two unmarked entrances, one on each street. The interior of the building lent itself to a clandestine drinking establishment with trapdoors and secret stairs. It was rumoured that in advance of a raid, the bartender would tip off the patrons, known as '86 the patrons' – that is, let them out of the 86 Bedford Street door while the police entered from Barrow Street.[12] The speakeasy became a favourite spot for influential writers, poets, playwrights, journalists and activists, including members of the 'lost generation': F. Scott Fitzgerald and Ernest Hemingway, E. E. Cummings, Willa Cather, Edna St Vincent Millay, Eugene O'Neill and John Dos Passos. Another alleged favourite haunt of Scott and Zelda Fitzgerald was the Beatrice Inn at 285 West 12th Street, which opened as a speakeasy in 1924. The back door leading to an alley was probably an easy escape route during enforcement raids.

T for Texas

In 1922 the rumrunner Larry Fay founded the El Fey Club, one of several establishments presided over by the legendary nightlife personality Mary Louise Cecelia 'Texas' Guinan, who got her speakeasy start at the El Fey. Before her new venture of nightclub hostess, Guinan had already had a colourful career as a stage and film actor. The daughter of Irish immigrant parents, she grew up on a ranch in Waco, Texas, where she learned cowboy skills, and honed her marksmanship at a local shooting gallery. In 1898 she won a scholarship to the American Conservatory of Music in Chicago, where she developed her singing voice as a soprano. After two years studying music, Guinan spent four years as part of a touring show that featured 'Wild West' entertainment. A brief marriage ended in divorce, and Guinan moved to New York to try her luck on Broadway. At this point she adopted the name 'Texas' to differentiate herself from the scores of other pretty girls with light soprano voices vying for roles. Within a couple of years she had achieved considerable success with roles in shows including *The Gibson Girl Review*, *The Hoyden* and *The Lone Star*.

In 1913 Guinan was a headline star of *The Passing Show*, on its national tour. As a well-known actor, she signed a deal for her photograph to be used to promote a weight-loss plan. However, the advertisements claimed she had lost 70 pounds on the plan. When journalists found this to be untrue, Guinan was accused of perpetrating a fraud. The postal service then investigated and declared it to be a swindle. As a result, the u.s. Postmaster General prohibited Guinan from receiving mail through the post. Although she continued acting, the episode damaged her stage career and was instrumental in her move to develop other professional avenues. These included film roles, and she appeared in numerous two-reel shorts in 1917–19, often with western themes, revising her cowboy skills in *The Gun Woman* and *Getaway Kate* (both 1918). She moved into film production as well as acting on *The Lady of the Law* (1919), *The Girl of the Rancho* (1919) and *A Moonshine Feud* (1920), among others. She formed Texas Guinan Productions in 1921, putting out more western-themed movies, including *The Code of the West* and *Spitfire* (both in that year).

Tired of being typecast, Guinan returned to New York and in 1923 was hired as a nightclub singer at the Beaux Arts club, for which she was paid the huge fee – for the time – of $50,000 a year. After a while, it became clear that there was even more money to be made as a club promoter and hostess, so she threw in her lot with Larry Fay to host the El Fey Club in return for 50 per cent of the takings. Over a period of less than a year they made more than $700,000, the equivalent of about $11.5 million today. Guinan made her mark by hiring the best chorus girls and ensuring that the club was always lively through her give-and-take dialogue with the patrons. The *New Yorker* reported in August 1925:

> The only other excitement of the week was the return of Texas Guinan to the Del Fey Club [*sic*] . . . greeted by what is popularly known as an ovation. There was the usual jamming of

Texas Guinan in her idiosyncratic style in the 1920s.

tables, the usual two-by-four dance floor, the usual arguments, the fervent singing of 'Boola-Boola' and 'Old Nassau' in happy impartiality, and the usual bland cuties in the entertainment, showing the most flagrant coats of tan in New York. At four o'clock in the morning when I departed, soaked to the skin by a glass of ginger ale that had been neatly deposited in my lap, the party was still going strong. No other person in the world can imbue a place with the hilarious vitality that Texas can.[13]

Guinan's over-the-top attitude was a huge draw, and she became known as 'Queen of the Night Clubs' with her famous greeting: 'Hello, suckers – come on in and leave your wallet at the bar!' After a year, she moved on to launch her own club, the 300 at 151 West 54th Street. The opening-night event was the marriage of the actor Wilda Bennett to the Argentine dancer Abraham 'Peppy' de Albrew.

An occupational hazard of running a club was being busted by Prohibition agents, an event that would be followed by the club being padlocked and a court appearance for the promoters, who faced stiff fines or a prison sentence if convicted. Guinan made a point of collecting the padlocks as a necklace (until it became too heavy to wear), and used the padlock as a design on her publicity. At three o'clock in the morning on 3 July 1926 a raiding party of Prohibition agents and officers from the New York Police Department entered the 300 Club. Acting on evidence gathered over previous nights by policewomen dressed as flappers and detectives in eveningwear, the late-night raiders seized four bottles of liquor and arrested a seventeen-year-old floor dancer for performing an 'objectionable dance'. More than four hundred patrons were crowded into the club when the raid commenced, including two senators and twenty members of a Georgia delegation travelling with the golfer Bobby Jones, who had just returned stateside after winning the British Open.[14] Like other club and speakeasy operators, Texas had a legal team on side who were adept at finding their way around the clauses of the Volstead Act, and, as on other occasions, she was not convicted after that particular raid. Despite numerous raids during her nightclub career Guinan insisted that she was not involved in selling liquor, proclaiming, in December 1927:

Texas Guinan, 'Queen of
the Night Clubs', in court
for selling liquor in 1928.

Texas Guinan, 'Queen of the Night Clubs', in court for selling liquor in 1928.

I never take a drink and I never sell a drink. I'm paid to put on an act and I put on an act. I once gave [u.s. Attorney for the Southern District of ny Emory] Buckner a certified check for $100,000 to give anyone who has ever seen me take a drink or sell a drink. That check is still good, so's my offer.[15]

Guinan was adept at reinventing herself as the situation demanded, becoming a businesswoman and promoter in the New York club life she described as 'an essential and basic industry'.[16] She seemed to know everyone in the Roaring Twenties – the Prince of Wales, Ruby Keeler, George Raft, Rudolph Valentino, Walter Winchell, Mae West, Aimee Semple McPherson and even President Warren G. Harding. Tired of the nightclub raids and court cases by the end of the 1920s, Texas tried to move to Europe, but she was banned from entering the United Kingdom and prevented from working in France by national labour laws. She built on these reversals by launching the revue *Too Hot for Paris* on her return to the United States. She took the show on the road, but contracted amoebic dysentery during an epidemic at the World's Fair in Chicago and died in November 1933, one month before the repeal of Prohibition.

Texas Guinan was a larger-than-life character who left such an impression that she was immortalized in contemporary stories, plays and films. She appears as Miss Missouri Martin in Damon Runyon's Broadway stories. The film characters Maudie Triplett (played by West) in *Night after Night* (1932) and Panama Smith (played by Gladys George) in *The Roaring Twenties* (1939) were based on her, while the film *Incendiary Blonde* (1945) told her story, starring Betty Hutton as Texas.

Illegal drinking was not the only type of increased 'substance abuse' that resulted from Prohibition. The use of marijuana also rose substantially. Prohibition had made alcohol less convenient to get hold of, raised the price and rendered the quality doubtful, so an increasing number of people were drawn to marijuana for recreational use. One of the unforeseen consequences of Prohibition was that a much wider section of the population was now in touch with the routes to gain illegal substances, and the social stigma of doing so declined significantly.

As well as speakeasies, 'tea pads' sprang up from 1920 and flourished by the hundreds. These establishments for the smoking of cannabis were especially common in Harlem, throughout which there were apartments that were known as places where people could pick up a supply of marijuana or stay and smoke, chatting with others. The style and clientele varied, some catering to the gay community, others having a more literary clientele and quite a large number popular with customers from the jazz scene. Most tea pads had low lighting, jazz on a gramophone in the background, and comfortable chairs and divans around the room. The price of marijuana was low compared to that of liquor, at about a quarter for two marijuana cigarettes. For those scraping by, it became a known dodge to raise the rent money by hosting a 'tea party'.[17] Marijuana could be bought even more cheaply to take away at the door of a regular tea pad, or if the host of the tea party had a connection to a 'wholesale' supplier. The host would let their friends know they were having a pay-at-the-door tea party. Limiting information to word of mouth and to a specific day meant that it was fairly unlikely that they would be busted, unless things got out of hand.

Let's Misbehave

There were regular raids on speakeasies, although some inconspicuous places that had secured an understanding with the local police served alcohol from the inception of Prohibition in 1920 to the repeal in 1933, with never a break. The patrons of those that were targeted would be rounded up and there would be a public disposal

New York City Deputy Police Commissioner John A. Leach, right, watching agents pour liquor into the sewer following a raid during the height of Prohibition.

of kegs of beer and bottles of spirits into the sewer, sometimes with a posed photograph for the official agency and to be circulated to the press. This was seen as a setback by the operators but only a pause in supply to the drinkers, not the end of the road. In April 1921 New York enacted even stricter local legislation with the Mullan-Gage Enforcement Law, which meant that possession of alcohol for drinking, even a hip flask, was a crime, and gave police and officers of other agencies powers to search for alcohol. Case after case came before the courts and the legal system was nearly overwhelmed, the courts clogged with cases involving people with no criminal record having been found in possession of alcohol. Sentences were handed out proportionate to the amount of alcohol found. The impact of the legislation was seen dramatically in 'the case of 77-year-old Nora Kelly. Just one month after enactment of the new law, the elderly woman stood before a New York City magistrate, charged with possession of a small flask of whiskey. The judge rejected her explanation and she was sentenced to five days in jail.'[18] The backlog caused by the Mullan-Gage law prevented courts from dealing with cases of serious and violent crime. Political pressure was brought to bear, and after a change of governor, the law was repealed as unworkable after two years.

Throughout the Prohibition years the enforcement agencies battled a combination of forces. There were previously law-abiding members of the public, who felt that the state interfering in their ability to have a drink was an infringement too far and 'thumbed their noses' at the Volstead Act. There were the organized crime gangs, who had gained enormous influence and resources through the explosion in demand for an illegal substance. There were also very high levels of corruption among the police and other enforcement agencies, partly because they did not believe in the ideals of Prohibition. It was therefore common for officers to be bribed to give advance warning of a raid or just happen to let significant gang members slip through when there was one.

However, there were those who would not accept bribes and continued the efforts to shut down the clubs, speakeasies and restaurants that were serving liquor in backrooms and cellars. One such man was Emory Buckner, Attorney for the Southern District of NY, who adopted a new strategy. It was customary to padlock the doors of a venue that had been raided and where liquor had been found in violation of the Volstead Act. Buckner exploited a clause of the law that allowed enforcement to keep the establishment locked for a year before having to go to court, instead of arresting a few hapless waiters and bartenders as before, then allowing the place to open again. This strategy cut into the core business for owners and operators. Buckner vowed to shut down 1,000 establishments in New York alone, and he succeeded in closing some of the most prestigious in the city. However, the drinking continued as the speakeasy owners abandoned the premises that had been padlocked and opened new places with cheap furnishings. Some of the more exclusive clubs continued to use the well-appointed venues but created new, hidden entrances, keeping the front doors padlocked and dark.

The thrill of the speakeasies and raucous jazz nightlife made the 1920s roar, and they have taken on an image of glamour and high spirits over time. There was an ugly side to the scene, though, since it created a power base for organized crime and corruption to thrive as never before. Prohibition triggered a surge in organized crime, with gangs fighting for control of the hugely profitable rumrunning, brewing and bootlegging trade. Organized crime became big business: the stakes were high and life was cheap. New York's homicide rate rose to an average of more than one per day. Many murders were linked to bloody vendettas between gangs, but gang members also killed cops, Prohibition agents, bartenders, watchmen and drivers at the industrial alcohol plants, as well as speakeasy customers and bystanders.

New York had had criminal street gangs for more than a hundred years before Prohibition. They were renowned for the violent fighting among themselves and for running various protection rackets, prostitution and organized robberies, such as stealing cargo from the docks. From the 1820s to the 1890s different groups came to prominence, always linked to a particular district of the city, such as the Bowery Boys and the Five Points Gang (the latter from an area near what is now Chinatown). The gangs also had strong national or ethnic ties. The Dead Rabbits gang was Irish, for instance, and there were Jewish gangs and Italian gangs, the last drawing from more recent immigration and coming to prominence at the turn of the twentieth century.

One of the first gangs to emerge was the 107th Street Gang from East Harlem. At this time Harlem was a mostly white neighbourhood, with new high-quality housing, an opera house and good schools in one part, while East Harlem consisted of poor tenements, with a large proportion of Italian immigrants. The 107th Street Gang was led by the Morello and Terranova families. By 1915 Ciro Terranova had set up a network of protection rackets among meat, fish, fruit and vegetable sellers in the street markets. If they did not pay up, their stall would be destroyed. The police patrolling the markets were bought off to turn a blind eye to the extortion. Terranova was also known as the 'Artichoke King', having cornered the market in artichokes by buying up the California crop to sell into New York. (Baked artichoke was a staple of Italian – particularly Sicilian – family meals.) Ciro set the price, thus making a huge profit on all sales of the vegetable.[19] He joined forces with Ignazio Lupo 'the Wolf' Saietta, who was one of the most feared gangsters, ready to eliminate anyone at the first sign of disloyalty.

Such rackets made a relatively easy living for the gangsters from the early 1900s until 1920. There were rivalries between gangs, leading to abductions, torture and murders, many at the notorious East Harlem 'Murder Stable', where an estimated twenty to sixty people were killed, many first hung up on meat hooks and tortured to extract information about rival gangs. However, all this was relatively small in scale and had little effect on life for many in the city, compared to what was to come with the explosion of criminality fuelled by Prohibition.

Just as the criminal opportunities were opening up, there was a fight for leadership of the Mafia gangs in New York. Key members of the 107th Street Gang had been convicted on forgery charges in 1912, leading to ongoing power grabs by rival gangs over the next few years, with a series of murders and revenge murders. By the mid-1920s Joe Masseria had become the boss of the New York Italian Mafia. He had arrived in the city in 1903, fleeing a murder charge in Sicily. He joined the 107th Street Gang and rose to prominence through a combination of treachery, luck and willingness to kill those vying for power in in his own gang as well as the bosses of rival gangs.[20] As 'the Boss' he had five crime families in Manhattan, Brooklyn and the Bronx operating under him. This consolidation rendered his operations more widespread and lucrative. However, Masseria was stuck in a tribal approach to crime, which meant that he steered clear of dealings with politicians and anything more than small-scale bribes to front-line police. He also hated those of other nationalities and would have nothing to do with gangsters of Irish, Jewish, German or other heritage. He missed opportunities to bring in millions of dollars from schemes that would have involved cooperation with non-Sicilian gangsters.

The Bronx-born Arthur Simon Flegenheimer, the son of German-Jewish immigrants, adopted the surname 'Schultz' from a trucking firm at which he worked as a young man. The forename 'Dutch' was bestowed on him as a corruption of 'Deutsch' (German). With Prohibition, he took control of the beer trade in the Bronx and then moved in on the Harlem numbers racket. But the bootlegger king of Harlem eventually grew too big for his boots, at least in the opinion of the Mafia's enforcement arm, Murder Inc., as it was dubbed by the media. The Mafia bosses had decided not to assassinate the crime-busting federal prosecutor Thomas E. Dewey, to avoid the inconvenience of having to deal with a massive crackdown on the

Mafia, but Schultz was outraged and declared that he would do the job himself. After six hours of deliberations, the Murder Inc. Commission decided he had become a maverick liability and ordered his elimination. A few days later a Mafia hit-squad burst into the Palace Chop House in New Jersey, where Schultz was relieving himself in the gents toilet. He took a bullet below the heart, but staggered out to sit at a table, which he deemed a more decorous place to breathe his last.

Irish-born Owen 'Owney' Madden emigrated to the United States to become one of New York's most powerful underworld figures. Within a few years of settling in what were then the slums of Hell's Kitchen, Madden joined a gang of thugs called the Gophers, whose five hundred members exerted an iron-fisted rule over Manhattan's West Side. By the time he turned twenty, he had become the Gophers' unchallenged leader by virtue of brute, merciless force. Despite his almost frail appearance, this convicted murderer earned the reputation of a tough and ruthless gangster worthy of the nickname 'the Killer'. As it did for Schultz, becoming the proprietor of a well-known jazz club catering to the gentry of white Manhattanites provided a cover of respectability that proved useful for Madden's criminal activities behind closed doors.

Madden's taste was as woeful as his murderous character. More than half a century after the American Civil War, New York's flashiest nightclub saw fit to boast the ornamentation of a mock southern plantation:

> The bandstand was done up as white-columned mansion, the backdrop painted with cotton bushes and slave quarters. The racial fantasy extended well beyond the décor. All the performers were black – or, in the case of the chorus girls, café au lait – and all the patrons white, if not by force of law, then by force of the thugs at the door.[21]

In the early twentieth century a new generation of gangsters were emerging who scorned the Sicilian Old World 'mumbo-jumbo' and the stress on respect and honour. These included Charles 'Lucky' Luciano, who despised Masseria and his focus on long-standing feuds with gangsters from this or that Italian town, who had crossed his family by word or deed in times past. As far as Luciano was concerned, this was a major distraction from securing the influence that enabled long-term routes to making money. He joined forces early in his career with the Jewish gangster Meyer Lansky, and both were protégés of 'the Fixer' Arnold Rothstein, a multimillionaire gambler and criminal financier. Rothstein is best known as the man who fixed the 1919 baseball World Series. He was more than a gambling fixer, however, and is credited with being the first criminal to understand fully the importance of 'organization' in organized crime and its links to extorting influence with police, politicians and judges. He was the model for the character 'the Brain' in Runyon's Broadway stories.

Just before Prohibition, Rothstein had spotted the opportunity for a network to distribute illegal drugs. The influenza pandemic resulted in an increase of drug-takers, as many people turned to drugs to get through it. In April 1919 the first federal drug agents raided physicians and druggists who were prescribing opium, cocaine and heroin. Soon afterwards, Bellevue Hospital set up its first drug treatment centre. Many doctors were reluctant to treat addiction, which was seen as a self-inflicted and morally reprehensible condition, and it was recommended that the Department of Health discontinue any sort of drug treatment programme. The problem was seen as a political matter, not a medical one. Politically, drug treatment was regarded as a clear vote-losing issue, one that might suggest the politician was not morally upright and in support of wholesome values, while illicit drug supply was not even a consideration in terms of campaigning on law and order. The journalist Jimmy Breslin reported:

Arnold Rothstein, the Broadway gangster who always heard the first moan of human weakness and rapidly calculated how he could earn money on it, sat on a bench in the waiting room at Bellevue and ate an apple and observed the derelicts writhing in the hallway outside the emergency room . . . 'Nobody here wants to be treated,' Rothstein decided. 'They just want some drugs.'[22]

He decided to provide the organized distribution of drugs through criminal networks.

Rothstein was known as a man who had influence everywhere, not just through alliances with many different gangs but also via a vast network of police and political contacts. These connections came to the fore when arrests were made and cases for bootlegging, prostitution or gambling were due before the courts. It is estimated that of 6,902 liquor-related cases connected to Rothstein, 400 never came to trial and 6,074 ended in dismissal. Rothstein was in very deep with the Tammany Hall leader at the time, Charles Murphy, and changed the way in which graft operated, moving from deals with front-line police officers to direct pay-offs for political leaders. The huge profits of the Prohibition era meant that the power had shifted from the politicians to the criminals – so much so that Rothstein was able to demand (and obtain) changes to police procedure to make his rackets more secure.[23]

Who's Sorry Now?

Key politicians in New York, at city and state levels, both Democrats and Republicans, were firmly against Prohibition. Al Smith, Governor of New York State from 1922 to 1928, was a Democrat who remained untainted by the corruption of Tammany Hall. He was a member of the New York State Assembly from 1904 until 1918, when he first became governor. He then lost the next election before winning three times in the 1920s. As governor, Smith offered alcohol to guests at the state mansion in Albany and was responsible for the repeal of Mullan-Gage in 1923. Smith supported the flamboyant Jimmy Walker in his attempt to become Mayor of New York in 1925, since they agreed on many political goals, including improved parks and playgrounds throughout the city, better sanitation, and the extension of the subway system. They were also in agreement in their

Mayor Jimmy Walker with Franklin Roosevelt in 1926, when they were political allies.

opposition to Prohibition, but Walker had a very different approach to corruption.

Smith used the backing of Tammany Hall to get Walker elected, but his backers required that he change his approach to obvious flouting of the Volstead Act. Walker did not agree to give up booze but consented to be more discreet about his drinking and about his extramarital affairs with showgirls. Such activities were mostly relocated to a penthouse apartment that was in part funded by Tammany Hall.[24]

Walker's period as mayor was noted for the growing number of speakeasies in New York, and the lack of enforcement after he replaced the police commissioner with a former state banking commissioner who had no experience of criminal law. Since Walker did not feel that drinking was a crime, he discouraged the police from enforcing Prohibition law or taking an active role, unless it was to curb excessive violations or would prove newsworthy. His political fortunes turned after the stock market crash of 1929, when Cardinal Patrick Joseph Hayes, Archbishop of New York, denounced him, implying that the mayor's immorality was a cause of the economic disaster. Franklin D. Roosevelt, who had replaced Smith as Governor of New York State the previous year, was less supportive of Walker. Feeling that Walker was a symbol of New York corruption, Roosevelt set in train the Hofstadter Commission, a joint legislative committee formed by the New York State Legislature, chaired by State Senator Samuel H. Hofstadter, with its investigations led by Samuel Seabury, ex-judge of the Court of Appeals, to probe deeply into the police, the operation of magistrates courts and bribes relating to the award of public works contracts.

In December 1929 Judge Albert Vitale was robbed during a dinner party by members of organized crime gangs, but the stolen items were swiftly returned after the magistrate made some calls to well-placed Mafia members. This prompted questions from the press about links between organized crime and the judiciary. It was then revealed that Vitale owed nearly $20,000 to Rothstein. The judge was investigated and asked to explain how he had built up a sum of $165,000 – four times his official salary – over just four years. After Vitale was removed from the bench, further official investigations revealed that the Brooklyn judge W. Bernard Vause had been paid $190,000 in return for obtaining pier leases for a shipping company, and that another city judge, George F. Ewald, had paid Tammany Hall $10,000 for the replacement seat of Vitale.

Meanwhile the Seabury investigation revealed a highly organized conspiracy between judges, attorneys and police to frame working-class people, often women, who had no knowledge of the law or funds to pay for legal defence, by paying false witnesses and extorting money from defendants. Victims were made to understand that conviction and a prison sentence were a foregone conclusion unless money was paid through certain attorneys to court personnel, police and others.

Charges of corruption were brought against those involved in the scheme. Walker brought about his own downfall by reneging on his agreement to pay the police commissioner's costs. This spread the net further into the workings of Tammany Hall after a judge was asked to stay the sentencing of the chief of the Bureau of Fire Prevention for taking bribes to award permits for garages and petrol stations. The use of the network of Tammany Hall-linked Democrat political clubs for gambling was investigated, as was the fact that clubs were routinely being tipped off before raids. It had been noted that a large number of Rothstein's associates had been present when Police Commissioner Lewis Joseph Valentine's Confidential Squad swooped on one of the clubs, for which members could not account. When questioned, Walker refused to give details of his personal bank accounts and claimed that payments he had received were not bribes but 'goodwill gifts' from supporters. Although Roosevelt was anxious about losing the support of Tammany Hall for his presidential bid, he also felt that if he were seen to be weak in dealing with Walker, it would influence voters. With his nomination for the presidential race censured, he persuaded Walker to resign in 1932.

By the end of the decade the tide had turned on Prohibition. It had proved to be a complete failure in terms of establishing a 'dry' society with temperance as the norm. The unintended negative consequences were plain to see in terms of the level of casual lawbreaking when it came to buying and selling alcoholic drinks, but also growing problems with gambling, drugtaking and corruption in public office, all of which were linked to the increased prevalence and violence of organized crime. The Volstead Act was dismantled piece by piece. The Blaine Act of 20 February 1933 put forward proposals for the Twenty-First Amendment, which would repeal the Eighteenth, while the Cullen-Harrison Act of 21 March allowed low-alcohol beer and wine to be manufactured and sold. The Blaine Act was passed by all states over the course of 1933, returning decisions on alcohol to state control. The individual states in turn passed legislation on alcohol down to county level, a circumstance that has resulted in some 'dry' counties, mostly in the southern states.

Unfortunately, dismantling the power of organized crime was not an easy undertaking. The circumstances of Prohibition had allowed a rapid rise in the money the gangs made, which translated to a huge increase in power and the establishment of networks, alliances and power-broking. The criminal infrastructure that grew up during Prohibition has proved ruthless, nimble and inventive in finding new ways to secure profits and influence to the present day.

3

Broadway Melody

It wasn't only the pursuit of booze that put the roar into the Roaring Twenties. From the streets of New York, a new tempo arose through the popular songs of Tin Pan Alley, the nickname for West 28th Street between Fifth and Sixth avenues, which was the hub of music publishers in the city. Eventually, 'Tin Pan Alley' took in the whole New York industry of songwriters, lyricists, composers and music publishers, who turned out the popular songs of the day. The city's enterprising publishers were the first music companies to specialize in popular songs, rather than hymns or classical music.

In the theatre world, it seemed that audiences had developed an insatiable appetite for comedies and musicals. New York stages hosted more than two hundred new productions each season. Manhattanites headed in droves for Broadway's famed 'Great White Way', named for the white lights that picked out the names of the shows and stars in front of each theatre. Immortal names burst on to the scene. Topping the stage reviews were Rodgers and Hart's *The Girl Friend* (1926) and George and Ira Gershwin's *Funny Face* (1927). The Gershwin brothers were the songwriting team whose voice became synonymous with the craze for musicals. The new vogue was embodied in their syncopation-mad triumph *Lady, Be Good* (1924), a rousing combination of jazz, blues and energetic dancing encapsulated in the new musical comedy show. Songs written by Broadway composers in the 1920s have become standards, among them the Gershwins' 'The Man I Love', Irving Berlin's 'Blue Skies', Rodgers and Hart's 'The Blue Room' and Cole Porter's 'What Is This Thing Called Love?'

The public's appetite for popular songs was fuelled by the constant creation of new shows for Broadway. During the 1920s, the phenomenon of Broadway (between 41st and 53rd streets) as the home of theatre in New York was consolidated. This was a result of the large number of theatres that were built around Times Square and along the cross streets in the early years of the decade. By 1927 there were 71 theatres in those streets alone.[1] They included the Apollo Theatre, which opened in 1920 and was home to the *George White's Scandals* revue shows for most of the decade, the Ambassador Theatre, opened in 1921, the Earl Carroll Theatre in 1922 (playing *Earl Carroll's Vanities* revue shows), Chanin's 46th Street Theatre (later the Richard Rodgers Theatre), opened in 1925, the Biltmore Theatre in the same year, and the Hammerstein and Royale theatres, which opened in 1927, to name but a few. Alongside the theatres staging plays and musicals, the area also boasted several cinemas, including the huge Paramount Theatre (1926) and the Roxy Theatre, the largest theatre in the world at the time of its opening in 1927.

The 1920s brought an explosion of musicals, many of them comic, that gratified the public's craving for light-hearted entertainment. A tidal wave of memorable songs swept the city, boosted by sales of sheet music, which was the primary route to popularization before the mass ownership of gramophones and radios. As we saw in Chapter One, the latter became a common household purchase in the 1920s, and between 1923 and 1930 some 60 per cent of families in the United States bought a radio set. The 'Broadway musical' as a distinct genre evolved over the first twenty years of the century, merging aspects of vaudeville shows – in which a series of speciality acts were increasingly linked by a loose narrative and songs sung by the different acts – with an Americanized form of the European romantic or comedy-romance operetta. The operettas were seen as reflecting a distant and old-fashioned culture and were often set in romanticized European historical eras. Broadway shows tended to have snappier plots, a contemporary (usually American) setting and songs with a new sound, featuring modern rhythms, often borrowing from ragtime and jazz, with catchy tunes and 'smart' lyrics.

Broadway musicals are all essentially love stories. As such, they celebrate women, but this is almost exclusively about feminine appearance or at least the traditional 'feminine' virtues of kindness, sympathy and homemaking. There is also a good deal of making fun of women as predictable, weak and confused. The new women of the 1920s to some extent demanded a different kind of love story, one in which the woman has a little more punch, sometimes comes out on top, and sometimes very actively pursues the man she wants. But even where the female is a genuine 'lead' role, there is the inevitable 'happy ever after' ending of matrimony for the couple.

One of the first Broadway musicals was *Irene*, which opened at the Vanderbilt Theatre on West 48th Street in November 1919. With lyrics by Joseph McCarthy (not to be confused with the notorious politician of the 1940s and '50s) and music by Harry Tierney, based on the play *Irene O'Dare* by James Montgomery, it is set in New York's Upper West Side. It tells the story of an Irish immigrant shop assistant who is introduced to high society when she is hired to help a leading socialite redecorate her mansion. The lightweight plot includes traditional romantic elements – poor, hard-working girl loved by rich tycoon, business success of outsiders, long-lost love and disguised identity – all in the contemporary early twentieth-century setting of New York. The songs are a mix of traditional reflective ballads, such as 'Alice Blue Gown', and jazzy numbers, among them 'Skyrocket' and the fast-paced 'Hobbies'. The *New York Times* declared that, along with girls, music and jokes, what *Irene* had to offer was a lot of catchy music and a scrappy title character whom audiences were quick to fall for, together with that rarity for Broadway shows at the time: a plot. The show was a huge hit and played at the theatre until

1921, with 675 performances, a run that set the record for more than two decades. 'Irene is pleasantly embodied by Edith Day, who is pretty to behold, who sings passably and who dances rather better than that,' the *New York Times* commented. 'Indeed, everybody in the company dances a little bit better than they do anything else.'[2]

Blue Skies

Despite the development of the distinctive 'Broadway musical', operettas continued to be popular with audiences throughout the decade, and one of the most successful composers in the genre was Sigmund Romberg, whose hits *Blossom Time* (1921), *The Student Prince* (1924) and *The Desert Song* (1926) continue to be produced for summer seasons and are popular with amateur operatic companies. Romberg served his musical apprenticeship pushing out songs for the early revue shows run by the Shubert brothers, Lee, Sam and JJ, the most prolific Broadway producers. At one time they owned 31 theatres in New York alone, along with numerous others across the States. Despite the pressure to keep churning out songs, Romberg managed also to write the music for full shows, including *The Magic Melody* (1919) with lyrics by Clare Kummer, one of the rare female lyricists and composers on Broadway. He followed that with the full score for *Blossom Time* with the librettist Dorothy Donnelly, adapted from a German original. Initially none of his full shows were an outstanding success. But the incredibly productive Romberg had a bumper year in 1924, writing songs for shows produced by the Shuberts, as well as *Annie Dear* for the impresario Florenz Ziegfeld and his biggest hit, *The Student Prince*, again in collaboration with Donnelly.

The theatre critics of the New York papers were hugely influential and could make or break a show with their reviews. Theatre was the main source of entertainment, and newspapers the primary medium through which the potential audience could learn about forthcoming shows. Two of the most powerful voices were Alexander Woollcott

Decorative cover for the sheet music of
Sigmund Romberg's operetta *The New Moon*.

and Robert Benchley, theatre critics who were both also known as
literary wits. They were members of the Algonquin 'Round Table',
a club of journalists, writers and critics who met every day for lunch
at the Algonquin Hotel on West 44th Street (see Chapter Eight).
Unusually for critics, Woollcott and Benchley later honed their skills
as performers, to an extent, performing monologues (Benchley) and
cameo parts (Woollcott). Brooks Atkinson, the *New York Times*

STRIKE UP THE BAND

theatre reviewer from 1925 through to 1960, was even more influential at the time but is less well known today, having stuck to his role of theatre critic for the leading paper. In contrast to Woollcott and Benchley, he aimed to focus on the shows, leaving his emotions out of his reviews. He did not find witty ways to highlight weakness, as many critics did, but it was noted that a short review was likely to be neutral or negative, whereas the more he liked a piece, the more he would write. In 1960 Atkinson had a Broadway theatre named in his honour – a rare accolade for a theatre critic.

Woollcott's reviews were an exhilarating mix of acerbic, witty comment and enthusiastic praise. He made no attempt to moderate his views, lauding to the skies what he enjoyed and trashing any productions that he regarded as 'hack' work. He was a literally larger-than-life eccentric among an assortment of unconventional characters. The entertainer Harpo Marx described him as something that had got loose from the Macy's Thanksgiving Parade, while the caricaturist Irma Selz said he resembled a great stuffed owl. There were no sacred targets when Woollcott unleashed his arrows. He once described Los Angeles as 'seven suburbs in search of a city', while for him the editor of the *New Yorker*, Harold Ross, looked like a 'dishonest Abe Lincoln'. Woollcott dismissed the famed pianist Oscar Levant as someone with 'nothing wrong that a miracle cannot fix'.

Woollcott joined the *New York Times* on leaving college and worked his way up from junior reporter to feature writer. He was always a keen theatregoer, and when the *Times*'s drama critic retired in 1914, Woollcott took on the role. From the start, he changed the style of reviewing, which until then had been little more than an edit of the producers' press releases, setting out the gist of the show and the brilliance of the starring actors. Woollcott's essays in the Sunday edition of the *Times*, 'Second Thoughts on First Nights', were the first reflective writing in the drama pages of the press. However, he also set a record for the shortest review of a Broadway play. The play was entitled *Wham!*, while Woollcott's review, in full, read 'Ouch!'

In 1922 Woollcott moved to the *New York Herald*, but two years later, when the *Herald* merged with the *Tribune*, he was shunted to the *New York Sun*, an afternoon paper which held little appeal for a drama critic. In 1925 he moved to the *New York World*. When the *New Yorker* magazine was started in 1925 by Algonquin Round Table members (and husband and wife) Harold Ross and Jane Grant, Woollcott joined as a contributor, having worked with Ross in France during the First World War on *Stars and Stripes*, an official newspaper to boost the troops' morale. In 1928 Woollcott quit newspapers and continued to write for the *New Yorker* and other magazines, while turning his hand (unsuccessfully) to play-writing and, more successfully, to hosting a radio show and later performing cameo roles written for him.

Benchley went into journalism after writing for the *Harvard Lampoon* while at that Ivy League college. Following a chequered history of editorial positions and freelance writing for a wide range of publications, including the *New York Tribune*, *Vanity Fair* and *New York World* magazine, he took up the post of drama critic for *Life* magazine in April 1920. He was therefore reviewing in the early heyday of the Broadway musicals and was known as a generous critic during his decade as a reviewer. He appeared on stage in 1922 with his monologue 'The Treasurer's Report' in the one-off satirical revue *No Sirree*. It was such a popular turn that its musical director, Irving Berlin, asked him to reprise the act for the *Music Box Revue* of 1923. This signalled a move into more performing, including forty short films and features for MGM, which Benchley continued alongside regular reviewing. He was a regular contributor to the *New Yorker* from its launch in 1925, working with fellow Round Table members Ross, Grant, Woollcott and Dorothy Parker.

One of the legendary Broadway characters in the 1920s was the producer, actor, singer and playwright George M. Cohan, known as 'The Song and Dance Man'. Born into a vaudeville family in the 1880s, he was performing from his earliest years and contributed his own songs and skits to the family act from his early teens. He had written and performed in his first Broadway play by the time he was 22 years old, just after the turn of the century. He continued to write, produce and perform in plays and musicals, and in 1907 he joined forces with Sam H. Harris as co-producer, putting on two or three Broadway shows per year for more than a decade. Their partnership was broken by Cohan's vocal opposition to the Actors' Strike of 1919 and his refusal to join American Equity. By the 1920s Cohan had been barred from acting as a non-union member, but he continued with his producing activities. He led the trend for musicals, producing the musical comedy *Mary* in 1920 and *The O'Brien Girl* in 1921. He wrote the story, music and lyrics for *Little Nellie Kelly*, his biggest hit, which opened in November 1923 and ran for 276 performances.[3] Altogether,

> the multi-talented Cohan, who contributed to 21 musicals and 20 plays, pioneered the natural transformation of vaudeville into song-and-dance shows with scripted characters and story lines, however lightweight. His pulsing tunes and swaggering street-wise attitudes offered refreshing counterpoint to the more sedate operettas with their ponderous romantic tales played out by castle-dwelling characters of privilege.[4]

Star Dust

To reach the top of the U.S. musical charts 25 times and have your songs rerecorded over the years by more than forty leading singers, from Louis Armstrong to Bob Dylan, your name has to be Irving Berlin. Undeniably one of the greatest songwriters of the twentieth century, Berlin composed popular songs for more than six decades, charting and changing public taste while influencing scores of composers. Having survived an impoverished childhood on the Lower East Side of New York, as a newly arrived Russian immigrant, Berlin made his start in Tin Pan Alley, having taught himself to play the piano while working as a singing waiter. After selling some early compositions, he obtained work with the Harry Von Tilzer music company and then as a lyricist for the songwriter and publisher Ted Snyder. His biggest early success was the song 'Alexander's Ragtime Band' in 1911, which was revived throughout the 1920s and '30s, with many stars recording hit versions. After a few years Berlin's songs began to be included in Broadway musicals, and in 1914 he wrote *Watch Your Step*, a revue to showcase the talents of the dancers Irene and Vernon Castle. By 1920 Berlin had written dozens of hit songs. He gained the attention of Florenz Ziegfeld and wrote songs for his lavish *Follies* shows, including 'A Pretty Girl Is Like a Melody', the lead song for Ziegfeld's *Follies* of 1919, which became the signature tune for all future *Follies* revues. It marks a leap of development in the style and sophistication of Berlin's music, which continued through his outpouring of songs in the 1920s. Realizing that he did not need to work for another publisher, he ended his connection with the firm Waterson, Berlin & Snyder to set up his own company, Irving Berlin Inc., and retained control of his publishing business for the rest of his life.

In 1921 Berlin partnered with producer Sam Harris to build the Music Box Theatre at 239 West 45th Street, expressly to stage musical revues devised by Berlin, for which he wrote the musical numbers and Harris was producer. As theatre owner, designer and composer, Berlin watched over every aspect of the Music Box Revue productions from 1921 until 1926: the themes, the music composition, the musical arrangements, the casting, the sets and the costumes. While the focus of many other revue shows was on the girls, at the Music Box it was on the music combined with the stylish stage designs and the refined setting of the intimate venue. Hit songs over the years included 'Say It with Music', 'Everybody Step', 'Shaking the Blues Away' and 'Pack Up Your Things and Go to the Devil'. Berlin also wrote songs for the *Follies* and other shows, including such enduring favourites as 'Always', 'Blue Skies', 'What'll I Do?' and 'All Alone'. He continued to compose songs and music from the 1930s to the 1960s, creating many classic film scores, when musicals moved to Hollywood from Broadway, including *Top Hat* (1935), *Follow the Fleet* (1936) and *Carefree* (1938), as well as the later Broadway musical *Annie Get Your Gun*, his greatest hit, in 1946.

The Gershwin brothers George (the composer) and Ira (lyricist and joint composer on some songs) worked their way into Broadway musicals from a variety of partnerships with other composers and lyricists from Tin Pan Alley. George spent several years working with the lyricist Buddy De Sylva on the long-running revue show *George White's Scandals* (1919–39), while Ira had contributed lyrics to several popular songs of the late 1910s and early '20s. In 1924 George shot to fame in musical circles when his ground-breaking orchestral jazz symphony *Rhapsody in Blue* was first performed on 12 February at the Aeolian Concert Hall, as part of bandleader Paul Whiteman's concert entitled 'An Experiment in Modern Music'. From then until George's death in 1937 the brothers worked exclusively together on their songs. Their first joint musical was *Lady, Be Good* (1924), with story by Fred Thompson and Guy Bolton, which included the title song as well as 'Fascinating Rhythm'. The story was a typical rags-to-riches tale of down-and-out brother-and-sister dancers who land jobs as entertainers for a social event on a millionaire's country estate. Through a number of contrived plot twists, both find true love and matrimonial happiness is assured by the end. It was sensational at the time owing to its daring use of syncopation and its encapsulation of contemporary sensibilities, including the style of stage dancing that the music facilitated.

Lady, Be Good was also notable for starring the dancing siblings Adele and Fred Astaire. They got into show business in 1905, at the ages of nine and six respectively, when their dancing teacher advised their parents that they showed 'promise'. The family moved accordingly from Omaha to New York, and after a year at stage school the Astaires had a vaudeville act and performed intermittently on stage, with gaps for full-time schooling until 1917, when they featured in their first Broadway musical, Lee Shubert's *Over the Top*. Their next Broadway hit was *For Goodness Sake*, which opened in February 1922 and earned them favourable reviews, but it was not until the show transferred to London's West End that the Astaires were hailed in notices as the stars of the show. The London run could have continued beyond its 418 performances, but the Astaires were keen to return to New York. They were signed up as the stars for *Lady, Be Good*, which sealed their reputation as leads who could carry a show. They went on to perform in further Gershwin musicals, including *Funny Face* in 1927. Their partnership continued until 1932, when Adele retired from the stage on her marriage to the British aristocrat Lord Charles Cavendish. Fred continued with stage musicals for another year but, following intense interest from Hollywood, felt that

George and
Ira Gershwin.

Adele and Fred Astaire.

he could reinvent himself better as a single performer in the medium of film. He went on to perform in many movie musicals, including *Top Hat, Carefree, The Gay Divorcee* (1934), *Shall We Dance* (1937) and *Silk Stockings* (1957).

Astaire's career in stage, film and television spanned more than three quarters of a century. He starred in more than ten Broadway and London West End musicals and made 31 musical films. Despite the many accolades for his unquestionable greatness, he remained as modest and elegant as the characters he portrayed. He once commented on his remarkable dancing ability, 'I have no desire to prove anything by it. I just dance.'

The Gershwins wrote for other musical stars of the day, including Queenie Smith in *Tip Toes* (1925), which satirized the Florida property boom of the time. This was followed in 1926 by *Oh Kay*, the story by P. G. Wodehouse and Guy Bolton, a Prohibition-era bootlegger comedy that originally starred Gertrude Lawrence. It was typical of the way in which the 1920s Broadway musicals were pulled together that Lawrence was selected as the star of the show before writing began. She had started performing on the London stage at the age of 10 and by 1920, at the age of 22, had worked her way up to become a leading actor in West End musicals. Her friendship with Noël Coward led him to write his musical revue *London Calling* in 1923 to showcase her talent. Lawrence first performed in New York on the tour of the subsequent *London Revue* of 1924. She was such a success in it that she was signed up for *Charlot's Revue* of 1926, which actually opened on Broadway in late 1925. Lawrence was singled out as the star of the show in a review by Woollcott, who called her 'the personification of style and sophistication' and 'the ideal star'.[5] She was therefore fairly well established on Broadway when the Gershwins wrote the score for *Oh Kay*, including songs that would suit her voice – all before Wodehouse and Bolton had written a word of the story that the songs were intended to carry. When the libretto was completed, eight songs from the Gershwins' score were cut because they could not easily be incorporated.

One of the great songwriting teams of the 1920s was Richard Rodgers and Lorenz Hart, the first team in which lyricist and composer received equal billing.[6] They started working together in 1919 with the number 'Any Old Place with You' for the show *A Lonely Romeo*. They followed it with eleven songs for the show *You'd Be Surprised*, put on by the amateur Akron Club in 1920, and composed the Columbia University Players' varsity show of that year, *Fly with Me*. That was seen by the Broadway producer Lew Fields, because his son was the choreographer, and Rodgers and Hart were asked to use three of their songs and write the rest of the score for Fields's next show, *Poor Little Ritz Girl*. However, trusting a Broadway show to such newcomers caused a rethink, and by the opening night in July 1920 eight Rodgers and Hart songs had been dropped and Sigmund Romberg commissioned to write additional numbers. The disparity between the two styles was picked up by the critics, who made such comments as 'the more serious songs are from Sigmund Romberg, and they are pleasing but hardly as striking as the lighter numbers,' and noted the contrast between 'Rodgers' hard, brisk tunes and Romberg's rich and syrupy melodies'.[7] Rodgers and Hart had an ongoing success with *The Garrick Gaieties* in 1925, with 'Manhattan' as the breakout hit that has become a classic. The *Gaieties* were reprised with a new edition in 1926, after which Rodgers and Hart composed *The Girl Friend,* which ran for 301 performances. They continued to write songs for revues and Broadway shows throughout the 1920s. Their success was mixed in terms of the reviews and runs of the shows, but they cranked out many popular songs, including 'My Heart Stood Still', 'With a Song in My Heart' and 'Ten Cents a Dance', before decamping to Hollywood early in the following decade to write a series of film musicals. They returned to Broadway in the mid-1930s.

West End Blues

Cole Porter's background – a wealthy establishment family in Indiana – was very different from that of Berlin, the Gershwins and the Tin Pan Alley hustlers. Few songwriters have ever travelled in the places and circles that Porter made his natural world. A Harvard Law School graduate who played the piano for anyone who would listen, he was educated to his manicured fingertips and spent his best years lounging in wing collars against exotic backgrounds with the sleekest peacocks. If there is truth to the adage that money attracts money, it was borne out by Porter when, after serving as a volunteer in the French Foreign Legion (where he had a portable piano made specially for him so that he could carry it on his back and entertain the troops in their bivouacs), he married a sparkling debutante, Linda Lee Thomas, whose wealth matched his own.

Porter had some early success writing songs and the score for the show *See America First* (1916). However, it was not a major hit, so he gave up composing for a while and devoted himself to travelling. While on board ship returning to the States, he met the Broadway producer and comedian Raymond Hitchcock, who hired him to compose songs for his revue *Hitchy-Koo*. One of the songs was Porter's first big hit, 'Old Fashioned Garden'. However, when he received an inheritance that allowed him to travel even more widely, Porter left the Broadway scene for several years. His next foray into musicals

Cole Porter.

was with the score of *Greenwich Village Follies* of 1924. Again, this was not a hit, and the songs he had contributed were gradually dropped during the Broadway run. Frustrated by the public response to most of his work, Porter nearly gave up songwriting as a career, although he continued to compose songs for friends. However, he went on to write numerous musicals, contributing both lyrics and score (unusually among Broadway composers), including *Paris* (1928), which included one of his most enduring hits, 'Let's Do It'. It had an approach to sex that was novel for the time, considering it fun and normal, rather than naughty or, conversely, coyly romantic, as in the usual contemporary musical treatments. This show was a hit and finally Porter was hailed as a top songwriter on Broadway.

Porter inhabited two worlds, Broadway and international high society, where he was famous for renting luxurious apartments in Paris and New York and palaces in Venice. These became fashionable salons that attracted the musical, theatrical and literary stars of the day. His apartment in Paris was famous for its walls of mirrors, and furniture upholstered in zebra skin. His home in Venice was where Robert Browning, the poet, had died. In New York he also kept up two apartments in the Waldorf-Astoria, one as a residence, the other to work in.

Porter threw these venues open to his circle of friends by holding lavish parties. Notable extravagances for these gatherings included hiring the entire Ballets Russes and, on another occasion, hiring fifty gondoliers as footmen. His experience of the exotic side of life came through in his urbane lyrics, with their witty phrasing and rhymes. This was coupled with his original compositional style, which was not influenced solely by the style or rhythm that was fashionable on Broadway that season, but rather grounded in his formal music studies (also undertaken at Harvard). By the 1930s Porter was one of the major songwriters on Broadway. He continued writing successful shows after a serious riding accident in 1937 left him with permanent injuries to his legs. Although he failed to secure major successes for some time during and after the Second World War, when his sophistication and high-society slant were somewhat out of fashion, his career revived with the score of *Kiss Me, Kate* in 1948. He continued to write hit stage and film musicals throughout the 1950s.

The musicals of New York continued throughout the 1920s in their wisecracking, fast-paced, dancing way. Hundreds of shows were never revived after their initial run, although the songs have endured as popular favourites and some were recycled into newer shows. The mould was broken at the end of 1927 with the opening of *Show Boat*, with lyrics by Oscar Hammerstein II and music by Jerome Kern, based on the 1926 novel of the same title by Edna Ferber, one of the writers who assembled at the Algonquin Round Table. Halfway through reading the novel in 1926, Kern called Hammerstein with the idea of a musical show based on the book. *Show Boat* had all the must-have ingredients of a hit show: great story, original and moving score, memorable lyrics. It also had a great production by Florenz Ziegfeld, who was known for his lavish revue shows: 'In a rare act of theatrical courage, Ziegfeld took a fancy to the Kern and Hammerstein work and invested it with his showmanly flair.'[8] It opened at the Ziegfeld Theatre on Broadway on 27 December 1927, to enthusiastic reviews. The story follows the lives of the performers, stagehands and dock workers on the *Cotton Blossom*, a Mississippi River show boat, over forty years of American history. The show's hit songs included 'Make Believe', 'Ole Man River', 'Can't Help Lovin' Dat Man' and 'Why Do I Love You?' The size of its ambition and its cast reflected the buoyancy of Broadway, which was at its peak in the 1927–8 season, when no fewer than 264 shows were produced in 70 theatres.

Show Boat took forward a style that had already been emerging in musicals, in which the songs are key to moving the plot along and illustrating character and motivation. Many of the frothy Broadway musicals, conversely, had to work hard to link together catchy songs and force them into a storyline. As Hammerstein put it, 'the song

The original production of Kern and Hammerstein's *Show Boat*, 1927.

is the servant of the play.'[9] Nothing like *Show Boat* had been seen
before on Broadway, and it was an important event in the history of
American theatre. However, this foray into a gritty and gripping topic
– the ongoing American conflict of racism, segregation and mixed
relationships – did not set the stage for a sea change in the direction
of the musical over the next few years. After 1929, as the reverbera-
tions of the financial crash continued, audiences who could afford
the price of a show ticket wanted not stories of social injustice but
rather glamour, escapism and light-hearted entertainment.

A Pretty Girl Is Like a Melody

For glamour alone, nothing could beat the Ziegfeld *Follies*, which were
hugely popular throughout the 1920s. They were staged for fifteen
years at the New Amsterdam Theatre, a renovated Art Nouveau gem
that later fell into disrepair to become the badly tarnished crown
jewel in a string of historic playhouses along 42nd Street, before its

later renovation in 1995.[10] Florenz Ziegfeld was acclaimed by his contemporaries as the inventor of show business, the visionary who laid the foundations for the musical galas that took the city by storm in the 1920s. The *Follies* he created were inspired by the Parisian Folies-Bergère cabaret music hall, which he had visited before the First World War. During the 1920s Ziegfeld created thirty elaborate productions, mainly in celebration of his fascination with feminine glamour. The trim, immaculately attired son of Belgian and German immigrants was a trendsetter in the world of entertainment, breaking with traditional Victorian burlesque and music-hall comedy routines to bring the genre of musical drama to its peak. His wife, the actor Billie Burke, saw in her husband a man in endless pursuit of pleasure: 'The world was a place created just for fun, and Flo Ziegfeld, of all people in the world in this peculiar era, was the best-equipped man for having that fun.'[11]

The revue shows started with the *Follies of 1907*, which shocked some critics as the revue girls showed their bloomers. By the 1920s the *Follies* were an established feature of Broadway and the girls were showing a bit more than bloomers, yet the shows retained an air of stylishness and glamour, rather than being tawdry or edging into burlesque. For Ziegfeld only the best would do for the productions, which were renowned for their lavish sets and costumes. Every dollar had to show when it was on the stage, and each show cost as much as $200,000 to produce (roughly $3.5 million today). Many of the elaborate settings were designed by the architect Joseph Urban, who also designed the classic interiors of the Ziegfeld Theatre. Ziegfeld hired the top performers, employed great designers to create the lavish costumes, and commissioned some of the most popular Tin Pan Alley songwriters to provide the music. Hit songs of the decade that started out as *Follies* numbers include 'Dreams for Sale' by James F. Hanley and Herbert Reynolds, 'Second Hand Rose', written by Grant Clarke and Hanley for Fanny Brice, and Berlin's 'Shaking the Blues Away', sung by Ruth Etting in the *Follies of 1927*.

Ziegfeld discovered many stars of the day, giving an early boost to the careers of Eddie Cantor, Mary Eaton, Will Rogers, W. C. Fields and Nora Bayes. Although he included them in the *Follies* line-up, Ziegfeld had neither time for comics nor much of a sense of humour:

> Half the great comedians I've had in my shows that I paid a lot of money to and who made my customers shriek were not only not funny to me, but I couldn't understand why they were funny to anybody. You'd be surprised how many of my expensive comics I've run out on and locked myself in my office when they were on stage.[12]

A great discovery of Ziegfeld's was Fanny Brice, one of the most versatile female performers on Broadway. Brice, a native New Yorker, was born to Hungarian Jewish immigrants. In 1908, at the age of seventeen, she dropped out of school to work in her first burlesque revue, *The Girls from Happy Land*. Two years later she began her almost thirty-year association with Ziegfeld. Brice was a comedienne, telling stories of Jewish life in the Bronx, but could switch to perform as a strong, soulful singer, introducing such songs as 'My Man' and 'Rose of Washington Square' to audiences. In 1924 she was earning $2,500 a week – which compares favourably with the average weekly income of $63 in the United States in the early 1920s. Her pay supported a Central Park West town house and a Long Island farmhouse for weekends.[13] If Ziegfeld failed to find amusement in her comedienne routine, he was at odds with an adoring public who packed the auditorium to overflowing whenever her name appeared on the bill. Brice appeared in the *Follies* from 1910 into the early 1920s. After the successful stage musicals *Fioretta* (1929) and *Sweet and Low* (1930), she returned to the *Follies* in the mid-1930s, before embarking on a long career in radio. She was a witty, bubbly, optimistic person who – as well as her stage career with Ziegfeld – is remembered as the creator and star of the top-rated radio comedy series *The Baby Snooks Show*.

Above all, Ziegfeld developed the concept of the 'showgirls'. Separate from the all-dancing chorus line, the showgirls were simply there to look beautiful and be admired for it. The couturier Lucile (Lady Duff-Gordon) had introduced the idea of the aloof model in her fashion shows during the First World War. The girls were required to walk haughtily through the room in a move known as the 'Lucile Slither', and never to smile. These fashion shows became so popular

Fanny Brice in the 1920s.

Dolores, the ultimate Ziegfeld girl, in a typically elaborate *Follies* costume.

in New York that they moved from reception rooms to theatres. Having attended one with his wife, Ziegfeld decided to base a scene for the next *Follies* on a fashion show. He hired Lucile to design the costumes and decided to use her models for the scene. The models were not required to sing or dance, but simply to model the costumes and move across the stage or down a staircase in a graceful way, using the 'Ziegfeld Walk' to carry the most awkward-to-wear creations with fluidity and grace. The model 'Dolores' became the star of the *Follies* from 1917 to 1923, owing to her commanding stage presence and her ability to carry off the most exaggerated costumes and headdresses. Her star status was reflected in her earnings, which rose from $75 per week when she started to $500 a week on her retirement in 1923.[14]

As the 1920s opened, Ziegfeld captured a new audience with his *Midnight Frolic*, starring Jessie Reed, whom he enticed away from appearing in the Romberg operetta *Sinbad*. Rather than going on to a nightclub, *Follies* patrons were encouraged to stay for this late-night show on the roof of the New Amsterdam Theatre, complete with box seats and a balcony. Ziegfeld mechanized the stage so that it rolled back to reveal a dance floor, and installed a glass walkway that allowed the chorus girls to strut their stuff right above the customers seated below. The show was a little racier than the *Follies*:

The girls shimmying down the glass walkway above the audience were reportedly cautioned to wear bloomers but oftentimes the rule wasn't followed very closely. Audience members were asked to vote for the young lady he or she considered the most beautiful and to state why on cards handed out by the usher. The young lady receiving the most votes during the run of that Frolic series had her salary doubled. One of the audience favourites was the 'balloon girls', who encouraged male patrons to use their cigars to pop the balloons covering the majority of their costumes.[15]

Many *Follies* girls became stars of stage and screen, including Irene Dunne, Louise Brooks, Marion Davies and Barbara Stanwyck. Others were the original entertainment celebrities, their photos in the gossip columns of the papers, accompanied by breathless accounts of their clothes, jewels and love affairs. Dark-haired, mercurial Jessie Reed starred in the *Midnight Frolic* and the *Follies* in the early 1920s and was the subject of extensive media coverage for her string of marriages, five in total, of which the last two were to millionaires. Unfortunately, all her spouses found her too volatile a companion, and every one of the conjugal relationships ended in a messy and acrimonious divorce. That set her on a downward spiral, and by 1936 she was acting as a hostess in a Chicago nightclub. Reed's topsy-turvy tour through life ended in 1940, at the age of 42, when she died of bronchial pneumonia, penniless, a charity patient in a Chicago hospital.

During the same period Imogene 'Bubbles' Wilson was also star of the *Follies*, but her revue career had an abrupt ending when she was fired by Ziegfeld over her much-publicized affair with the married comedian Frank Tinney. Their tumultuous liaison was reported in the press from May to August 1924. This included the police attending a bust-up in Wilson's apartment, a subsequent case of assault brought by Wilson against Tinney, their reconciliation in August and her tearful farewell to Tinney when he sailed to Europe, as he was handed legal separation papers from his wife. Wilson was forcibly escorted off the ship when she ignored the departure whistle. This was all too much for Ziegfeld, who disliked what he felt was negative publicity for the show and feared 'disruption of the morale of my cast'.[16]

One of the most famous and colourful showgirls was Peggy Hopkins Joyce, who was on the stage only briefly but was famous for her flamboyant love life, before and after her stage interlude. This included numerous engagements, marriages to four incredibly wealthy men, and subsequent divorces. Joyce was written about for her series of scandalous affairs, her collection of diamonds and furs, and her generally lavish lifestyle. By the time she was twenty, she had been married twice and left her second marriage, to the lawyer Sherburne Hopkins, to pursue a stage career, making her debut in the Ziegfeld *Follies* of 1917. While travelling with the Ziegfeld show in 1919, she met the millionaire Chicago timber merchant J. Stanley Joyce, and in 1920 he became her third husband, with Peggy adding his name to that of Hopkins in her surname. The newly married Mrs Joyce was reported in the press to have gone on a $1 million shopping spree over the course of a week. Within the year, she left Stanley for the Parisian playboy and multimillionaire newspaper owner Henri Letellier. She sued Joyce for divorce, demanding $10,000 a month in alimony and attorney fees of $100,000. Joyce countersued, claiming that she had married him only to defraud him of money. Peggy was awarded $600,000 in the divorce settlement. She was also allowed to keep all the jewellery she had acquired during the marriage and was given stock in Joyce's timber company that gave her a monthly income of $1,500 for life.[17]

Peggy Hopkins Joyce.

By 1922 Peggy Joyce's romantic escapades had made her one of the most written-about women in the American press. She seems to have welcomed the publicity, since she granted many interviews and was happy to receive reporters in her bedroom, wearing the trailing, semi-transparent negligees that were fashionable at the time. She returned to the stage in 1923 in that year's edition of *Earl Carroll's Vanities* revue. Her fame was such that a reference to her in a song or revue dialogue was sure to get recognition and a laugh. 'I've Got Five Dollars' (1931) by Rodgers and Hart is one example, and Porter got in on the act with 'Why Shouldn't I?' from *Jubilee* (1935). As early as 1925, Anita Loos included a reference to Peggy's notoriety in her novel *Gentlemen Prefer Blondes*:

> And all of we girls remember the time when he was in the Ritz for luncheon and he met a gentleman friend of his and the gentleman friend had Peggy Hopkins Joyce to luncheon and he introduced Peggy Hopkins Joyce to Mr Spoffard and Mr Spoffard turned on his heels and walked away. Because Mr Spoffard is a very very famous Prespyterian [*sic*] and he is really much to [*sic*] Prespyterian to meet Peggy Hopkins Joyce.[18]

Makin' Whoopee

George White's Scandals started its long run in 1919. White, a dancer, actor, lyricist, choreographer and composer, had appeared as a dancer in the Ziegfeld *Follies* in 1915. He decided to start his own revue from the experience and proceeded to raise the production money while also writing lyrics and choreographing the show, as well as appearing in it. White's trademark style was a snappy, risqué show with a score heavily influenced by jazz. George Gershwin contributed five scores for the *Scandals*, and his enduring songs from these shows include 'I'll Build a Stairway to Paradise' (1922) and 'Somebody Loves Me' (1924).

Famous performers appeared in several of the annual shows, among them Ann Pennington, Ethel Merman, Paul Whiteman and His Orchestra, and Bert Lahr. The *Scandals* also popularized the dances that have become synonymous with wild Jazz Age parties: the Charleston and the black bottom.

Ziegfeld's and White's shows were by no means the only ones in town. Earl Carroll was another producer of extravagant musical revues throughout the 1920s, rivalling the *Follies* and the *Scandals* for their celebration of the female form and their humorous interludes. A showman, theatrical producer and director, Carroll – who could boast of a New York theatre bearing his name – was celebrated for his songs, dances and flamboyantly costumed ladies.

The *Vanities* got off the blocks a little later than the *Follies* and the *Scandals*, with its first show in 1923, continuing for eleven series. Carroll's shows tended more towards burlesque and humour, with less emphasis on the music and more on nudity, the girls picked for 'vivacity' rather than statuesque beauty. Carroll's affairs, wild parties and stunts made headlines in the gossip columns, boosting ticket sales. One of the first stories to get widespread attention was when he was arrested for exhibiting indecent pictures of the girls outside the theatre. Rather than posting the modest bond, he went to trial and the *New York Times* printed an editorial against the 'censorship' by which the pictures were required to be removed. The longer the debate went on, the more the box office takings improved. At the start of his trial, Carroll cited the various public places in the city where the nude female form was on display, such as the classical figures on the facade of the New York Public Library. He won the case, and the *Vanities* continued to push the limits of public decency laws.

The number of girls involved in the *Vanities* increased and the routines became more elaborate as time went on, and Carroll engaged Busby Berkeley as dance director, to design and choreograph the chorus numbers. During the 1920s, Berkeley was dance director for more than twenty Broadway musicals. He was known for his full-stage patterning, getting effects from geometric lines of dancers, and his numbers were among the largest and the best-regimented on Broadway. (He moved in the 1930s to Hollywood, where he was able to take his approach to its logical conclusion in the medium of film.) Between the tableaux and the chorus-line numbers, the shows consisted of vaudeville comedy routines largely based on conventional comic 'types'. By the time of the fourth *Vanities* edition, in 1926, Brooks Atkinson described these comedy turns as 'the same old stuff' in his review for the *New York Times*.[19]

One of Carroll's stunts turned into a scandal that resulted in his conviction and imprisonment for perjury. At 4 a.m. during an after-show party at the Earl Carroll Theatre in February 1926, a bathtub was wheeled on to the stage and champagne poured in, although Carroll later claimed that it was only ginger ale (Canada Dry, to be exact). The model Joyce Hawley climbed naked into the tub.

Earl Carroll with dancers from the *Vanities,* January 1925.

Carroll, standing on a chair, announced to the guests that they should grab a glass and form a queue to take a drink from the tub.[20] After a few minutes Hawley said she was too cold (according to her testimony, there was less than 1½ inches of wine in the tub), and Carroll called the drinkers away from the bath, handing the girl a towel. Hawley redressed and began to dance with the others again, the tub was rolled off to the side of the stage, and that would have been that – a risqué incident at another debauched Jazz Age party – had not one of the three hundred guests broken the unwritten rule that such goings-on were not to be reported in the gossip columns. Philip Payne, editor of the *New York Daily Mirror*, published a front-page story about the night. Immediately federal agents were called upon to act. Following the trial – a huge media circus – in May, Carroll was found not guilty of the liquor charges. It wasn't, after all, illegal to have alcohol at private parties: it was only illegal to buy or sell it. However, the judge found that Carroll had lied to the court about what the tub was filled with, and there were at least four witnesses to refute his claim that no one sat in the bath. He was sentenced to six months in prison for perjury.

Bye, Bye Blackbird

In May 1921 the new musical *Shuffle Along* became the unlikeliest of hits. It was written by the black musicians and vaudeville stars Eubie Blake and Noble Sissle, who performed as the Dixie Duo. The libretto was by Flournoy E. Miller and Aubrey Lyles, consisting of jokey dialogue based on their earlier play *The Mayor of Dixie* (1910). Despite being seasoned writers and performers, the four had never written a musical or performed on Broadway. The plot revolves around two crooked business partners, Steve and Sam, who run for Mayor of Jimtown, USA. They agree that if one wins, he'll make the other chief of police. They win – through a crooked campaign – and subsequently fall out, and a long comic fight is a central feature of the show. As they fight, the losing candidate, the honest, virtuous Harry Walton, vows to end their corrupt regime. Harry gets the people behind him, wins the next election, and runs Sam and Steve out of town.

Shuffle Along opened at the 63rd Street Music Hall, somewhat out of the way of the main theatre district, but with such infectious, jazz-inspired hits as 'I'm just Wild about Harry', 'Love Will Find a Way' and 'In Honeysuckle Time', audiences flocked to see it. Famous fans included George Gershwin, Fanny Brice, Al Jolson and Langston Hughes. Over its two-and-a-half-year run, the show launched or boosted the careers of Paul Robeson, Florence Mills, Fredi Washington and Adelaide Hall. Josephine Baker saw the show as her entry to the big time from a small touring vaudeville group. She joined the company at fifteen as a dresser, learning all the chorus routines and steps, and when a chorus girl fell ill, she stepped in. She then made the part her own by clowning on the end of the line, pretending to get the steps wrong, stealing the scenes. She was not popular with her fellow chorines, but the audiences loved her.[21] *Shuffle Along* contributed to the desegregation of theatres in the 1920s, giving many black actors their first chance to appear on Broadway. Once it left New York, the show toured for three years and was, according to the historian Barbara Glass, the first black musical to play in white theatres across the United States.[22] It popularized the black American musical, proving to producers and managers that audiences would pay to see black talent on Broadway. President Harry S. Truman even picked a *Shuffle Along* song, 'I'm Just Wild about Harry', for his election campaign anthem in 1948.

The downside of its success was that *Shuffle Along* became the model for all black musicals of the 1920s, and it set certain boundaries. Any revue that followed the model was assured of reasonable reviews and audiences, yet if a show left

what had become the standard formula for the black musical, disastrous reviews became almost inevitable . . . The result

Lyricist Noble Sissle with cast members from *Shuffle Along*, 1921.

of this critical stranglehold on the black musical was that *Shuffle Along* imitators swiftly became commonplace, as black authors and composers prepared shows within extremely narrow constraints.[23]

In 1926 the first of a series of *Blackbirds* revues was launched by Lew Leslie, a white nightclub director. The show featured the talents of the singers Florence Mills and Adelaide Hall with the dancer Bill 'Bojangles' Robinson in an all-black cast but with an all-white writing and production team. This pattern was repeated in numerous musicals featuring black performers over many years.

It is not surprising, considering the times, that the composition of Broadway musicals was dominated by white male writers and composers. However, as well as people of colour, a small number of women succeeded in getting into the business of music publication. They include Dorothy Donnelly, May Singhi Breen, Nora Bayes, Clare Kummer, Dorothy Terriss and Elsie Janis.

Most of these women started out as actors or singers. Female lyricists and composers tended to work with a male mentor and promoter, usually somebody who was already established within Broadway circles. Several women wrote with their husbands, and it was usually the wife writing the lyrics and the husband composing the music, as was the case with Terriss and Bayes. However, as their songs gained popularity, these women achieved authority and independence. For example, Terriss wrote with her husband, Theodore Morse, but also with the composer Julián Robledo. Bayes, who had collaborated on many occasions with her husband, Jack Norworth, continued to gain fame as an actor, singer and lyricist after their divorce.[24]

A few women were truly superstars by the time they turned their attention to writing, and many were noted for visiting the troops overseas during the First World War. Janis, Bayes, Donnelly and Ruth Etting were well known throughout the United States and Europe. Janis, who had been a star of Broadway since 1906, was dedicated to entertaining the troops on the front lines in Europe and raising funds for war bonds. Her wartime work was so highly acclaimed that she became the only honorary captain of the American Expeditionary Force. She had many talents, and also enjoyed a career as a Hollywood actor, screenwriter, production manager and composer. She continued singing and acting into the 1920s and diversified into writing lyrics and screenplays. She even produced an early Hollywood musical revue, *Paramount on Parade*, in 1930.

A small number of female composers did not rely on an established stage presence or collaboration with their husbands in order to gain recognition. May Singhi Breen was a divorcee and single mother during the 1920s and was one of the most prolific female composers of the era. Dubbed the 'Ukulele Lady', she arranged the ukulele accompaniment for many popular songs and was largely responsible for the recognition of the ukulele as a serious instrument. She successfully advocated for the inclusion of ukulele players into the American Federation of Musicians.

Clare Kummer was a professional playwright and composer who had a successful career from 1900 until the 1940s. As a songwriter, between 1900 and 1944 she published 44 songs. She also had thirteen plays produced, ran a theatre production agency, and was a scriptwriter for Metro and Paramount. Her plays produced on Broadway during the 1920s included *The Mountain Man* (1921), *The Robbery* (1921), *One Kiss* (1923), *Annie Dear* (1924, a musical with songs by Sigmund Romberg) and *Pomeroy's Past* (1926).

The two-act musical *Just Because*, set in New York, was written and composed entirely by women and ran for just over a month in the spring of 1922 at the Earl Carroll Theatre on Broadway. It has never been produced again. The book was written by Helen Smith Woodruff and Anna Wynne O'Ryan, with lyrics by Woodruff and Annelu Burns. During preparation of the production, Woodruff helped to organize funding for the show. Burns apparently sold her rights to some of the songs to Woodruff before the show opened, so it is no longer clear who wrote what. The music was composed by Madelyn Sheppard, who is credited with more than fifty published songs, several of which were recorded by many different singers in the 1920s. Woodruff, Burns and Sheppard collaborated on a number of projects over several years. A photograph from 1918 shows the three with the operatic tenor John Barnes Wells and sailors recruited for the photo opportunity, all singing from the sheet music to 'When Your Sailor Boy in Blue Comes Sailing Home to You', with lyrics by Burns and music by Sheppard.

Alongside the musicals on Broadway, there were also straight plays, which were generally regarded as more 'highbrow' entertainment. As well as revivals of the classics, there were many new plays each season, totalling an incredible 1,463 over the decade.[25] The outstandingly long run of the 1920s was that of *Abie's Irish Rose* by Anne Nichols, which ran for 2,327 performances. The second-longest run, *The Bat* (867 performances), was also by a female playwright, Mary Roberts Rinehart, with Avery Hopwood. *Abie's Irish Rose*, a comedy romance about a Jewish boy marrying an Irish Catholic girl against the will of their bigoted fathers, had had a reasonable run in Los Angeles but could not find a backer for Broadway. Nichols mortgaged her home and pawned jewellery to raise the cash to produce the play herself, opening in 1922 at the Fulton Theatre. It had mixed reviews from the critics, owing to its stereotypical portrayal of Jewish and Irish immigrants (long the stalwart of vaudeville comedy acts), but the public loved the show. Robert Benchley, one of its strongest critics, asked, 'Where do the people come from to keep this going? You don't see them out in the daytime,' as the show reached its 2,000th performance.[26] The answer appeared to be that the audience came in from immigrant neighbourhoods. They were people who would not normally venture to buy tickets for a Broadway play but were drawn by the pride in seeing their culture portrayed on stage, no matter that it was in comic-strip fashion. Advertising also played a part, with large billboards in predominantly Jewish areas of the city.[27] As it went on, the play itself became a phenomenon, as is reflected in the lyrics of the 1925 Rodgers and Hart hit *Manhattan*.

4
Crazy Rhythm

If the spirit of New York City in the Roaring Twenties could be embodied in a single word, it would unarguably be 'jazz'. This new, syncopated dance music erupted on to the New York music scene as an antidote to the gloom of years of global war and pestilence. Before long, the Cotton Club and other newly opened Harlem music venues were featuring such performers as Count Basie, Bessie Smith and Fats Waller. Jazz became the backdrop to a host of genres of popular culture. In literature, F. Scott Fitzgerald's *This Side of Paradise* (1920) confirmed the author as the philosopher of the 1920s flapper. Al Jolson belted out the music in his film *The Jazz Singer* (1927), while Eubie Blake and Noble Sissle's hit musical *Shuffle Along* packed in crowds of theatre-hungry New Yorkers.

The origins of this distinctively American style of music stretch back to the late nineteenth century and the community of black musicians performing in New Orleans. The first American jazz ensemble is acknowledged to have been the cornetist Buddy Bolden's Ragtime Band, which began to perform in 1893 as a grouping of street and marching bands. Elements of jazz existed at the turn of the twentieth century, but the actual development of the genre did not begin until around 1910 and the word itself was not widely in use until a few years later. This new music might well have remained a local speciality were it not for the mass migration northwards of black people in

Al Jolson in the 1927 film *The Jazz Singer*, the first 'talkie' movie.

1910, including a number of musicians, to escape the lynch-mob culture that prevailed in the Deep South well into the twentieth century.

There is a consensus among researchers seeking the roots of the word 'jazz' that it is a term of uncertain etymology. There are theories to suit every persuasion. A prevalent hypothesis is that it is related to 'jasm', a slang term dating back to 1860 meaning pep or energy. Others credit the Italian poet Filippo Tommaso Marinetti and his Futurist followers with the new word – they began using 'jazz' in about 1909 as an adjective to describe anything new. They believed it was the first Modernist word, since it used what they deemed to be the most modern letters in the Roman alphabet, j and z.[1] There are even those who claim that the word's earliest appearance in written English was in a newspaper article in 1912, quoting the baseball pitcher Ben Henderson, who had dubbed a new, wobbly curve ball the 'jazz ball'.

The mass relocation – a flight, one might rightly call it – in the early years of the twentieth century brought thousands of black people from the South to such safe havens in the North as Detroit and Chicago. There, if not exactly being welcomed with open arms, they at least enjoyed a measure of protection under the law. Boll-weevil infestations had left the cotton fields in ruin, and the North held out the promise of jobs for these former agricultural workers in flourishing industries, among them meatpacking and manufacturing. Chicago, in particular, was home to a variety of ethnicities, allowing more personal expression in the form of music. Manpower was in decreasing supply in the lead-up to the First World War, when the United States government instituted a ban on immigration from Europe, so assembly-line jobs were available in munitions factories in Chicago and several other cities. Even domestic work in northern cities offered higher wages and greater personal autonomy than in the South. Most urgently, southern lynch mobs were showing no mercy to any black person suspected of defying the rule of white supremacy. Small wonder, then, that the black population of Chicago soared from about 40,000 in 1910 to more than 100,000 ten years later.

Refugees from racial persecution arriving in Chicago and other cities of the North brought with them a musical heritage that, until that time, was almost unknown outside the clubs of New Orleans. Their music was Dixieland, an early style of jazz that developed in the Louisiana music capital's jamming venues from about 1910 onwards. It was, in effect, a fusion of ragtime, Negro spirituals and blues, and it first gained notoriety thanks to the Original Dixieland Jass Band, which later changed the spelling of 'Jass' to 'Jazz'.[2] Chicago's South Side became home to numerous clubs for performing jazz artists, creating sounds that varied between Dixieland and Mississippi Delta styles.

For the time being, New York City was consigned to the side-lines, while Chicago rose to become the undisputed jazz hub of the North. This was the preferred destination of black southerners during and immediately after the First World War, when tens of thousands of migrants flocked to what became known as the city's Black Belt area. Jazz made its debut in the Windy City in the guise of small ensembles, entertaining in bars along State Street and in other neighbourhoods in vogue with music buffs. In response to the enthusiastic response, show bands, radio groups and grandiose ballroom orchestras emerged to commandeer the limelight. Jazz Ltd, Dixie Hokum, the 11-11 Club, and the Basin Street Club (which played host to Danny Alvin and His Kings of Dixieland) were a few of these fashionable nightspots. Top billers, such as the pianist Jelly Roll Morton, drew crowds that spilled into the streets. So dense were those crowds that passing trolley traffic often had to be halted.

The moment was approaching for New York City to step up to centre stage, to be crowned the largest and most competitive community of jazz musicians to be found anywhere in the country. This came about largely in the wake of another migratory movement: the exodus from Chicago of young musicians who suddenly found themselves out of work after the city police initiated a crackdown on the city's speakeasies, most of which offered late-night jazz-band sessions. They had had a taste of the big time, and there was only one other big-time spot for them to ply their trade. Musical unemployment tempted many jazz virtuosos to board the Greyhound Supercoach for the 800-mile journey to the East Coast. As history was to attest, Chicago's loss was New York's gain.

The south–north journey that eventually led jazz talent to move to the East Coast had its counterpart in an east–west movement, one that washed up on the shores of New York Harbor from across the Atlantic. Russian-born Irving Berlin and Al Jolson from Lithuania are two names that resonate strongly in the jazz world, and most of the pre-eminent figures in jazz history who were not African American came from families that had immigrated from Italy, Ireland, Germany and Russia. Jewish people from Middle Europe, already familiar with a style of music that involved a bluesy use of the pentatonic (five-tone) scale and a feel for improvisation, were especially drawn to jazz.[3] By the 1920s, New York had become home to America's largest communities of black and Jewish people, who collaborated as musicians and songwriters respectively. An outstanding example of these European immigrants' enrichment of the New York music scene was Jolson, whose dynamic style of singing jazz and blues catapulted him to the top spot among the famous and highly paid entertainers of his day. Jolson popularized traditionally black music for white audiences with memorable hits such as 'My Mammy', first performed in 1918, and 'Swannie', written in 1919 by George Gershwin. Born Asa Yoelson to a Jewish family from rural Lithuania, he also acquired celebrity as an actor, in particular by reviving the Broadway hit *The Jazz Singer* (1925) for the big screen in 1927. This sell-out film holds the distinction of being the first motion-picture 'talkie', thus laying to rest the era of silent films.

New Yorkers were by no means strangers to innovative as well as classical music. Chicago played host to the jazz virtuosos from New Orleans and other parts of the Deep South in the years leading up to the 1920s, but once Prohibition had kick-started the move eastwards, the new arrivals who alighted at one of the several West Side bus terminals found themselves in what was indisputably the world's music capital. Carnegie Hall, the Metropolitan Opera House and the Broadway theatres had been offering entertainment to a savvy musical audience since the 1880s. As early as 1920, blues singers and Harlem stride pianists were making their first recordings.[4]

The significance of this relocation en masse to the Big Apple was reflected in the person of the 23-year-old cornetist Louis Armstrong, who set off on the eastbound journey in 1924. Armstrong established himself in New York and there, along with Duke Ellington, Fats Waller and others, he attained something akin to divinity with fans for performances that displayed a profundity of tone, technique and improvisation never before heard in the realm of jazz. The critic and historian Ted Gioia explains:

The superiority of Armstrong's musicianship, the unsurpassed linear momentum of his improvised lines, could only serve to make the whole New Orleans ensemble tradition look passé, a horse-and-buggy cantering by Henry Ford's assembly line. The New Orleans pioneers exit stage left, Armstrong on trumpet enters stage right, heralding the New Age of the Soloist.[5]

It was not long before Armstrong's talents began attracting widespread acclaim across the nation and even beyond its shores. European devotees took up the new musical craze with gusto, and for many jazz enthusiasts, Armstrong was its primary exponent. On a visit to New York, the celebrated Swiss-French architect Le Corbusier found himself in ecstasy after attending an Armstrong concert. His eulogy verged on poetry:

> Let's listen to Louis Armstrong on Broadway, the black Titan of the cry, of the apostrophe, of the burst of laughter, of thunder. He sings, he guffaws, he makes his silver trumpet spurt. He is mathematics, equilibrium on a tightrope. He is Shakespearean!... Nothing in our European experience can be compared to it.[6]

I'm a Jazz Baby

Satchmo (short for 'Satchel Mouth'), as Armstrong was affectionately known to friends and fans for his toothy smile and distinctive expression when playing the trumpet, stood out as a game-changer in the jazz world. The New Orleans native's career spanned five decades, during which he reigned supreme as one of the most influential figures in jazz. Armstrong never turned his back on his southern roots, yet without doubt he buried its traditions forever to fashion a new dynasty in his adopted New York. He ushered in the age of the soloist, and other musicians would sit at his feet in rapture, feeling the heat of his rising star. Many of his musical creations contained jazz solos of such compelling brilliance that the emphasis in a jazz performance was changed from the ensemble to the soloist.

In 1924, when he was still playing in a band in Chicago, Armstrong got a call that was to transform his life and, in consequence, the entire domain of jazz. Fletcher Henderson, a key figure in big-band jazz and one of the most prolific black arrangers and bandleaders of his time, invited Armstrong to play with his ensemble in New York. When Satchmo arrived in Manhattan, the biggest jazz name in town was that of the now all-but-forgotten trumpeter Johnny Dunn, who played with the Jazz Hounds, a noisy five-piece band. To their own astonishment, they had scored an unprecedented triumph when 75,000 copies of 'Crazy Blues' (1920), with vocals by Mamie Smith, were distributed to Harlem record shops in less than four weeks. Dunn remained a top biller on the New York entertainment scene throughout the 1920s, performing for Harlem audiences at the Lafayette Theatre and other uptown venues. He was a tall, immaculately tailored dandy who made little effort to endear himself to his fellow musicians. Few tears were shed when Armstrong descended on New York City like a force of nature, to blow Dunn out of the water. It was also Armstrong who provided the spark that made the big jazz band viable. His presence in Henderson's orchestra in 1924 changed a dance band similar to other dance bands of the period into a jazz band, the first of its kind.

Armstrong also gained enormous fame as a vocalist, his gravelly voice punctuated by bouts of wiping his sweaty brow with a handkerchief. He subsequently referred to his performances as a musician and singer in the 1920s as 'those awful glorious days', when he and his fellow musicians would rehearse almost every day in their own style of improvisation, with no reference to the diktats of musical arrangers.

Slowly but steadily, Armstrong began to exert an influence on the New York musical community. 'Brass players were the first to feel

Louis 'Satchmo' Armstrong, one of the most
influential figures in jazz, with his bandmates.

the heat of Armstrong's rising star,' Gioia continues. 'As with Charlie
Parker's innovations twenty years later, Armstrong's contributions
eventually spread to every instrument in the band. Don Redman's
arrangements, Coleman Hawkins' saxophone work – one by one,
the converts were won.'[7]

The broad-grinned fireball from New Orleans drew huge crowds
at such prominent venues as the Roseland Ballroom, the Cotton

Club and, in later years, Carnegie Hall itself. Recording studios lost no time in signing this dynamic new arrival to the jazz stage. Armstrong had been in the city little more than a year before he was scooped up by a multitude of studios, supporting such great singers as Ma Rainey, Maggie Jones and the queen of vocalists herself, Bessie Smith. He and Smith dazzled fans with their classic Parlophone recording of W. C. Handy's 'St Louis Blues' in 1925.

Armstrong was possessed of boundless energy for performing before his fans. In 1943 he moved to the working-class neighbourhood of Corona, Queens, with his fourth and last wife, Lucille Wilson, a dancer at the Cotton Club. It was there that he spent the last 28 years of his life. On Sunday mornings traffic would often come to a standstill in front of the house, when Armstrong emerged for an improvised al fresco jamming session.[8]

Armstrong was more than a great jazz virtuoso. It was he who moved this style of music on to the path along which it has developed for decades. Through the sheer power of his musical imagination and personality, he reshaped the limited urban folk music of his childhood in the Deep South, unlocking the potential that has made it part of a global culture. The testimonials that poured in from the biggest names in music leave no doubt that he was the unchallenged king of jazz from the 1920s onwards. For Ellington, 'If anybody was a master, it was Louis Armstrong. He was and will continue to be the embodiment of jazz.' Fellow trumpet virtuoso Miles Davis said, 'You can't play anything on a horn that Louis hasn't played.'[9]

Side by Side

By 1920 Harlem was home to more black residents than any city in America or, for that matter, in sub-Saharan Africa. Between 1910 and 1920 the city's black population soared by 66 per cent. With more than 300,000 new arrivals during that decade, New York's black community was soon twenty times larger than that of any of the city's other ethnic minorities. The number of black people living in Harlem almost trebled within ten years from 12 to 35 per cent of the total residents. Most of those who had joined the pilgrimage from the South eventually settled in that district, where a black community had been in existence since the nineteenth century. The result was that over the course of a quarter of a century Harlem's social profile reinvented itself.

In the first half of the 1920s Harlem was aglow with musical residents. It was largely working-class, but 'one only had to walk down Seventh Avenue to meet any number of black celebrities, like Ethel Waters, Florence Mills, Noble Sissle or Eubie Blake. And of course, Fletcher Henderson was a familiar face in the streets of Harlem.'[10] There was a Harlem Symphony Orchestra and a Harlem String Quartet, and black musicians were no strangers on the stage of that icon of Midtown entertainment, Carnegie Hall.

While Harlem was gaining prominence as the nucleus of black music and nightlife, white New Yorkers began to venture uptown to indulge in what in the early 1920s became known as 'slumming'. They were inspired to seek out black music, thanks to a run of theatrical productions staged in the familiar territory of Manhattan's Theatre District. When *Shuffle Along* premiered in May 1921 at the 63rd Street Music Hall (see Chapter Three), it had the distinction of being the first all-black show or musical to be presented in the Broadway area, written, composed and played exclusively by black entertainers. It became a landmark in the history of New York theatre. Along with the first Irving Berlin *Music Box Revue*, it also turned out to be one of the most memorable musical scores heard that season. It was the springboard for some of America's enduring classic numbers, from 'I'm Just Wild About Harry' and 'Love Will Find a Way' to such prancing, dancing pieces as 'I'm Just Simply Full of Jazz'.

The surge in the number of black virtuosos on the jazz scene demanded venues to accommodate an equally fast-growing number

Harlem was not only the home of jazz. The Universal Negro Improvement Association (UNIA) march through Harlem in 1920.

of fans from well-heeled Midtown, as well as the less affluent crowd from above 125th Street. Harlem was the jazz Mecca of the globe, and it was there that the nightspots catering to whites-only audiences established themselves. This was the sad irony of Harlem nightlife in the 1920s, during the height of the neighbourhood's creative powers: that the top clubs featured the nation's top black musicians, but only a white audience could take in the shows. Nonetheless, this was for many performers an exceptional forum to kick-start their livelihoods, for this strip of establishments soon became the hottest entertainment spot in New York. They were located in what came to be known as 'Jungle Alley', along 133rd Street between Lenox and Seventh avenues, so named for what became popularly known as 'jungle music'. The unique sound of jungle music was achieved by using horn mutes to imitate the growls and cries of wild animals.

Jungle Alley was a place for affluent Manhattanites to dabble in the saucy sounds of jazz, as performed by some of the most talented people on the scene. Gleaming Pontiac and Franklin sedans lined the streets, delivering partygoers to the Cotton Club and Connie's Inn, both of which opened their doors in 1923. Of the two, the Cotton

Irving Berlin, celebrated ragtime and Broadway musical
composer and lyricist, with his wife Ellin Mackay.

Club featured the most extravagant shows, charged the highest prices
and enforced the colour barrier most strictly. When the writer and
photographer Carl Van Vechten was once turned away by a Mafia-
hired bouncer, he vowed to boycott the club until black patrons could
hear Ethel Waters singing on stage. Connie's Inn was tucked away in
a basement near the Lafayette Theatre. The club had been a desegregated venue since 2013 and this is where a decade later Duke Ellington
made his New York debut. These were two of the biggest names
among dozens of establishments in Jungle Alley. Smalls Paradise was
another nightclub in Harlem, also to be found in a basement on 134th
Street. It was opened in 1925 by the black entrepreneur Ed Smalls,
and showcased revues that featured the club's permanent staff of
entertainers.

There was no love lost between the Cotton Club and Connie's
Inn. Unlike Smalls, the Cotton Club catered exclusively to white
audiences. Connie's was the inspiration of the Latvian immigrant
and notorious bootlegger Connie Immerman, who set it up in
partnership with two of his brothers. This nightspot boasted acts
by Armstrong and other greats. Its steep cover charge of $2.50, its

intimate atmosphere and its ability to hire famous entertainers made it unique among Harlem nightspots. Its rival the Cotton Club, at 142nd Street, also featured many of the most popular black entertainers of the day, Armstrong among them. There was an unsavoury link between both establishments, in that both thrived under the protective wings of two of New York's most notorious mobsters, Dutch Schultz (the power behind Connie's) and Owney Madden (founder and proprietor of the Cotton Club). Madden purchased the club – previously the Club Deluxe, owned by the first black heavyweight boxing champion, Jack Johnson – while Madden was doing time in Sing Sing Prison.

An assortment of other less stylish dives lined the streets of Jungle Alley. These suggestively nicknamed 'lap joints' numbered up to ten per square block. Typical among them was the Sugar Cane, a subterranean rendezvous also owned by Smalls, which could accommodate up to a hundred revellers, or twice that number on a

Jazz orchestra at the Cotton Club, a favourite Harlem venue of the 1920s.

Saturday night. The audiences were a racial mix, but generally most of the tables were occupied by black patrons, this being one of the few desegregated clubs in Harlem. Moonlighting jazz performers, such as the Bon Ton Buddies or 'Jazzlips' Richardson, would stroll in, fresh from playing at Connie's, to do a set in exchange for a bite to eat, washed down with an illegal whisky or two.

Drop Me Off in Harlem

'The whole world revolves around New York.' So exclaimed one of the most illustrious names in jazz history, the offspring of pianist parents, who turned up in Gotham the year Harlem's clubs began to make their appearance around Lenox Avenue. In 1923 Edward Kennedy Ellington boarded the Baltimore and Ohio Railroad 'Marylander' to seek his fortune in New York, encouraged to leave his home in Washington, DC, by none other than the famed pianist and singer Fats Waller. At the age of 24, Ellington had already acquired the sobriquet 'Duke', from his patrician demeanour. Something of a child prodigy, he played his first piano engagements while in his teens, at an ice-cream parlour in his home town. The piano was meant to fill his leisure hours, while he worked towards completing a degree in commercial art. But the die was cast when he joined up with friends to form a band whose drummer, Sonny Greer, had intriguing tales to tell of time spent playing in New York. Inevitably, the commercial art plans were cast by the wayside and the Duke set off for Gotham.

The Hollywood Club, a Midtown Manhattan entertainment venue between Seventh Avenue and Broadway, was in the early 1920s one of the chosen meeting places for jazz enthusiasts. After a brief closure, it reopened in 1925 under a new name, the Kentucky Club, and was said to have the hottest band in town, the Washingtonians, which later became known as the Kentucky Club Orchestra. By this time Ellington was attracting enthusiastic audiences to hear his piano talent there as leader of the Washingtonians, a group of exceptional quality that opened up unique opportunities for some of the greatest names in jazz, including the Duke himself. He was now welcomed by Harlem stride pianists as one of their own. This was the catalyst for his earliest recordings, such as the rare Blu-Disc and Gennett discs, featuring first-class soloists and sidemen, such as Greer, the trumpeter Bubber Miley, the trombonist Charlie Irvis and the arranger Don Redman.

Ellington and his five-piece Washingtonians were the main feature at the Kentucky for two more years before they got their big break and moved their act uptown to play at the Cotton Club. It was there that Ellington was given the chance to expand his talents. The club employed him to arrange and compose for a variety of dancers, singers, miscellaneous acts and theatrical revues. The five-man ensemble of the Kentucky Club now grew to an orchestra a dozen strong. Armstrong remained at the Cotton Club for five years, performing as Duke Ellington and His Famous Cotton Club Orchestra.

Ellington was in every sense of the word a pioneer in music. He infused his jazz compositions with Latin musical forms, creating a unified melody that became known as the Big Band sound. His innovation later became the hallmark of big-bandleaders of renown, such as Benny Goodman, Artie Shaw, Tommy Dorsey and Chick Webb.

For Ellington, the big band was not simply a group of musicians unifying an ensemble of instruments into one voice. He believed in letting the dissonant voices of each musician play against the others, and wrote music that capitalized on the particular style and skill of his soloists.

Ellington can be credited with creating a musical dynasty, but he was always generous in his praise of other Harlem jazz stars. His admiration stretched even to the likes of the clarinettist Sidney Bechet, a dyed-in-the-wool maverick whom Ellington upheld as 'one of the truly great originals'. The Duke even managed to bring this notoriously unclubbable individual into his band for a few months in 1926. Bechet, a native of New Orleans, was one of the

The Cotton Club in Harlem brought a white audience up to the streets of Harlem to see stars like Duke Ellington and Bill 'Bojangles' Robinson.

earlier pilgrims to New York, where he settled in 1919. He was taken on by Will Marion Cook's Syncopated Orchestra, and in that same year he joined Cook's band on a tour of Ireland and the United Kingdom, where they played a command performance for King George v. Bechet's temper was fearsome. He was sent to Brixton Prison for brawling with some women in a London hotel room, and was deported back to New York after serving a brief spell behind bars. In Paris in 1928 he became involved in a heated confrontation over a woman with the banjoist Gilbert McKendrick. Bechet pulled out a gun and fired at McKendrick, missing him but wounding several bystanders. This earned him eleven months in a maximum-security French jail, after which he was once again deported back to New York, where he blithely left his transgressions behind him and went on to lead a band with the jazz trumpeter Tommy Ladnier at the Savoy Ballroom.

Ain't Misbehavin'

When it came to volatility, Bechet stood in a class of his own among the jazz greats who made their mark in New York in the 1920s. That is by no means to deny the striking individuality and eccentricity that characterized other stars of those days, whose personalities were reflected in their nicknames, such as Thomas 'Fats' Waller, Bill 'Bojangles' Robinson and Bessie 'Empress of the Blues' Smith. Waller, a New Yorker, began his career at the keyboard as a child, playing the organ for Sunday services in a Harlem Baptist church. By the time he reached his fifteenth birthday, in 1919, he was displaying his talents as resident organist at the Lincoln Theatre, in what was at that time a predominantly white area of Harlem. His big break came the following year, when James P. Johnson, a celebrated pioneer in stride piano, adopted Waller as his protégé and schooled him in the art of swiping the ivories left-hand style.

Waller became a regular attraction at Connie's Inn. As a teenager he had once been hired by the Immerman brothers to work as a delivery boy for a delicatessen business they ran in 125th Street. Waller was one of the most colourful of the idiosyncratic artists in the Harlem entourage of the 1920s. At Connie's, he would park his considerable bulk on a piano stool, a bottle of whisky close at hand and a bowler hat or crumpled trilby perched on his head, as he flashed a pair of Eddie Cantor eyes as big as saucers at the audience. There he sat, expounding his musical talent as well as an inevitable touch of clownish wit, his white admirers lapping up every moment of the show. If by the end of the gig he found himself the worse for drink, as was often the case, rather than struggle to find his way home he would stumble across Seventh Avenue to a local flophouse, or doss at the nearby church. Slapstick antics aside, Waller produced legendary compositions for New York stage revues, songs such as 'Honeysuckle Rose' and the unforgettable 'Ain't Misbehavin', which premiered in the musical *Hot Chocolates*, the show in which Louis Armstrong made his Broadway debut.

Waller chalked up nearly 200 recording sessions, 450 compositions, and hundreds of radio shows and musicals during his relatively brief career, which spanned less than three decades. He was one of, if not the, most successful among his contemporaries in terms of his takings from musical compositions, but he nonetheless lived his life short of disposable income, a fact that can be explained by his nickname. Waller consistently frittered away his money on boozing and binge eating. Hamburgers six at a time, fifteen hot dogs or four steaks constituted a regular meal, washed down with as many as a dozen bottles of beer. Once, while dining out with Fletcher Henderson, he wolfed down nine hamburgers then said he didn't have enough money to pay the bill. Waller repaid Henderson by composing nine songs, which he gave to his dinner companion, including the famous 'Henderson Stomp'.

BRASS AND KEYBOARD formed the backbone of 1920s jazz, but feet and voice featured big in the picture as well. The remarkable tap-dancing maestro Bill Robinson became well known as 'Bojangles', a nickname that connoted a cheerful and happy-go-lucky demeanour for his white fans, despite its nearly polar-opposite meaning in the black community. 'Jangler', in the Harlem vernacular, described a contentious or irritating person. Bojangles lived up to his handle: he was an inveterate gambler in possession of a quick temper and a gold-plated revolver, who nevertheless adopted as his own the cheerful catchphrase 'Everything's Copasetic', meaning tip-top. Although he worked regularly as an actor, Robinson was best known for his spectacular dance routines. He pioneered a new form of tap, shifting from a flat-footed manner to a light, swinging style that focused on elegant footwork. The most beloved of tap dancers in the first half of the twentieth century, as well as the most highly paid black entertainer, Robinson claimed he could run backwards faster than most people could go forwards.

When Bojangles arrived in New York in about 1900, he challenged the tap dancer Harry Swinton, star of the stage comedy *In Old Kentucky*, to a buck-dancing contest at Brooklyn's Bijou Theatre. Bojangles won, hands down. This was a type of folk dance that originated during the era of slavery. Buck or time steps were inserted with skating steps or crossover steps on the balls of the feet that looked like a jig, a routine that Robinson executed while he chatted and joked with the audience. His star was now dazzlingly in the ascendent. He became an icon of black musical comedies, later a top vaudeville performer, and finally a leading figure of motion pictures, appearing in fourteen films. He was one of the few black performers to headline at New York's prestigious Palace Theatre. His unique 'stair dance', introduced in 1918, was distinguished by its showmanship and sound, with each step emitting a different pitch and rhythm. Onstage, his open face, twinkling eyes and infectious smile were irresistible, as was his tapping, which was delicate and clear. Robinson was noted as a philanthropist and a champion of racial equality, well ahead of his time. When he died, in 1949, almost 100,000 people lined the streets of New York to pay homage to their treasured, up-on-his-toes entertainer, as the hearse carried his body to Evergreen Cemetery in Brooklyn.

THE POWERFUL VOICE OF BESSIE SMITH set the tone for the eclectic assemblage of musicians and dancers that dominated New York's Jazz Age. 'She used to thrill me at all times,' said Louis Armstrong. 'It's the way she could phrase a note, a certain something in her voice that no other singer could get.'[11] Armstrong and Smith made several recordings, most notably the 'St Louis Blues' of 1925, which became a major hit, selling more than 800,000 copies. The song remains a fundamental piece of the jazz repertoire, and with Smith's deep resonance and drawn-out tones, it marks the differences between jazz and blues. It is said that the recording became the financial salvation of Columbia Records, which quickly offered her an exclusive recording contract. By 1919 she was leading her own *Liberty Belles* song show, and in 1923 her recording of 'Down Hearted Blues' brought her widespread fame.

Before that year had ended, Smith had recorded 26 more songs for the label, including the famed 'Ain't Nobody's Business'. The title was very much in line with the character of this no-nonsense woman, whose commanding 6-foot, 200-pound presence could be as overpowering as her voice. 'I don't want no drummer. I set the pace,' she was once quoted as exclaiming to a bandleader. She appeared alongside Bechet in the revue *How Come?* in 1923, but her explosive temper resulted in her being dropped from the show. Woe betide anyone who provoked Smith's wrath. The story goes that at a cocktail party at the home of Carl Van Vechten, she turned down a dry martini, shouting that she didn't drink dry martinis, or wet ones either. Whisky was her tipple. She then proceeded to floor her host's wife with a punch when the unfortunate lady tried to plant a kiss on Smith's cheek.

Smith's career ended tragically in 1937, when she was just 43, the victim of a car crash on Route 61 in Tennessee. Her grave remained unmarked until a tombstone was erected in 1970 by an admirer, the singer Janis Joplin, who herself died two months later.

Three O'Clock in the Morning

The Cotton Club might claim to be New York's undisputed venue of choice for late-night live music. But it was to the Savoy Ballroom in Lenox Avenue that couples headed to let off steam on the dance floor, which was known as 'The Track' because of the grooves worn by the shuffling of foxtrotting and Lindy-Hopping feet. Located between 140th and 141st streets in Harlem's heartland, the Savoy was

Bessie Smith, whose powerful voice earned her the title of 'Empress of the Blues'.

a block-long bubbling rhythm factory that, from its opening in 1926, set New York's jazz-fuelled tempo. On any given night of the week, hundreds of merrymakers packed the spacious dance floor, as such luminaries as Duke Ellington, Ella Fitzgerald and Count Basie supplied the tunes and style of moves that inspired the actor Lana Turner to acclaim it as 'the home of happy feet'.

Whitey's Lindy Hoppers was a professional group of exceptional swing dancers first organized in the late 1920s by Herbert 'Whitey' White in the Savoy Ballroom. White, who began his career at the Savoy as a bouncer and graduated to dancing waiter, began organizing exceptional ballroom prodigies in his spare time. The Lindy Hoppers ensemble took on different forms and a variety of names and subgroups, including Whitey's Hopping Maniacs, Harlem Congaroo Dancers and the Hot Chocolates. The name Lindy Hop itself is derived from Charles Lindbergh's record-breaking 'hop' from New York to Paris in 1927. The choreographers Frank Manning and Norma Miller (the latter of whom was known as the 'Queen of Swing') were the group's brightest stars throughout the 1920s. 'The Savoy

The Savoy Ballroom was a Harlem Mecca for music and public dancing.

opened the doors for all people being together,' said Miller. 'We were the first people anywhere who were integrated. We didn't have segregation at the Savoy.' In 2018, a year before her death at the age of 99, she appeared for the last time at the Herräng Dance Camp in Sweden, an annual gathering of Lindy Hop lovers from around the world, first held in the 1980s. 'A place like this is unbelievable,' she exclaimed. 'It's like Brigadoon' (the musical about a Scottish village that magically reappears once every hundred years).[12]

NEW YORK'S MUSIC FRENZY of the 1920s extended beyond the cluster of Harlem jazz clubs. The ballrooms that began popping up across the city epitomized the compulsion to shake off those gloomy years of war and epidemic. Their role models were Fred and Adele Astaire (see Chapter Three), the brother-and-sister duo who in the 1920s were hailed as dancing royalty and mobbed wherever they went.

After watching a dance session at New York's Grand Central Palace, the Philadelphia entrepreneur Louis Brecker was determined to start his own club. He partnered with a local brewer, Frank Yuengling, to open the first Roseland Ballroom in 1918. It was only a matter of months before Philadelphia's 'blue laws', prohibiting the sale of alcoholic drinks on Sundays, caused Brecker and Yuengling to move to New York.[13] After surveying several sites on Manhattan, they agreed to acquire the second floor of a run-down five-storey building at 51st Street and Broadway. Several months of restoration work later, the gala inauguration of the Roseland Ballroom on New Year's Eve 1919 attracted hundreds of foot-tapping fans, waiting anxiously for the doors to open. The appearance that night of the celebrities Billie Burke, Florenz Ziegfeld and Will Rogers, in addition to two hundred attractive, scantily clad hostesses braving the winter chill, plus the promise of hot music and dancing, acted as an irresistible magnet for the event. The two owners' business acumen paid off in spades. Their first-night receipts totalled $18,000, more than $300,000 in today's money.

Proving himself a skilled practitioner in outfoxing legal constraints, Brecker came up with a brilliant ploy to bypass a New York City law that banned competitions lasting more than 12 hours in a 24-hour period. In 1923 he announced that Roseland would be hosting a six-day dance marathon. He haughtily thumbed his nose at the 12-hour limitation by chartering a 60-foot sloop, docked in New York Harbor. At dawn, just before the 12-hour cut-off, eighteen marathoners strutted their way out of the ballroom, boarded a van and, gyrating all the way, were driven to the waterfront. From there, they sailed 3 miles out to sea into international waters, to carry on their dance competition beyond U.S. legal jurisdiction. (Brecker later dispatched a distressed telegram to the newspapers to report a hasty return to shore after dancers began dropping from seasickness.)

THE PENCHANT SHARED BY many New Yorkers for uninhibited whirling and gyrating in public places was not everyone's Prohibition cup of tea. There was a sizeable core of starchy – one might call them outright puritanical – members of society who demanded what they considered a higher standard of decorum on the dance floor. Bowing to pressure from this troop of moralists, who had taken their complaint to the police, in December 1922 the owners and managers of several top dance halls and cabarets met in the Hotel Astor to form the New York Ballroom Association. The choice of venue was not without a touch of irony, that hotel's bar being New York's pre-eminent gay rendezvous. Their brief was to act as supervising agent of all dancing in the city's clubs.

The final accord was submitted to NYPD Special Deputy Commissioner George W. Loft by committee members from the Roseland, Bluebird, Rosemont and Danceland ballrooms. It stated,

A high standard is a dance in which no position or step is over-suggestive, immoral or improper. Observation and experiment have convinced us that dancers, no matter how well-trained and refined, cannot keep time with some interpretations of current dance music without lapsing into movements undoubtedly similar to those now facing regulation by the police.[14]

Whether the carousers were ever made aware of any curbs being imposed on ballroom excesses, it was patently obvious that little if anything was done to enforce the new code of behaviour. To the popular Lindy Hop, Charleston and foxtrot were added a raft of newer, even more audacious dances. As was the case with these classics, the Texas Tommy was born in post-traumatic times, shortly after the San Francisco earthquake of 1906. The New York version was described by the dancer Ethel Williams as 'a kick and a hop three times on each foot followed by a slide'. Then came the turkey trot, a technique that involved hugging, accompanied by copious risqué swaying to and fro. Another popular leg-shaker was the Peabody, a brisk one-step swing routine named after the NYPD officer Lieutenant William Frank Peabody, a cop who was light on his feet despite his portly physique.

The party was far from over. In fact, 'moving into high gear' would be a more accurate description, taking into account the ever-expanding array of madcap indulgences, most remarkably that of dance marathons. In the years leading up to the Depression and, indeed, well beyond the Wall Street Crash, these giddy human endurance competitions flourished in New York City ballrooms. It was common for participants to take the expression 'dance 'til you drop' a little too seriously. In some instances, nursing staff and hospital cots were deployed to attend competitors who literally danced themselves into a stupor and collapsed on the floor. Pushing through the pain of hours on the trot, couples would often prop each other up as the numbers dwindled, with judges making their way around to enforce the rule that anyone whose knees touched the floor would be disqualified. In one case, a contestant named Homer Morehouse dropped from exhaustion and died of heart failure after dancing non-stop for 87 hours.

The bacchanal was by no means confined to crowds of revellers shuffling their feet across the dance floor. While Bessie Smith was belting out 'Alexander's Ragtime Band' and Louis Armstrong was trumpeting 'Hotter than Hot' to entranced audiences at Harlem nightclubs, high above the skyline the four flying boats of the newly formed NYPD Flying Squad were chasing daredevil aviators, who soared ecstatically over Manhattan's rooftops. It was symbolic of the sounds and rhythms that were transported in the 1920s from New Orleans to New York, there to be transformed into a high-flying style of music that injected vitality into the Big Apple, the launch pad for the world's greatest names in jazz.

5
Oh! Lady Be Good

The Roaring Twenties gave birth to a new kind of woman, one who drank, smoked and (gasp!) danced with members of the opposite sex in illegal speakeasies. The type most readily associated with the 1920s is the 'flapper', an impetuous, often reckless woman personifying youth and confidence, dressed in the new fashions and taking a carefree rush at the uproarious social life of the age. These headstrong damsels were beginning to exercise new freedoms, some of which – such as the increasing presence of women in the workplace – had started with the First World War. After the war, the major political change was women winning the right to vote.

Emancipation did not happen overnight. The flappers were a highly visible and vociferous minority, and age, family responsibilities, religious sensibilities and financial constraints meant that for many the 1920s were not markedly different from what went before or came afterwards. However, there is no doubt that for a decade young women were in the spotlight and making waves in a way not seen before. Despite changes brought about by the Wall Street Crash in 1929 and the subsequent Depression, the spirit of independence and fun was out of the bottle and would not be pushed back in.

Who was the 'flapper'? The term tends to be associated today with *Great Gatsby*-style parties, beaded evening shift dresses, cigarette holders and dancing the Charleston, an image based on the notoriously wild parties of Prohibition-era New York. But there were many different types of young woman who were considered flappers. These ranged from socialites, for whom life was one long party spent rebelling against propriety and Emily Post's celebrated guide *Etiquette in Society, in Business, in Politics and at Home* (1922), to college girls going out to make their way in professional roles, to working-class women who were making a bit more money as better job opportunities become available and were thus able to engage in the new pursuits of leisure and consumerism.

The term 'flapper' seems originally to have been a description of a young girl, compared to a young bird that is learning to fly. An article in the London newspaper *The Times* in 1910 stated: 'A "flapper", we may explain, is a young lady who has not yet been promoted to long frocks and wearing of her hair "up".'[1] By the 1920s the flapper had grown from a gawky girl into a brazen young woman.[2] This poem published in the *Brooklyn Eagle* in 1922 and entitled 'The Flapper' summed up one view:

> There is a girl who dresses neat,
> And takes a fellow off his feet:
> She wears low shoes and woollen socks.
> Sometimes the ones with the coloured clocks.
> And wears a hat with a turned up brim.
> She wears a scarf and striped tie,
> And certainly winks with a wicked eye.
> Of course, she wears a very short skirt.
> And all in all she is a flirt:
> This girl who is so very dapper
> Is my idea of the modern flapper.[3]

The description is very focused on clothes, and it is interesting that, other than the 'very short skirt', the garb is all quite masculine. This androgynous look is set off by 'winks with a wicked eye' and the estimation that she is a flirt. The girl is characterized as smart in both clothes and personality, and admired for being lively and flirtatious, rather than innocent. She is not lauded for the traditional female virtues of gentleness, grace and prettiness.

F. Scott Fitzgerald claimed for his wife, Zelda, the title 'The First American Flapper'. Zelda had certainly adopted many of the aspects of the party-girl persona early in the development of the flapper phenomenon, and sometimes took her social antics to extremes. She was the flirtatious belle of Montgomery, Alabama, the most popular girl at every dance, and already famous for her practical jokes when

Young Zelda Fitzgerald, *c.* 1919.

she met Fitzgerald in the summer of 1918. Once his novel *This Side of Paradise* was accepted for publication, Fitzgerald pushed for marriage, since he now had some money and standing in the literary world to offer her, and Zelda accepted. They married just after the novel was published in 1920, moving to New York to be at the centre of the literary world.

The Fitzgeralds partook of the metropolitan life of shopping sprees, Broadway shows and drinking in speakeasies and at private parties. Rivers of gin and champagne flowed and Zelda threw herself into the social whirl, identifying strongly with the spirit of the age. In the *Metropolitan Magazine* in 1922, she wrote of flapperdom as something that was already past the iconoclastic, trendsetter phase, under the heading 'Eulogy on the Flapper'. She recognized that elements of the trend were now becoming mainstream, adopted by schoolgirls and shopgirls, who were imitating the behaviour they read about in magazines and decking themselves out in flapper fashions through the copy designs and mass marketing of the style. Although elegiac in tone, her article set out a manifesto that many women would follow throughout the decade:

> How can a girl say again: 'I do not want to be respectable because respectable girls are not attractive' . . . the Flapper arrives at the knowledge that 'boys do dance most with the girls they kiss most' . . . Perceiving these things, the Flapper awoke from her lethargy of sub-deb-ism, bobbed her hair, put on her choicest pair of earrings and a great deal of audacity and rouge, and went into the battle. She flirted because it was fun to flirt and wore a one-piece bathing suit because she had a good figure; she covered her face with powder and paint because she didn't need it and she refused to be bored chiefly because she wasn't boring. She was conscious that the things she did were the things she had always wanted to do.

Now audacity and earrings and one-piece bathing suits have become fashionable, and the first Flappers are so secure in their positions that their attitude toward themselves is scarcely distinguishable from that of their debutante sisters of ten years ago toward themselves. They have won their case. They are blasé . . . Flapperdom has become a game; it is no longer a philosophy.[4]

While most of the flappers would not have recognized a 'philosophy', there was something in their approach that went beyond fashion and was more about attitude. Many women wore drop-waisted dresses with shorter skirts – after all, that was what was in the smart shops – but they were not flappers. The flapper attitude was to be seen and heard socially and to partake of what had previously been the solely male pleasures of smoking, drinking, driving and having more leeway to 'play the field' (a little) without losing one's reputation and becoming unmarriageable.

FOR WOMEN, SMOKING IN PUBLIC was completely unacceptable before the 1920s. As late as 1904, a woman had been arrested on Fifth Avenue for lighting up a cigarette, and some railway companies maintained a ban on women smokers in the dining cars to as late as 1929. The tobacco companies were much quicker on the uptake, however, and swiftly adapted their publicity to appeal to women. A wave of tobacco marketing targeted at women used advertising copy designed to prey on female insecurities about weight and diet. Many of these campaigns strived to entice women to smoke by using mainstream beauty and fashion standards to portray smoking as feminine. 'I do prefer Lucky Strike' assures a fresh-faced, bobbed-haired girl in an advertisement from 1923. In the late 1920s that particular brand was sold as a route to thinness for women by the 'Reach for a Lucky instead of a sweet' campaign. In 1927 this was fronted by a movie celebrity:

Lucky Strike advertisement from 1929: 'Reach for a Lucky instead of a sweet'.

'*Light a Lucky* and you'll never miss sweets that make you fat', with a picture of Constance Talmadge captioned 'Charming motion picture star'. Sales of Lucky Strike increased by more than 300 per cent during the first year of the campaign, from 14 billion cigarettes in 1926 to 40 billion in 1930, making Lucky Strike the leading brand nationwide.[5]

In New York, Prohibition had brought about a change in social life as men and women went out together to clubs and speakeasies. Women had previously not been allowed in bars at all, and it was acceptable for them to drink only in private homes or at private parties, where the usual offering would have been a punch or 'fruit cup' of fairly dilute alcohol. Many of the era's cocktails were designed to appeal to women, with added colour and sweetness from such exotic liqueurs as the violet parfait d'amour and vivid green crème de menthe.

Lois Long wearing a short dress and pearls at the *New Yorker* office,
in a staged photo contrasting her clothes with those of the 1890s.

Lois Long, writing as 'Lipstick' in the newly launched *New Yorker* magazine, wrote a nightlife column, 'Tables for Two', which included advice about coping with a hangover and the correct amount to tip the cab driver ($2) if you threw up in the car.

Long was taken on by Harold Ross, editor of the *New Yorker*, at just 23, having done a brief stint as theatre critic at *Vanity Fair* after graduating from Vassar College. Ross recognized that, as a committed flapper, Long could bring vitality and an 'In with the In-Crowd' vibe to the magazine. She was living the lifestyle, sharing a small apartment with the actor Kay Francis. She dressed in the latest styles and spent her evenings out on the town, going from one hot nightspot to another, smoking, drinking and staying out as late as she liked. Long continued in this vein after taking the job at the *New Yorker*, but now all paid for on the magazine's expense account, sharing her weekly adventures with its readers. According to the historian Joshua Zeitz, 'She became one of America's most insightful chroniclers of the new middle-class woman who seemed to embody the flapper's spirit and style.'[6]

Long was a firm believer in exhaustive first-hand research. Her nights were devoted to jazz, gin and jitterbugging, and she was known to appear in the office at four o'clock in the morning, usually inebriated and still in her evening finery. She would climb jauntily over the semi-partition to her office in her gown (having left her key at home when she set off for the evening) and start to type out a column, with the night's revelry fresh in her mind. Lipstick's columns would talk about how an evening that started at the 21 Club would progress to other Broadway clubs when the 21 closed, often finishing at a Harlem jazz venue in the early hours of the morning. This work routine continued every night, with Long developing a massive tolerance for alcohol, drinking cognac for preference, since she had been assured by bootleggers that it was harder to fake the taste and smell of brandy. In her columns, Lipstick made little mention of alcohol, tending to refer to ginger ale or glasses of 'White Rock', a popular mineral water. Those reading between the lines would be clear that she was visiting speakeasies, clubs selling liquor, and restaurants with 'private lounges' in which alcohol was served.

The 'Tables for Two' columns are full of dry humour, name-dropping of the celebrities that Long had seen at restaurants and clubs, and a knowing overview of the trends in dancing, fashions and entertainment. The columns brilliantly capture the feel of the Jazz Age and the frenetic drive to have a good time to the exclusion of all else. 'All the great minds who used to be absorbed solely in worrying about whether or not to order chicken salad, whether or not to Ask Him In, and the correct method of serving asparagus,' commented Lipstick on 17 October 1925, 'now seem to have concentrated on but one vexing problem – "Are they dancing the Charleston at the smart night clubs?"' She went on, 'the answer is No. And the reason, undoubtedly, is not that nice people disapprove of this pastime, but that nice people do not yet know how to do it.' She then writes of people 'almost' dancing the Charleston at the Mirador, where

> the dance floor is comfortably filled with very attractive people, the music is good ... I would go there more frequently were it not for the fact that at least five night clubs are opening daily, and each announcement sounds more alluring than the last. And what are you going to do if you happen to be the kind of person who wants to see everything that is going on?

In the same column, Lipstick describes an evening when, after the theatre, she and her escort went to the Rues de la Paix,

> the largest night club in town and[,] despite the presence of Venus covered with silver radiator paint, shuddering in a grove of lilacs at one end, one of the most attractively decorated ... the music is very good, and the show, which appears quite casually at intervals until quite late at night, is fair enough.

Frankly I do not know what the place lacks, but it is not very stimulating to me at present . . . As for the Club Caravan – *sacre bleu*, and all that sort of thing!

Club Caravan advertised daring stars of the stage in 'continental' costumes, but, despite first-night reports of a young woman clad only in a single red rose, 'what had they gone and done but draped her in green chiffon by the time we got there!' The column ends with the disappointing news that, having gone to check out the club at 10 East 60th Street, 'I walked up there one balmy evening at one forty-five and found it closed for the night – at a quarter to two!'[7]

Long was aware of the singular nature of her job, noting in one of her columns the two comments that offended her the most: 'The first is "How do you ever stand the strain of going out every night?" And the second is "Gosh, what a soft job you have, nothing to do but go out dancing!"'[8] On her salary, which had been raised to $75 a week (equivalent to about $1,125 today), and with her college background and connections, Long was in the upper echelons of working women. That said, she personified the flapper aspirations that appeared everywhere, in advertisements, magazine short stories and movies, of independence, stylish living and a social life on her own terms. With the Depression and the repeal of Prohibition, the 'Lipstick' columns lost their edge. Long became the fashion correspondent for the *New Yorker*, the first to bring intelligent critique to the role, and continued with it until her retirement in 1970.

In the Jailhouse Now

A minor celebrity of the 1920s who made a name for herself in a man's world was Celia Cooney, the 'Bobbed Haired Bandit'. In 1924 the diminutive, twenty-year-old Celia carried out a series of robberies of New York grocery stores, armed with an automatic pistol and aided by her husband, Ed Cooney. From the time of their first heist, of

Roulston's grocery, the fact that a woman was involved in a routine shop robbery made the Sunday papers. The *Brooklyn Eagle* reported 'Woman with Gun Holds up Six Men', describing it as a 'startling holdup'. The *Brooklyn Citizen* led with 'Six Employees in Grocery Store Held Up by Pretty Girl'. The police at first refused to accept that the culprit had been a woman, suggesting to the grocery clerks that it must have been a man in girl's clothes. The whole affair seemed like something out of the movies.[9]

The Cooneys found a new apartment to rent, instead of the one room they had been living in, furnishing it on the instalment plan and starting to buy nursery equipment for the baby they were expecting. In a week, the $680 haul from the first robbery was gone. They carried out two more hold-ups the following weekend, robbing a second grocery store, since the first place they hit had little cash in the register. Again, the Sunday papers headlined with Celia's gender. The *New York Telegram and Evening Mail* coined the name by which Celia would become notorious: 'The Bobbed Haired Girl Bandit Terrorizes Brooklyn'. It was a gift from heaven for the press: melodrama, moral outrage and the novelty of a gun-toting, smartly dressed female.

The couple continued their robbery spree in Brooklyn through early 1924, with the newspapers avidly reporting each heist and adding several that the couple did not commit. Newspaper reporters made up more and more, filling their columns with speculation on who the 'Bobbed Haired Bandit' was, her character, her motives and where she would strike next. They turned it into an entertainment story, rather than crime reporting. This kept Celia in the public eye and enabled her to become a sympathetic character, admired for her pluck and daring, rather than being dismissed as another two-bit criminal, stealing money from hard-working shopkeepers. She played up to the role by delivering notes to the police, including a teasing one when they arrested the wrong suspect: 'Leave this innocent girl alone and get the right one.' In February, when she and Ed had not committed a robbery for more than a week, she apologized for 'taking a vacation which deprived the police of their Saturday night diversion'.[10]

Other than the first one, the robberies had not been very lucrative, and the Cooneys were running out of money. In April they became over-ambitious, planning to steal the wages of the National Biscuit Company warehouse and disappear from Brooklyn. They made mistakes that drew attention to them by moving out of their apartment, checking into a hotel, hiring a car and tying up the driver, and letting themselves be seen by more than twenty employees of the biscuit company. During the robbery the cashier made a grab for Celia, and Ed shot and wounded him. They fled to Florida, leaving $8,000 in the safe. They arrived in Jacksonville broke, with Celia heavily pregnant, and took a shabby room, worse than the one they were living in when they decided on robbery as the way to get money for nice things for their baby.

Celia gave birth in mid-April, but the baby died after a few days. Meanwhile, the couple had been identified by witnesses at the National Biscuit job and the police intercepted a letter from Celia to Ed's mother, begging for money. They were brought back to New York by rail, and crowds gathered as they passed through the stations on the way, trying to get a glimpse of the girl bandit. The train was besieged by a crowd when it arrived at Penn Station. Everything was over in May, when the *Daily News* headline screamed 'Ten Years for Bobbed Bandit', carrying a front-page picture of the Cooneys being sentenced. The *Telegram and Evening Mail* gave an account of Celia's demeanour on being sentenced and led from the court:

Game to the last, the young woman whose crimes stand almost without parallel for coolness and impudence heard the sentence without the flicker of an eyelash . . . Not once from the time she entered the room did she give the slightest indication that her pulse had increased by so much as a single beat or that her nerves were less steady than when her hand held a revolver.[11]

The press continued to dig into Celia's background of deep poverty, parental neglect and a violent father. For some, the story became an emblem of a society that was failing to care for and nurture children from the slums. For others, she symbolized a permissive society that gave too much freedom to young women, prompting them to go off the rails. The Cooneys were released after seven years and went on to have two sons, before Ed died of tuberculosis in 1936. Celia struggled with poverty as a widow before finding stability and better pay doing factory work during the Second World War.

Look for the Silver Lining

Working-class women in New York had laboured outside the home in previous centuries in a limited number of occupations, such as market gardening and dairy work, and as seamstresses, laundresses and domestic servants in the homes of the wealthier middle and upper classes. As factories and sweatshops became established in the nineteenth century, there were more opportunities for women, particularly in garment-making, which started to move into the mass production of cheap men's suits and work overalls. There was also a large market for accessories, such as artificial flowers, for the assembly of which the nimble fingers of girls and young women were required.

During the First World War women were in demand to make up the shortfall of male workers who had joined up to fight, for example from the Brooklyn shipyards, and to undertake war work in munitions factories. While there was initial resistance to women taking men's jobs, the war requirements for labour meant that they were hired in large numbers and the government actively ran recruitment drives for women in war-related industries. As a result, women not only began working in heavy industry, but also took other jobs traditionally reserved for men, such as railway guards, ticket collectors, bus and tram conductors, postal workers, police officers, firefighters and clerks.[12] However, in 1920–21, once the men returned from the Front and were demobilized, there was an economic recession as the economy adapted from a war footing to peacetime production, while struggling to reabsorb the demobilized troops into the workforce. One rapid adjustment was that women were removed from the jobs they had gained, and female employees were banned from taking a number of roles. But other avenues were opening up.

In 1918 New York passed local legislation to allow women – excluding Asian Americans and Native Americans – to vote, based on existing federal laws. More than twenty women stood as candidates in New York State primaries in 1918, and two were elected, Mary Lilly and Ida Sammis. Both held positions during their term of office on various committees of the New York State Assembly. Lilly was a progressive who had been active in social reform movements for more than two decades before her election. She was one of the first women to complete a law degree, graduating in 1895. She was an advocate of prison reform, while Sammis introduced several bills relating to women's employment. However, neither woman stood for re-election.

The Nineteenth Amendment to the Constitution (1920) provided a national extension of the vote to women, yet it was not until 1925 that a female candidate, the Republican Ruth Sears Baker Pratt, was elected to the New York City legislature (at that time called the Board of Aldermen). Pratt had been active behind the scenes in the Republican Party and, once she was persuaded to stand for office herself, her combination of wealth, social standing and knowledge of local politics gave her a powerful political base. As Alderman, she clashed repeatedly with Tammany Hall, particularly over the budget, which she believed could be slashed by millions if spending, patronage positions and rampant corruption were curtailed. After retaining her seat as Alderman for four years, Pratt stood for Congress and in 1929 became the first woman to represent New York State in the national legislature.

In the 1920s one in five women in New York was earning a salary, typically as factory workers in clothing, printing and food production, trained teachers, nurses, midwives and social workers, or clerks, typists, waitresses and telephone operators. Teaching was considered a natural extension of motherhood. In the nineteenth century it had been a male profession, but industrialization brought more lucrative jobs for men, leaving education to women. By the 1920s three quarters of teachers in New York were female. At the same time, the attitude persisted that women should not work outside the home if their husbands were employed, and that working women were taking jobs away from men who needed them more. Many positions were kept out of women's reach, and they were mostly expected to quit their paying jobs if they married.

As the economy picked up, modernization meant that there were new openings for women, particularly in New York, which housed the head offices of large corporations and had the highest intensity of telephones in the United States. The city's rapidly growing network of business and private telephones required an army of female switchboard operators, the 'hello girls' who connected calls at central telephone exchanges. Telephone users would pick up the phone, connecting immediately to the switchboard. 'Hello. Number, please?' the operator would ask, then, 'Hold the line, please,' as she expertly removed and inserted jack plugs to connect the call. If the number was on the operator's switchboard, they would connect the call by plugging the ringing cable into the relevant jack. If not, they would transfer the call to the correct exchange, where another operator would be able to connect the caller. The job of a switchboard operator took concentration, good interpersonal skills and deft hands. The telephone companies soon realized that women and girls were much more skilled and reliable than the messenger boys who had first taken on the job. These teenage boys were prone to boredom and would start to mess

Switchboard operators.

around among themselves. 'When some other diversion held their attention, they would leave a call unanswered for any length of time, and then return the impatient subscriber's profanity with a few original oaths,' wrote the historian Marion May Dilts in her book *The Telephone in a Changing World (1941).*[13]

Meanwhile, the number of offices in the city was rising fast. Builders tore down twice as many buildings as went up, with the new buildings occupying two or more old plots and rising much higher. The result was that the amount of office space in New York City increased by 92 per cent by the end of the 1920s. The city was the centre of financial services, transportation, the growing communication, marketing and design sectors, and legal services. Floor upon floor of offices were given over to rows of female clerks doing bookkeeping using adding machines, and secretaries working at typewriters. Again, women's nimbler fingers gave them an edge over men in using the new technology. The office buildings also provided employment for charwomen to clean them, dusting, polishing brass fittings and mopping floors. Many were paid less than $9 a week (about $135 today), well below the weekly $11.65 ($175 at today's rates) that was considered minimum pay.

On the streets of the city, low- and moderately priced cafeterias and luncheonettes grew popular, and both were considered suitable eating places for women. It became more common for families to go out for meals, especially on Sundays. In these less formal eateries, women instead of men were hired as cooks, waiting staff and counter servers, taking over the majority of food-service jobs. Prohibition meant that concerns over women serving alcohol were no longer valid, and waitresses were considered friendlier and more attractive to customers.[14]

IN THE FASHION SECTOR, the increased mass production of clothing meant that more working-class women were employed as seamstresses, often in large workshops. Some manufacturing moved out of the traditional New York Garment District to reduce production costs through cheaper labour in areas like Cincinnati and Baltimore, where they could build larger, more efficient factories and pay lower wages. The functional button-down blouse called a 'shirtwaist' became the popular staple for working women, so large resources were devoted to its production. Shirtwaists were embellished on the collars and cuffs with lace or detailed stitching that required a high level of technical skill with industrial sewing machines. An office worker in a crisp, tailored shirtwaist became a lasting image of the new woman at work.

One of the highest areas of employment for women was in laundries. Demand for laundry to be done outside the home rose as urban areas grew more industrialized and polluted. Laundries became mechanized over the decade, but many still did washing by hand in the early 1920s. The labour involved in washing, starching and pressing men's shirts and women's blouses, in an era when the domestic washing machine was an expensive innovation (costing $81.50 in 1920, about $1,300 today), meant that working people in particular relied on linen services and laundries to ensure they looked business-smart. The writer Kate Simon, who arrived in New York with her family as an immigrant from Poland at the age of four during the First World War, grew up in the Bronx in the 1920s. She describes how she held down a laundry job throughout her high-school years, ticketing bundles of washing, to get for herself the pocket money her family could not provide. This meant she could buy Cokes with friends in the local ice-cream parlour, or buy a cheap ticket for the cinema or theatre.[15]

In addition to manufacturing and laundering, clothing sales and the rise of department stores offered another employment opportunity for women. The way clothing was bought changed dramatically for the middle classes. Going to a dress shop or department store for ready-made clothes and underwear was very different from buying lengths of fabric as had been done before. Women were much more comfortable trying on and buying clothing from female shop assistants than male assistants, leading to a greater volume of sales as more female shop assistants were employed. The growth of the cosmetics and beauty market also required women to sell products to other women. Shop work was considered respectable and the hours decent, compared with factory or catering work.

The first department stores had been established in New York in the mid-nineteenth century. The Marble Palace was opened at

280 Broadway in 1856 by Alexander Turney Stewart, while Blooming-dale's was established in 1861. Macy's, which started as a dry-goods store, moved through several locations before evolving into a true department store when it opened its iconic building in 1902 at Herald Square, Broadway and 34th Street. The department stores hit their stride after the First World War. The rise of consumerism in the United States and the emphasis placed on the monetary value of nearly every-thing were in part replacing traditional values of family, religion and tradition with new secular values of acquisition and consumption as the means of achieving happiness. Citizens at every level of income were encouraged to buy and become consumers of the more readily available factory-made goods. Department stores became a reflection of the new culture of consumption. Unlike the specialized stores that preceded them, they aimed to meet all the shopper's wants. As those requirements expanded with awareness of the array of new types of product through the power of advertising, so did the variety of goods available in department stores.

The expansion of these new areas of business brought employment opportunities for women, giving them some economic independence and an identity outside the home. However, wages were low, and for most working women, who were paid less than men in similar roles, those wages only just gave them enough to live on if they lived outside the family home. Young women working as telephone operators, typ-ists or sales assistants, who lived with their parents, were expected to contribute to the household's expenses, and most retained a very small proportion of their wage for 'spending money'. For single working-class women, living independently on a low wage was a constant exercise in budgeting. The average rent for a room was $7 per week (equivalent to $100 now), while subway fares – which remained at 5 cents for decades from the opening of the subway in 1904 until 1948, when fares rose to 10 cents – also had to be found. Groceries and fresh food were relatively much more expensive as a proportion of earnings than they are today, but in many lodgings any sort of apparatus to heat food was banned. Cheap diners and automats were popular, since a complete meal of main course, dessert and coffee could be had there for about 35 cents. The working woman also had to pay for suitable clothes or uniform, plus laundry. Even though a cinema ticket was relatively cheap at 15 cents, there would be little left over for entertainment.

I Wish I Could Shimmy Like My Sister Kate

A woman who wanted to live the flapper life to the full on an average female salary really needed to enter the world of 'dating', with its new vocabulary and manners. Before the 1920s, most courting between couples had taken place in the family home or on walks in the park, since there were very few other places to go – hence the older term 'walking out' with someone. The growth of leisure activities and entertainment options opened up a new array of possibilities – movie theatres, amusement parks and sports events – and therefore the idea of 'making a date' for which to purchase tickets. Dance halls and nightclubs were two of the favourite outings for young women. Dancing was a popular activity, moving away from the sedate waltzes and jolly polkas of the past to the close-hold, exciting rhythm and fast steps of the turkey trot, the black bottom and, above all, the Charleston. In the mid-1920s a quick way to social success was to know the Charleston and be able to teach others the moves.

In New York, two new theme parks were developed at Coney Island. They introduced more daring rides, such as the first roller-coasters, as well as the 'Canals of Venice' and the 'Tunnel of Love', which gave couples the chance to sit in a boat or carriage for two and be ferried through darkened tunnels, allowing the novel opportunity for hugging and kissing. Professional sport took off in the early years of the twentieth century, and attending the games became a regular part of social life. Baseball with the Brooklyn Dodgers at Ebbett's Field, for example, was easily accessible by public transport.

Yankee Stadium opened in 1923 with 67,000 seats, double the capacity of the Yankees' previous home, the Polo Grounds. The huge stadium was testament to the growing popularity of sports spectating and the draw of such stars as Babe Ruth.

To partake of these delights, the flapper needed a man to treat her, paying for dinners and show tickets and taking her dancing in jazz clubs. In return, she needed to look fashionable, exude a 'fun' personality, and understand a whole new currency: how much physical attention to permit and how much romantic investment to make in the man of the moment. Girls who did not 'get it' could find themselves dropped after a couple of dates, and noted as 'no fun' by the young men of their social circle. Equally, young men could get tired of being seen as the funder of a night on the town, when there was no real romantic interest from the girl. However, the new opportunities of leisure meant that men and women were able to get to know each

Flappers dance the Charleston at the Parody Club in 1926.

Luna Park, Coney Island, lit up at night in 1927.

other properly, without chaperones and free of the rigid structure of social conventions that had meant couples in the past often became engaged after the briefest of social encounters in formal settings.

Before the First World War it was still unusual for any respectable woman to have premarital sex (estimated at about 14 per cent of women in 1900). By the 1920s surveys suggested that around 38 per cent of unmarried women were sexually active.[16] But what still held true was the fact that for most women, this premarital sex was with the man whom they would marry. Lois Long of 'Lipstick' fame embraced the greater sexual freedoms of the day, along with the smoking and drinking of the flapper. She was known to have carried on an affair for more than a year with Peter Arno, chief cartoonist for the *New Yorker*, before they were married. Her reminiscences may have been a little more blasé than the behaviour at the time, but in later years she stated: 'You never knew who you were drinking with and who you'd wake up with.'[17] Birth control was known but highly controversial. Margaret Sanger, the famous birth-control advocate, was arrested repeatedly in the 1920s for disseminating information on contraception. *Vogue*, reviewing Sanger's book *The Pivot of Civilization* (1922), called her subject 'a vitally important phase of the new feminism'.[18] Meanwhile, as Kate Simon, an adolescent attending Hunter College in New York, recalled:

> Birth control clinics existed ... [we] didn't know where the clinics were and didn't try to find them, much too afraid of potential trouble since we heard that they were from time to time attacked by the law ... Though illegal, abortionists were not difficult to locate; everyone had a friend who had an address and telephone number ... Brave as we were and as brightly, offhandedly *New Yorker*ish in our manner when we mentioned it, our stomachs turned to burning knots as one week, a second, a third passed without a period. Money money, money – where were we to get it? The fear of not finding the money almost obliterated the fear of the operation itself. At least one hundred and fifty dollars and more frequently two hundred.[19]

Someone to Watch Over Me

From the start of the 1920s onwards a record number of young women were going to college. While most still aimed to get married, it was increasingly expected that female college leavers would get jobs and have a desire to put their education to use in a professional role before they retired from the workforce on marrying. The glamour of flapper life included negotiating a career alongside such excitements as the growing delight of being a consumer in the Manhattan department stores, dinner out at discreet restaurants, and dancing at the growing number of nightclubs. However, to enjoy this lifestyle the young lady needed a place to live, somewhere that allowed her a degree of independence in her comings and goings. Women's boarding houses were looked down on by college girls as old-fashioned and restrictive.

The traditional landlady would have a strong regard for propriety, and many imposed an early curfew on evenings out, a ban on visiting friends and a general lack of privacy for the boarders.

One alternative to the boarding house and a way to accommodate the ever-growing number of city workers was the high-rise residential hotel. This could fit in many more rooms than a tenement house for the same street-level 'footprint', and was profitable for developers owing to a loophole in the Tenement House Act of 1901 that exempted buildings containing apartments without kitchens from New York City's height and fireproofing restrictions. Developers could build multistorey layers of rooms on rooms, while selling the glamour of the fully serviced 'hotel' with dining facilities. Club-hotels for men had operated since the turn of the century, and in 1903 the first hotel for business and professional women opened, the Martha Washington Hotel on East 30th Street. At this time many New York hotels stipulated that no single female traveller could be offered a room after 6 p.m. unless she was accompanied by heavy luggage to demonstrate that she was legitimately travelling.

The Barbizon Hotel for Women on Lexington Avenue and 63rd Street was built in 1927 and opened early in 1928 in response to an influx into New York of young women, whose families were concerned that they stay somewhere respectable. Women who wished to stay at the Barbizon were vetted for their references and suitability, which until the 1950s included being white. No man was ever permitted beyond the lobby. Each guest had a single room at a weekly rate that covered daily maid service, a dining room and coffee shop, plus several lounges and club rooms. Each bedroom had a chest of drawers, an armchair, a desk and a lamp, a single bed with a flowered bedspread, and matching flowered curtains. It was not the cheapest accommodation, with rates starting at $10 per week, but, in offering the security of a 'chaperoned' environment, it provided the promise of independence that would otherwise be hard to obtain by young middle-class women who wanted to leave the family home and make their own way in New York. The ground floor of the hotel contained shops with their entrances on Lexington Avenue: a dry-cleaner, hairdresser, pharmacy, hosiery store, milliner and bookshop – everything a 'certain class of woman' might need. All these shops had entrances from inside the hotel, so that the residents did not have to venture out into the street if they did not want to.[20]

The Barbizon was not the only women's hotel aiming at the young professional market. Allerton House for Women on East 57th Street, near Central Park, opened in 1920. It offered rooms for female physicians, decorators, lawyers and writers, and boasted a homely atmosphere that included a sewing room, a modern, fully equipped laundry, a ballroom and lounges. Its five hundred bedrooms were fully booked before it even opened.

The establishment of female-only club-hotels was a physical manifestation of women stating their right to take up space in the world and to exist independently of the protection of a father, husband or family. New women could socialize as they wished, shop for pleasure and make their own way at work. The American Women's Association set up the largest accommodation for women on West 57th Street, which it called a 'movement', not a mere hotel: 1,250 rooms with baths over 28 storeys, with facilities including restaurants, lounges, a patio with four fountains, and a cafe where modern girls could have their coffee and smoke as freely as men. The club-hotels also catered to the more rigorous exercise that was now acceptable for women, with fully equipped gyms, full-size swimming pools and, at the Barbizon, squash courts.[21]

Lookin' Good but Feelin' Bad

One of the most immediate things that we recognize in looking back to the 1920s is the distinctive 'look' of the fashions, hairstyles and make-up. Fashion in the 1920s was dramatically different from previous styles, with the dropped waist, loose cut and shorter skirts that immediately made older clothes in the wardrobe look hopelessly outdated. The flapper look of shorter skirts was partly made possible by the introduction of rayon or 'artificial silk' stockings, which showed the legs to advantage. Rayon also mimicked luxury silk and satin fabrics in dressmaking and enabled the latest styles to be made quite cheaply, as mass-produced clothes, many still made in the sweatshops of the Garment District. This meant the new styles were within the means of any woman earning a moderate salary, or whose husband or father could afford her a 'dress allowance'.

The new style of less restrictive clothing, lighter underwear and medium-height heels meant that women were able to move differently, both during their daily lives and as required by the energetic dancing of the Charleston and the black bottom. As with other changes, the revolution in clothing had begun earlier. Brighter colours were available at the turn of the century owing to advances in dyeing, the straighter silhouette was first seen as early as 1907, and boyish elements came into women's styles in the 1910s. In the 1920s fashion in New York was still massively influenced by that of Paris, and it was the designs of Gabrielle 'Coco' Chanel that set the direction, particularly when wealthy Americans took to holidaying on the French Riviera and welcomed her elegant sportswear inspired by fishermen's clothes. Chanel's fluid designs in jersey – a fabric that had previously been used only for workwear and undergarments – and the simple chic of her shorter black evening dress (the 'little black dress') were revolutionary.[22]

One reason why more women could afford to be fashionable was the fact that the new styles were simpler than the elaborate dress of earlier times. As anyone knows who has put together a costume for a 'Roaring Twenties' party, a length of artificial silk, some chiffon and a sewing machine are all that is needed to get 'the look'. The true couture fashion of the day was of much more sophisticated construction, of course, but then – as now – it was possible to get away with a cheaper imitation. There was a rise in home dressmaking, since a woman without training as a seamstress could make a skirt or simple dress. Sewing machines were relatively affordable and advances in printing made paper patterns, invented at the end of the nineteenth century, more robust and easier to follow. Advertising and the new style of magazines aimed at women drove interest in and acceptance of fashion as something that was desirable and part of modern life, rather than a frivolity that all but the rich could ignore. Advertisements for patterns, fabric and sewing accoutrements encouraged women to view fashion as achievable in a thrifty way, by making their own. Being fashionable was sold to women as acceptable, and a responsible part of domestic economy.

The straight silhouette favoured slim, small-busted women, who experienced a new level of comfort in their underwear, needing to wear only drawers, a chemise and a slip beneath a straight dress, rather

Models for the National Association of Cotton Manufacturers showcase designs in cotton at the Waldorf-Astoria in 1927.

than the elaborate layers required by Victorian fashions. By 1928 this style of underwear had become even simpler with the introduction of the 'step-in' chemise, all-in-one camisole and knickers, or a simple crêpe de Chine bandeau bra and scallop-edged 'abbreviated panties'.[23] However, for those with natural curves, the corset – which in previous decades had been laced tight to give the smallest possible waist – was replaced with the elasticated long corset, which aimed to flatten bust, belly and behind wherever the curves threatened to disrupt the graceful fall of a straight dress. The new-style corset was still an unforgiving garment, promising to 'hold the figure firmly'.

In addition to the shorter skirts, the other main innovation in fashion was the style known as sportswear. Women were participating in sports, which were fast evolving in the period. Tennis and golf became widely played by men and women, skiing was increasingly popular as a newly developed activity, and sailing and motoring became leisure activities for the wealthy. Beach holidays became very fashionable and also accessible to the masses. The new fabrics and manufacturing techniques transformed swimwear, introducing the one-piece bathing suit for women replacing the cumbersome knee length tunic and bloomers. The Jantzen brand advertised 'The suit that changed bathing to swimming', highlighting that swimming was a sport. The term 'sportswear' covered everything from women's tweed golfing suits and tennis dresses, which allowed the freedom of movement to indulge in these sports, to a wide range of generally more comfortable, non-formal leisurewear. The development of machine knitting and new types of yarn meant that knitwear took on a much more stylish aspect in the popular 'jumper suit' of a long semi-fitted sweater or cardigan with a toning skirt in wool flannel. However, much of the sportswear was still very formal by today's standards. For example, a long-sleeved silk dress with intricate pintuck details, lace and pleating was described as a 'beach dress' in B. Altman & Company's catalogue in 1927.[24] Although some daring society women were starting to wear trousers as part of casual holiday attire for the beach in southern France, it was still not socially acceptable for women to wear trousers in 'normal' life, and they are not to be seen in the mainstream magazines or clothing catalogues of the period.

The style of the period was depicted in the lavishly illustrated, high-end glossy magazines that came to prominence in the 1920s. *Harper's Bazaar* and *Vogue* were the most influential in creating New York style. *Harper's*, which was first published in 1867 as a weekly paper aimed at women, had by the early twentieth century become a monthly magazine with a strong focus on fashion and reporting on high society. The publisher Condé Nast put *Vogue* on a similar path when he purchased the title in 1905, focusing on the New York upper class, the events of their social season, their leisure activities, the places they frequented and the clothing they wore. The magazine provided a window on this world to everyone who wanted to look like them and imitate their exclusive circle. Advances in colour printing were such that by the 1920s each edition was full of illustrations of impossibly glamorous, slim figures in the style pioneered by Georges Lepape, André Édouard Marty, Eduardo Benito and Romain de Tirtoff (Erté). The competition between the magazines led to exclusive agreements with contributors, such as Erté's ten-year contract with *Harper's*, which prevented him from supplying any artwork to *Vogue* during that period.

Photography was also becoming more sophisticated, and alongside the pictures of society beauties and social events, there was more use of photographic models to show off the fashions. One of the most sought-after models of the mid-1920s was Lee Miller, who at the age of nineteen had literally fallen into the arms of Condé Nast when she was nearly hit by a car on a Manhattan street. Nast befriended Miller, taken with her unruffled attitude and classic chic. He saw potential in her quintessential 1920s looks: the symmetrical face with curling lips and a long neck that suited short hair and the severe cloche hat. Within a few weeks he had engaged her as a model for *Vogue*, posing for a cover illustration by Lepape. She became a hit with the *Vogue* illustrators and photographers alike for her ability to hold a pose. She had been photographed by her father, a keen amateur photographer, from an early age, so she was used to staying still, as positioned, and could adopt at will the distant expression that was required. The fashion photographs of Miller show an inner radiance with a statuesque quality. All the time she was in the studio, working with the leading photographers Edward Steichen and Arnold Genthe, she was observing and learning.[25] In 1929 she made her next move, to become a photographer, declaring that she would rather 'take a picture than be in one'.[26] Travelling to Paris, she presented herself to the most famous avant-garde photographer of the day, Man Ray, as his student, despite the fact that he did not take students. Through an intense three-year relationship with Ray, she learned the technical skills of fashion photography and portraits, and developed with him the Surrealist technique of solarization.

Bobbed-Haired Bobby

In the 1920s short hair for women became the fashion and with the democratization of fashion, it was not confined to the wealthy elite. Short hair was taken up by young women across the social classes and was as much a statement about being a 'New Woman' as having a new look. It is hard to appreciate now how revolutionary this was, and the level of discussion and debate it engendered. This was not just within individual families, when young women wanted to have their hair cut in the fashionable style, to the dismay and outrage of their parents. Broken romances and engagements were also blamed on the hairdresser's scissors snipping off long locks. In Fitzgerald's early short story 'Bernice Bobs Her Hair' (1920), the conversational gambit of the teenage Bernice in asking her dance partner's view on bobbing her hair, is manipulated by her jealous cousin into making her follow through in the barber's chair.[27] Social consequences follow, as the boys she is trying to impress disapprove of the look and she is considered 'fast' by her aunt. Bernice takes her revenge by snipping off her cousin's luxuriant blonde plaits as she sleeps, then walking off into the night to catch a train home. There were numerous articles for and against the new haircuts in newspapers and magazines, all on the theme of 'a woman's glory is her hair'.[28]

The ballroom dancer Irene Castle, who was credited with introducing bobbed hair to American women, defended her hairstyle in an interview with the *Ladies' Home Journal* in 1921:

There has been so much controversy over the bobbed-hair craze that I feel I ought to put some of the world right, as to my side of it at least. I do not claim to be the first person to wear bobbed hair; in fact, I believe there are a number of people who, like myself, picture Joan of Arc with shorn locks! There have been several periods in history when women wore short hair. It is easier to be the first person to do a thing than the first to introduce it, and I believe I am largely blamed for the homes wrecked and engagements broken because of clipped tresses ... Don't think I am knocking those who may have followed in my footsteps; I am indeed honored, and in four cases at least that I know of it has been the making of a very individual and even beautiful person out of one who would not have attracted attention before.[29]

The *Brooklyn Eagle* posed the question 'To bob or not to bob?' in 1924, and the debate was still running in 1927, when the opera star Mary Garden and film actor Mary Pickford gave the views for and against in the April edition of *Pictorial Review*. In her opinion piece, 'Why I Bobbed My Hair', Garden expressed the broader sentiments that fuelled the debate:

Why did I bob my hair? For several reasons. I did it because I wanted to, for one thing; because I found it easier to take care of; because I thought it more becoming; and because I felt freer without long, entangling tresses. But above and beyond these and several other reasons I had my hair cut short because, to me, it typified a progressive step, in keeping with the inner spirit that animates my whole existence ... You may say that it matters very little whether a woman wears her hair long or has it cut short, but that is really not true ... Bobbed hair is a state of mind and not merely a new manner of dressing my head. It typifies growth, alertness, up-to-dateness, and is part of the expression of the élan vital! It is not just a fad of the moment either, like mah jong or cross-word puzzles. At least I don't think it is. I consider getting rid of our long hair one of the many little shackles that women have cast aside in their passage to freedom. Whatever helps their emancipation, however small it may seem, is well worth while.[30]

In a piece entitled 'Why I Have Not Bobbed Mine', Pickford responded:

In the epidemic of hair-cutting which has swept the country I am one of the few who have escaped. That does not mean that I have been inoculated by the germ, but that I have resisted valiantly. It has been a hard-fought battle, and the problem has occupied many of my waking and sleeping hours ... I suppose almost every woman in the world has had a moment of trepidation before she made the final and momentous decision to part with her crowning glory.

Pickford recognized that her curls were part of her screen persona:

my curls have become so identified with me that they have become almost a trademark ... I think they mean more than that – in some strange way they have become a symbol – and I think shorn of them I should become almost as Samson after his unfortunate meeting with Delilah . . . I think I should never be forgiven by my mother, my husband, or my maid if I should commit the indiscretion of cutting my hair. The last in particular seems to take a great personal pride in its length and texture, and her horror-stricken face whenever I mention the possibility of cutting it makes me pause and consider. Perhaps I have a little sentimental feeling for it myself. I have had my curls quite a while now and have become somewhat attached to them. Besides, there is no use denying the fact, no matter how much I should like to do so, that I am not a radical.[31]

However, two years after this article was published Pickford appeared on screen with bobbed hair, having succumbed to the scissors after the death of her mother.

Over the decade a range of short hairstyles came into vogue. The straight-cut 'bob', usually worn with a full fringe or 'bangs', was popularized by many stars of screen and stage, including the Hungarian-born twin dancers known as the Dolly Sisters (Rózsika and Yansci Deutsch), whose sleek, dark bobs were in place from 1920. The classic bobbed hair is today epitomized by the 'shiny black helmet' of the movie actor Louise Brooks, precision-cut to the level of her jaw, with a fringe just above the line of her eyebrows and the sides shaped into points, accentuating her perfect cheekbones. Variations of the bob could be longer, but never below the shoulders, and were worn with or without a fringe. The bob was followed by the somewhat softer, wavy 'shingle' cut, often helped along by the new Marcel wave 'permanent' treatment. Around the middle of the decade the more severe 'Eton crop' came in. In this style the hair was cut to reveal the ears and short all over, and styled with brilliantine to keep the sleek shape, creating a dramatic image that complemented the edgy silhouette of the fashions. Short hair went hand in hand with the cloche hat that

Classic 1920s bobbed hair epitomized by Louise Brooks
with her 'shining black helmet' of hair.

is so instantly recognizable as '1920s style'. These hats fitted so tightly around the head that they almost forced women to cut their hair, leaving no room for long hair to be styled underneath.

The short hairstyles added to the expense of maintaining the flapper look, since – unlike long hair, which could be managed at home by its owner or, for the wealthy, a maid – they required professional styling. The dramatic first cut to establish the style would cost about $5 ($80 at today's prices), and these short, precise styles needed regular trims at about $2 a time. In the early 1920s the bold young ladies getting short hair would go to a barber. Opportunities for hairdressers subsequently opened up, since women were more comfortable getting their hair done by women, and a whole new industry of beauty salons was established. In the 1920s nearly 25,000 hair salons opened in the United States, and women enjoyed such innovations as electric hairdryers, permanent waves, hair colour, and nail varnish applied by a manicurist.

Painted nails, along with noticeable make-up, were another part of the flapper look that would have been considered outrageous in smart society in previous decades, worn only by prostitutes and by actresses on the stage. Dorothy Parker in her short story 'The Diary of a Lady' (1933) intersperses almost daily visits from Miss Rose the manicurist into the account of the hectic social whirl:

> Miss Rose came about noon to do my nails, simply *covered* in *the* most divine gossip. The Morrises are going to separate *any minute*, and Freddy Warren *definitely* has ulcers, and Gertie Leonard simply *won't* let Bill Crawford out of her sight even with Jack Leonard *right there in the room*, and it's all *true* about Sheila Phillips and Babs Deering. It *couldn't* have been more thrilling. Miss Rose is *too* marvelous; I really think that a lot of times people like that are a lot more intelligent than a lot of people. Didn't notice until after she had gone that the damn fool had put that *revolting* tangerine-colored polish on my nails; *couldn't* have been more furious.[32]

While women in 1920s New York were owning the town with a new confidence and style, the beauty and fashion industry that had in part enabled the new freedoms – or at least helped to give them expression – was increasingly undermining this confidence through the insidious power of advertising. During this decade was born the 'never good enough' style of copy. To achieve the necessary slender look for the fashions of the day, women were encouraged to diet, take pills to dissolve fat from the inside, use massage machines to rub it away, or eat manufactured foods that promised to be 'slimming'. Beauty was becoming big business, with an ever-growing range of face powders, skin foods, lotions, hair tonics, hair removers, lipsticks, hair dyes and hand creams that no self-respecting woman could do without. Advertisers constantly drove home the message that appearances count, that the world was ready to judge the woman who wore a 'cheap' lipstick or the same dress too often. Even the indomitable flappers, in their all-out fight for independence of style, eventually fell victim to the market forces of commercialism and homogeneity. Yet the image of those glamorous bobbed-haired women in short skirts will always symbolize a freewheeling, audacious lifestyle unmatched to this day.

6

The Sidewalks of New York

New York underwent a dramatic facelift during the boom years of the 1920s, at a pace and intensity that could not fail to impress even the most hard-bitten Manhattanite. By the end of the decade, the novelist and newspaper columnist R. L. Duffus could proclaim, 'Perhaps the nearest a New Yorker ever comes to civic pride is when he contemplates the skyline and realizes that there is and has been nothing to match it in the world.'[1]

Twenty per cent of all new housing in the United States in that decade was built in New York City. Apartment buildings grew from 39 per cent of all construction in 1919 to 77 per cent in 1926. Along with a huge increase in suburban building in the four boroughs other than Manhattan, the city's public transport infrastructure expanded to accommodate the growing population. The city had been building overground urban and suburban railways since the mid-nineteenth century, followed by the elevated lines that ran over the roads and between buildings following the street pattern and known as the Third Avenue El, Ninth Avenue El and so forth. The El rapidly became fully used by commuters, who valued the reliability and speed of the lines, which were not held up by traffic and street crossings. The success of the elevated lines convinced developers that the high projected cost of creating an underground railway system would be profitable in time, despite the enormous difficulty and outlay required to tunnel through the Manhattan granite. The first subway lines opened in 1904 and there was significant further development in the 1920s. The first subway to Coney Island began operating in 1920, and the Pelham Bay Line was also extended to Pelham Bay Park that year. This made the New York subway system the largest in the world, at 202 miles, surpassing the 156 miles of Tube lines under London at that time. Other lines were also extended during the decade, among them the Flushing Line to 111th Street in 1925 and the Queensborough Line from Times Square to Flushing in 1928. The latter was celebrated with a parade on Fifth Avenue, with floats depicting the history of transport, and another parade in Flushing itself. Mayor Jimmy Walker addressed the crowd from the Commodore Hotel, near Grand Central station, but skipped the trip to Queens.[2]

Meanwhile, the road network was overhauled to cope with the huge rise in motor traffic. Between the end of the First World War and the end of the 1920s, more than half a million new motor vehicles hit the streets of New York City. Automobiles had been in development since the end of the nineteenth century, and in the early twentieth century were available for the rich to purchase as a luxurious novelty. Henry Ford's revolutionary idea to mass-produce cars and trucks changed everything. By taking advantage of interchangeable parts and the concept of the assembly line, Ford was able to exploit economies of scale, so that the car became affordable to people on middling incomes, providing personal rapid transport. In 1909 a new Model T cost $850, but by 1924 the price had gone down to only $260 (equivalent to about $4,680 today), while a top-of-the-range Chevrolet Superior Sedan cost $825 in 1926. To cope with the increase in motor traffic, new rules had to be introduced for the roads, and in 1920 the first traffic light was installed in New York, at 42nd Street and Fifth Avenue.[3]

There was also a rapid increase in the construction of business premises. Boosted by the economic boom, more than one hundred buildings of twenty or more storeys were added to the Manhattan

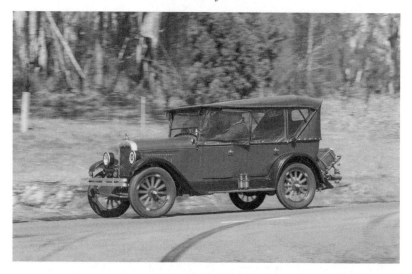

1926 Chevrolet.

skyline. Indeed, the growth of the car was tied up with that of the city's skyline, since Manhattan's office buildings housed companies selling financial, marketing, technical and legal services to the car industry. This, in turn, boosted car sales, which increased the demand for those commercial services, and so on. A section of Broadway near Columbus Circle became known as 'Automobile Row' as many Detroit companies set up offices and showrooms there. The development of the car industry was exemplary of the type of relationship that was coming into play between New York City and the American economy more broadly. In 1928 and 1929, respectively, developers signed contracts for the Chrysler and Empire State buildings, which – although completed early in the 1930s – came to symbolize the passion for construction of the Roaring Twenties. The reason for the building boom was that, adjusting for inflation, commercial rents were at an all-time high. Businesses were willing to pay because being in New York increased their profits, and the high rents motivated developers to keep building offices into the sky.

As for the residential market, in 1922 alone new homes went up for 38,363 families. Samuel B. Donnelly, secretary of the Building Trades Employers' Association, said, 'We have had building booms in New York City, but no man living ever saw so much building in one- and two-family houses as there is underway at the present time.'[4]

Contrary to the popular image of the maverick millionaire developer, the vast majority of builders were born in New York City or had emigrated as small children with their families from Eastern Europe. Many had begun their careers in the Garment District, evolving from clothing manufacturers (or a milliner, in the case of Abe Adelson), to builders, to real-estate developers. It was there that the frenzy of building was seen to start to change the look of the city dramatically. The largest concentration of factory skyscrapers in the world was in the eighteen square blocks comprising the Garment District from 35th to 41st streets, supporting 100,000 jobs in clothing manufacture that produced nearly three quarters of all women's and children's clothing in the United States.

An example of this type of developer is Abraham Lefcourt. Born in 1876 to Russian immigrant parents in Birmingham, England, he emigrated to America with his family in 1882. Lefcourt started out hawking newspapers on the streets of the Lower East Side and later worked in the garment industry, taking over his employer's business early in the century. In 1910 he built his first structure, a twelve-storey loft building for clothing manufacturers on West 25th Street. The first two floors housed Lefcourt's own women's clothing company, and above were offices rented to other companies. The success of the endeavour prompted him to move full-time into the real-estate business. Between 1910 and 1930 he constructed 31 commercial and residential buildings in the city.[5] Surviving examples include what was opened as the Seville Towers Hotel (and is now Essex House) at 160 Central Park South, one of New York's largest apartment hotels. This was designed by Frank Grad, a New Jersey-based architect who had already designed two towers in that state for Lefcourt. The building was designed in the modern style with setbacks, plus geometrically patterned brickwork and stone ornamentation. Among the loveliest features of the decoration are the gilded frozen fountains at the second and third storeys, and the gilded floral design rising four storeys above the main entrance.

In the boom years of the 1920s more than 125 setback buildings were built in the Garment District alone by a handful of little-known architects, mainly Jewish, including Ely Jacques Kahn, who designed more than a dozen buildings there in less than ten years. These were all in the ziggurat style demanded by New York City's zoning law of 1916. This had a direct impact on the shape and look of the new buildings by restricting uses by district and, especially, by limiting the mass of a building allowed on a given site. This was entirely different from the simple height limitation that had already been imposed by many cities, including Paris, London, Boston and Chicago. Instead of setting an absolute cap on height, the effect of the New York law was to sculpt individual buildings and the skyline in three dimensions. There were a number of different formulas, but in general terms the law required that after a prescribed vertical height above the pavement (usually 90 feet for cross streets and 150–200 feet for avenues), a high-rise had to be stepped back within a diagonal plane projected from the centre of the street. This was to ensure that adequate air and light could reach the surrounding buildings and streets. Designing structures to meet this requirement enabled the development boom and confirmed the architectural identity of New York as a city of towers, since unlimited height was permitted over one-quarter of the area of the plot. Examples still to be seen in the Garment District include the Bricken Textile Building at 1441 Broadway and 41st Street, designed by Buchman & Kahn in 1929. Different colours of brick, gold and dark brown emphasize the vertical columns of the windows and contrast with the grey stone used for the lower five storeys.

The resulting stepped-pyramid or 'wedding cake' massing typified the city's high-rises from 1916 until 1961 (when the zoning law was dramatically revised), shaping the look of whole districts. Downtown, more than 35 new setback buildings squeezed into the already densely built-up streets, several with towers of sixty or more storeys. Such

Bricken Textile Building, by architects Buchman & Kahn, 1929.

soaring landmarks as the Chrysler Building, 40 Wall Street and the Empire State Building – the world's three tallest buildings in 1931 – took their shape from the zoning law of 1916.

The Sunny Side of the Street

What we now know as the Art Deco style of the period started to appear in buildings early in the decade. The American Radiator Building was one, constructed in 1924 to a design by the architect Raymond Hood at 40 West 40th Street and now the Bryant Park Hotel. It was described in the *New York Times* as a 'daring departure': 'Unlike any office building in the country, the new structure is faced entirely with black brick and golden coloured stone trimming, worked together to give a rich black and gold decorative effect.'[6] The building shows a transition from the decorative style of niches, gargoyles and spires of the nineteenth and early twentieth century, harking back to the architecture of the European past, to the modern and in some ways futuristic skyscraper look of paired windows rising in uninterrupted vertical lines and the bold use of colour in the black brick facing and gold decoration. The gold colour was developed using bronze powder on cast stone, a technique that was devised after a number of experiments by Hood and his team. Hood had visited Brussels in the early 1920s and observed how gold highlights made otherwise gloomy buildings stand out, especially if their facades were darker. He deliberately designed the building in a different style from the existing approach to towers in Manhattan, based on his earlier success with the Chicago Tribune Tower, completed in 1922. The American Radiator building attracted a huge amount of attention in the architectural and wider press, with celebrated photographs and paintings by artists of the day, including Georgia O'Keeffe. The building was illuminated with dramatic floodlighting at night and this raised interest among the public, who would stop to admire the lit-up, gilded top of the tower.

The Art Deco style drew on a range of influences, most notably the Exposition Internationale des Arts Décoratifs et Industriels Modernes (International Exhibition of Modern Decorative and Industrial Arts), which was held in Paris in 1925 and from which the style later took its name (the term was first applied in the 1960s, when there was a resurgence of interest in the style – it was not known as Art Deco in the 1920s). Others include French Art Nouveau, the Vienna Secession and German Expressionism. Interior design, jewellery and other decorative objects were greatly influenced by the craze for Egyptian motifs sparked by the discovery of the tomb of Tutankhamen by archaeologists in 1922. Several of the architects working in New York and most closely associated with the style had trained in France, at the École des Beaux-Arts in Paris, and would have been familiar with the stylistic developments taking place in Europe. Architects described Art Deco at the time as the 'vertical style', a hallmark being to design the features of a building, particularly the windows, to highlight the soaring structure, rather than emphasizing the internal, horizontal arrangement of stacked floors.[7]

One of the most original features of the new buildings was the use of colour in the actual building materials to provide decoration, rather than adding decorative colour touches on top. This includes the use of brick in different colours, as in Hood's Daily News Building (1929), in which the contrast between red and white bricks highlights the vertical lines of the structure and terracotta provides architectural detail. Other buildings used new materials, such as the rust-resistant nickel-chrome-steel alloy Nirosta, which was used to great effect on the tower of the Chrysler Building by the Brooklyn-born architect William Van Alen. At street level, Art Deco details come into their own with highly ornate archways over entrances, intricate decoration on doors, stylized botanical designs as a frieze (often between ground and first floor, so as to be visible from the street), and decorative detailing around windows. These elements can be seen to great effect in the Chanin Building at 122 East 42nd Street and Lexington Avenue,

The American Radiator Building, by architect Raymond Hood, 1923–4.

built as the headquarters of a cost-conscious construction company, rather than to publicize a major corporation. The structure is a plain rectangular tower rising above symmetrically setback lower blocks. It is ornamented with shop windows at ground level framed in black marble and bronze, and above them a bronze relief depicting the story of the evolution of plant and animal life. A terracotta band of stylized abstract floral patterns, suggesting an exuberant, overgrown tropical jungle, wraps around the third storey of the building.[8]

The dramatic developments in the design of buildings and the resulting impact on the cityscape led to public interest in architecture and admiration of architects, along with condemnation from those who disliked the modern building styles. The architect as celebrity had hardly been known before, and the profession came to be seen in a romantic, dramatic light. This is reflected in Edna Ferber's Pulitzer Prize-winning novel *So Big* (1924). One of the main characters, Dirk DeJong, trains to be an architect, a profession that is presented as thrilling:

> Putting a building down on paper – little marks here, straight lines there, figures, calculations, blueprints, measurements – and then, suddenly one day, the actual building itself. Steel, stone and brick, with engines throbbing inside like a heart, and people flowing in and out. Part of a city. A piece of actual beauty conceived by you![9]

When he gives up architecture to make money as a bonds salesman, Ferber presents it as a sell-out, deserting beauty and self-expression: 'Someday you'll want [it] and it won't be there.'[10]

Another writer who saw architecture as a romantic and fascinating endeavour was the novelist Ayn Rand. Arriving in New York as an immigrant from the Soviet Union in 1926, she was greatly impressed by the skyscrapers of the Manhattan skyline, which she saw as symbols of freedom, and resolved that she would write about them. Her first attempt was in 1927, when working as a junior screenwriter for the filmmaker Cecil B. DeMille on a story about construction workers on a skyscraper being rivals in love. Rand rewrote it, transforming the rivals into architects. One of them was an idealist dedicated to erecting the skyscraper despite enormous obstacles. DeMille rejected Rand's script, but she continued to work on the idea, building on it to write her famous novel *The Fountainhead*. Although not published until 1943, the novel covers the 1920s and the development of the new style of architecture, which Rand presents as a hymn in praise of the individual. The book had an immense impact on the public perception of architects and architecture, although it has been criticized as:

> The perfect representation of everything that's wrong with the profession. Consider the plot. Here's the most popular story – maybe the only popular story – ever written about an architect, and in it the hero defends his right to dynamite a building because it wasn't made the way he wanted. 'I destroyed it because I did not choose to let it exist,' declares [the main protagonist, Howard] Roark. At best, this is like a kid throwing a tantrum and smashing his toy blocks. At worst, it's terrorism masquerading as free speech.[11]

The new industries were particularly keen to have modern-looking buildings with novel elements in their architecture and interior design. An example is the headquarters of the New York Telephone Company (the Barclay-Vesey Building), completed in 1927 at 140 West Street, a recognized Art Deco gem by the architect Ralph Walker. The company wanted to define its public image as progressive and modern, and the building was required to provide the technical efficiency for the call exchange infrastructure. Walker's firm, McKenzie, Voorhees and Gmelin, had already designed more than thirty phone-company buildings around the United States since 1885, and he had originally intended to design something more traditional, influenced by the Gothic Revival and Italian Renaissance styles, but for Manhattan it was decided to go with a design that signalled modernity. The building takes up the whole of a small, irregular city block, with a square tower set at an angle to the base block, giving the structure the sculptural quality that is such a distinctive feature of Art Deco buildings. It also exemplifies a particular trope of including references to the building's function in the exterior and interior decoration. The New York Art Deco expert Anthony Robins explains:

> The only suggestion on the building's exterior that it might house the New York City headquarters of the New York Bell Telephone is a small but clearly sculpted bell above the main entrance. Inside, however, telephone company imagery takes over completely, in a gently curving vaulted ceiling emblazoned with a dozen hand-painted scenes showing the development of communications across the ages. West African drums, Chinese carrier pigeons, Egyptian megaphones, and Native American smoke signals all converge from east and west onto a central painting that in earlier times might have been entitled *The Apotheosis of the Telephone*: a handsome, black standing phone with detachable earpiece (the kind on which reporters always frantically phone in their stories in 1930s movies), with the sun blazing forth behind it, surrounded by sun rays intertwined with the telephone cables of the modern world.[12]

The One Wall Street Building, designed in 1929 by Walker for the Irving Trust Company and opened two years later, was built on reputedly the most expensive piece of real estate in Manhattan, on the corner of Broadway and Wall Street. The company was looking to make its mark when it moved there from the Woolworth Building. The structure is almost unique among skyscrapers in combining features of Art Deco design with what can be termed 'Gothic Modern',

featuring curving limestone walls and tall windows echoing the traditional gothic arched windows of the nineteenth-century Trinity
Church, which stands nearby. The windows are matched by the tall
entrance with its pointed arch. One Wall Street was so connected
with Walker's persona that he dressed as the building itself for the
Society of Beaux-Arts Architects' ball in 1931. In the design Walker
celebrated the precision of the machine age, which is reflected in
the relief sculptures and pattern of the limestone-clad facade of his
creation.

THE INTERIORS OF ONE WALL STREET were treated with equal
attention. The entrance leads straight into one of the most dramatic interiors in New York, the three-storey Red Room lined in
sparkling mosaic tiles of red, orange and gold to designs by the
muralist Hildreth Meière, who worked on some of the most iconic
Art Deco buildings in New York as well as major religious and civic
buildings of the period across the United States. The tiling was pre-
fabricated in pieces in Germany, each stamped so that the installers,
the Ravenna Mosaic Company, could put it all together. It is one
of very few abstract mosaics by Meière, possibly responding to
the architect's concept for an abstract design. The Red Room was
designed as a private banking hall for the wealthiest clients, and is
now retail space for luxury brands. Inside there were originally desks
with matching lamps for the bankers and chairs for clientele.

Meière was one of the most prolific and creative artists to work
on the integral decoration of Art Deco buildings, exterior and interior ornamentation that declared the purpose of the building and was
part of the overall conception. These artists are little known today,
partly because it is the architects who are commemorated, and partly
because, with changing styles and the move towards minimalism
from the 1950s onwards, decoration was no longer considered integral to the overall design of a building. Meière was born in New

York in 1892 and started her artistic education at the Academy of the Sacred Heart in West Harlem. She studied art first in Europe. Later, while studying in San Francisco, she sketched Anna Pavlova dancing and the actor Margaret Anglin. The latter bought all the drawings of her and invited 23-year-old Meière to design costumes for the 1916 theatrical season in New York. During the First World War Hildreth studied mechanical drawing and surveying at the School of Applied Design for Women in New York to obtain a post in the Brooklyn Navy Yard, where the experience in tackling technical projects was invaluable.

From 1920 to 1922 Meière continued to study and won design competitions that resulted in her first mural commissions, working with architects to design murals for the homes of wealthy Manhattanites. Her first two significant commissions were for murals for the Nebraska State Capitol in Lincoln and the National Academy of Sciences in Washington, DC, both with the architect Bertram Goodhue. She worked on these major projects for four years. In the same period, she also won commissions for murals in ecclesiastical buildings, including Temple Emanu-El and St Bartholomew's Church in Manhattan.

Mural commissions involved a huge range of technical challenges, from translating two-dimensional cartoons of the design into the three-dimensional space required, to working across a wide range of media, including glass mosaic, ceramic tiles, marble, terracotta, metal, wood, enamel, stained glass and brick. The technical aspect of the work meant that Meière ran a large studio of technicians and had to deal with architects, clients, suppliers, craftspeople and builders for every commission, combining business and management skills with her artistic talent. She was celebrated in her day, winning such accolades as the Gold Medal in Mural Decoration from the Architectural League of New York in 1928, and newspaper and journal articles recognized her talent and unique representational style. Her stylized figures and geometric patterning introduced modernity to buildings across the country, pioneering a distinctive Art Deco

Mosaics designed by Hildreth Meière for the Temple Emanu-El,
a section of the design on the arch illustrating the creation.

approach that blended influences as diverse as early Byzantine mosaics,
classical Greek vase painting, Art Nouveau and Native American
beadwork. She believed that murals (which could be on walls, domes,
ceilings or floor) had to be integral to the structure they decorated.
A good mural, she maintained, was 'something that cannot be taken
away without hurting the design of the building. If the building looks
as well without it, it shouldn't be there in the first place.'[13]

Meière went on to provide some of the most iconic Art Deco
decoration of Radio City Music Hall as part of the Rockefeller Center
in the 1930s. Times got tougher during the Depression, when fewer
large buildings were commissioned, but she was successful in getting New Deal art contracts from the mid-1930s into the 1940s.
Established by the United States Treasury Department's Section of
Fine Arts, the New Deal programme awarded commissions for the
decoration of federal buildings. When the style for public buildings
became more severe and minimalist, her talents continued to be

employed in the decoration of religious buildings, including the National Cathedral in Washington.

Waiting for a Train

One area of Manhattan that changed the most during the 1920s was Midtown, between the main railway depots: Pennsylvania (Penn) Station (1910) on the west side at 33rd Street, and Grand Central Terminal (1913) on the east side at 42nd Street. These two transportation hubs, combined with the expansion of the subway system, drew millions of people to Midtown each week to work, play and shop. Around Penn Station were the offices and factories of the Garment District. Eastwards, near Herald Square, was the retail zone, including the giant Macy's department store, which opened in 1902 and had significant Art Deco additions in 1924 and 1928. To the north, Times Square was the city's entertainment centre, while the streets east of 5th Avenue were home to the gleaming new office towers that housed the corporations producing America's goods and services.

When Grand Central Depot was built in 1872 and was later redeveloped as Grand Central Terminal in 1898, the huge train yards were on the surface, with tracks fanning out from the station, creating a barrier to other traffic and taking up a huge amount of land. The lines into Grand Central stretched northwards from 42nd to 56th streets for nearly three-quarters of a mile, obliterating cross streets and forcing pedestrians to cross the yard on iron catwalks, braving swirling smoke and ash. After a terrible crash at Grand Central in 1902, when one train ploughed into the back of another because the signal had been obscured by smoke from the engines, the state legislature forced the New York Central Railroad, which owned the station, to electrify its steam locomotives. The introduction of electric trains made it possible to enclose the rail lines within tunnels. William J. Wilgus, the railway company's brilliant chief engineer, oversaw the electrification of the trains and the burying of the tracks. He then convinced the railway company to build the new station as a state-of-the-art terminal, with shop-lined underground passages leading to the subway system and to adjacent hotels and commercial buildings. His vision did not stop there. With the rail lines below ground, there was a huge real-estate opportunity. He suggested that the company build a new Park Avenue by leasing land to commercial builders where the old rail yard had stood. This would be on the roof of the new terminal's smokeless tunnels.

The New York Central Railroad changed its unsightly rail yard, an urban eyesore, into a new commercial and residential district that contemporaries called Terminal City. The project was completed with the building of the Waldorf-Astoria in 1930–31. The company accomplished this transformation by selling its 'air rights' above the ground that housed the tunnels – a new thing at the time – to property developers.

The plans for Terminal City provided for the efficient movement of cars as well as trains and people. An elevated roadway, or viaduct, ran over East 42nd Street and connected with a 'collar' road that encircled the terminal. When completed in 1927, the road carried north- and southbound traffic. Cars entered or left north Park Avenue by passing through arched portals built directly into the New York Central's new headquarters building. This was designed in high Beaux-Arts style, wedded to the most advanced building technology at the time of its completion in 1929. It was the world's first 'drive through' building, and it also has pedestrian walkways and a splendid through-block lobby. The building had a profusion of classical detail, including a pyramid roof and a magnificent lantern, floating above the city.[14]

Into the Wild Blue Yonder

Who could take a stroll through Manhattan and fail to be awed by the grandeur and magnificence of the tower soaring into the sky at Lexington Avenue and 42nd Street? There stands the Chrysler

Building, arguably the supreme icon of Art Deco New York, with the most instantly recognizable tower and spire:

> Built for an out-of-town automobile executive, designed by an architect whose other work is generally ignored, the tallest building in the world for barely twelve months before being eclipsed by the Empire State Building – yet here it is, the Chrysler Building: one of a kind, staggering, romantic, soaring, the embodiment of 1920s skyscraper pizzazz, the great Art Deco symbol of New York.[15]

Walter Chrysler personally financed the construction with his income from his car company, so that his sons could inherit the building. The Chrysler took the setback requirements to new heights of elegance in its series of receding parabolic arches, and exceeded all other designs in the way clues to its founding fortune are proclaimed in the form of automotive motifs incorporated into every feature of the decoration. The famous gargoyles thirty floors up, at the base of the upper setback of the tower, are modelled on the Chrysler Motors' bonnet ornaments. They are connected by grey and white mosaic circles representing tyres, which surround metal discs, representing hubcaps. The eagles at the corners of the tower on the 60th floor represent flight, embodying the machine age. The entire crown is clad with Nirosta, ribbed and riveted in a radiating sunburst pattern with many triangular vaulted windows, reminiscent of the spokes of a wheel.

At street level, the building exemplifies the Jazz Age love of zigzag decoration in the paving, the ways in which the walls of the entrances are stepped in, and the polished metal designs above the doors. The interior was equally lavishly decorated. Chrysler wanted the design to impress other architects and automobile magnates, so he imported various materials, such as African marble, regardless of the extra cost. The interior design incorporated many typical Art Deco themes, including abstract geometrical patterning and stylized

The spire of the Chrysler Building, by architect William Van Alen, 1928–30.

floral forms, although sadly throughout the leased offices much of this has been updated to 'modern' taste and office requirements in the late twentieth and early twenty-first centuries, and is now lost forever.

The highly unusual triangular lobby remains unchanged, its walls faced with polished stone in tones of red, yellow and amber. The dramatic design features include huge red marble pillars set with Van Alen's custom-designed lights. The lobby has dim lighting that, combined with the appliqués on the lamps, creates an intimate atmosphere and dramatizes the space. Vertical bars of neon lights are sheathed in the same Nirosta metal as the tower. An extraordinary ceiling painting by Edward Trumbull, *Transport and Human Endeavour*, pays homage to the machine age, road transport and aviation, including several silver aeroplanes and a depiction of the Chrysler Building itself. The ceiling paintings portray the task of creating the building, with pictures of surveyors, masons, carpenters, plasterers and builders, which are portraits of the actual workmen. The decoration also includes many typical design features of the era, with Art Deco triangles, sharp angles, gently curved lines, chrome detailing and a multitude of patterns.

There are 32 elevators in the skyscraper, clustered into four banks, giving the building three of the longest lift shafts in the world at the time of its completion. The elevator doors are one of the most painstaking parts of the interior design, and notably influenced by ancient Egyptian motifs. Made of metal and covered with eight types of exotic wood, they have ziggurat-shaped Mexican onyx panels above them. When the doors are closed, they resemble tall fans set off by metallic palm fronds rising through a series of silver parabolas, with the edges set off by curved lilies. Each lift is an exquisitely designed miniature Art Deco room. Both the doors and the lift interiors were considered works of extraordinary marquetry. According to the writer Vincent Curcio, 'these elevator interiors were perhaps the single most beautiful and, next to the dome, the most important feature of the entire building.'[16]

Walter Chrysler had been looking for a suitable plot since 1925 as the site for the global headquarters of his Detroit-based Chrysler Motors. By 1927 he had purchased the 84-year lease for the plot on Lexington Avenue, after long negotiations, for a reported $2 million. William Van Alen, who had been working on designs for the plot with the previous owner, William H. Reynolds, was retained by Chrysler. The architect had an original style, expressly his own, eclectic and adventurously modern. On 6 March 1928 Chrysler announced his plan to build a 68-storey tower 809 feet tall, twelve storeys higher than the massive Chanin Building being constructed across the street. Chrysler secured a $7.5 million loan from the mortgage specialist S. W. Straus & Co. to finance his dream. Some start-up work for the previous plans was demolished and construction of the building proper began on 21 January 1929. The steel structure had risen a few floors by June 1929. It was 35 floors high by early August and completed by September. Despite a frantic pace of about four floors per week, no workers died during the construction of the steelwork. The Chrysler Building was aiming to be the tallest habitable structure in the world, exceeding by 17 feet the Woolworth Building in Lower Manhattan.[17] Chrysler intended the building as a massive monument to himself, with his own office suite, bathroom and exquisite dining room right at the top, so that he could look down on the rest of the world.

Chrysler had begun his professional career as a humble machinist and railway mechanic. Pulling himself by his bootstraps up the corporate ladder, he developed an ego as large as one of his opulent 1928 Imperial sedans. At the age of 55 and the pinnacle of his career, now was the time to secure himself a bricks-and-mortar niche in the pantheon of business immortals. Reynolds had envisaged a building flowing with romantic imagery. Chrysler had different thoughts, with the building representing the triumph of the automobile, America's supreme success symbol.

This sparked competition, and by April 1928 a syndicate led by the investment banker George L. Ohrstrom had commissioned Van Alen's former architectural partner H. Craig Severance to design 'the tallest bank and office structure in the world', at 40 Wall Street. At a planned height of 840 feet, it would be 31 feet taller than the Chrysler Building. At the close of the 1920s these two buildings were in a skyscraper race.[18] The 40 Wall Street building was completed in 1929, standing at 927 feet in total with seventy storeys of office space above the Bank of Manhattan banking hall and a distinctive pyramidal crown, to create a typically romantic tower of the Roaring Twenties. Van Alen surprised everyone by making the Chrysler Building, completed the following year, taller than the announced plans had indicated, with an event that was to become a legend in architectural one-upmanship. Without fanfare, Chrysler unveiled his secret weapon. A spire 185 feet tall was furtively assembled inside the building's tower, and emerged from its chrome 'cocoon' and was bolted triumphantly into place on 23 October 1929. The 27-ton pinnacle was raised and secured in a breathless ninety minutes, a feat that had never before been achieved at that altitude. The gleaming silvery spear took the Chrysler Building's overall height to just over 961 feet, nearly 34 feet taller than its Downtown rival. Van Alen's acclaimed masterpiece had in the course of an afternoon become the game-changer in the New York skyline. However, it too was put in the shade by the sheer mass of the Empire State Building, which rises to 1,250 feet, with 102 storeys. Construction of the Empire State Building began on 17 March 1930 and was completed in a record-breaking one year and 45 days. Over just three years some of most iconic and tallest buildings had been designed and completed, changing the New York skyline dramatically.

You've Got to Be Modernistic

The seminal event that shaped Art Deco design was the Paris Exposition in 1925, a World's Fair-type exhibition designed by the French government to highlight the Style Moderne of architecture, interior decoration, furniture, glass, jewellery and other decorative arts in Europe and throughout the world. Many ideas of the international avant-garde in the fields of architecture and applied arts were presented for the first time at the Exposition. However, it is interesting to note that the fair had originally been planned for 1915. The First World War and its aftermath meant that it had to be postponed for ten years, and so not all the design ideas it put forward were totally new.

The programme for the Exposition stated that it was to be a celebration of modernism, not of historical styles. The organizers intended it to be 'open to all manufacturers whose products are artistic in character and show clearly modern tendencies'. A second purpose was attached to the Exposition by the French government: to honour the Allied countries after the First World War. For this reason, the new Soviet Union was invited, although its government was not yet recognized by France, while Germany was not included. There was much debate about the United States taking part. The contribution of $80,000 to sponsor national participation in the Exposition was a problem, and while designers and museum directors were keen that the USA be represented, they did not prevail, and the country officially declined to participate. Herbert Hoover, as Secretary of Commerce at the time, declared that there was no modern art in the United States. The Commerce Department did appoint an official delegation to attend the exhibition and issue a report. That report, which came out in 1926, stated that the USA had clearly misunderstood the purpose of the event, and that at least some participation should have been arranged to honour the French–American wartime alliance. While the USA did not have a pavilion, hundreds of American designers, artists, journalists and department-store buyers came to Paris to see the Exposition.

The official report and the American design professionals who attended the Exposition could see that the designs shown there would be influential in manufacturing in the United States, although the report was sceptical about the suitability of many of the exhibits for mass production. As a follow-on from the Exposition, four hundred of the more 'transferable' objects were selected for an exhibition to be held in America. These included glass, ceramics, textiles, lighting and some furniture. It is noteworthy that the American curators passed over the more avant-garde, strictly modern designs of Eileen Gray and Le Corbusier, and stuck with the designs that reflected the more traditional 'decorative' element. This may be one reason that Art Deco took off so strongly in New York, as the more challenging aspects of the Style Moderne did not make it across the Atlantic.

Macy's hosted an exhibition in 1926 in which the items were displayed in room settings, but not for sale. This attracted 50,000 visitors, signalling a huge increase of public interest in design as a discipline and something to be considered when making purchases for the 'ideal home'. Based on this success, and the subsequent development of the production of objects for the home influenced by the modern style, Macy's next exhibition in 1927 presented an entire house of modern design, with all the items for sale being American mass-produced ceramics, furniture, glassware and textiles based on French designs. These were cheaper than the artisan-executed objects from the original Exposition, but still relatively expensive. However, sales were higher than expected. Other stores followed suit, and in 1928 Lord & Taylor set up a new department, French Modern Design, featuring modern furniture and decorative items for the home. Although stylish, the furniture was liveable and practical, designed for 'smart city living', made from American woods and replacing the traditional 'added on' ornamentation with decoration that was integral to the design. Again, this department was a huge success for the store. People were convinced that it was important to have modern objects in their homes, and sales boomed, accounting for 20 per cent of Lord & Taylor's furniture sales in the department's first year.

Not to be outdone, in 1928 Macy's put on a new exhibition, 'The International Exposition of Art in Industry', featuring 5,000 designer objects for the home, again not directly for sale. The exhibition included a lecture series, fifteen room settings featuring designers from different countries, and ceremonies involving ambassadors from the contributing countries. It was so popular that Macy's had to employ special attendants to keep people moving through. One of the u.s. designers to be featured in the exhibition was Kem Weber, a furniture and industrial designer, architect, art director and teacher, who created several iconic designs in the 'Streamline' style. Weber's designs for a three-room apartment were featured in the November 1928 issue of Condé Nast's interior-design magazine *House & Garden*, which asked:

> Modernism – what about it? Should one loathe it? ... or love it? How to make use of it? *House & Garden* gives you a yardstick. Shows you modernist contrasted with classical ... What the Viennese and Germans are doing, and the

Kem Weber suite of furniture for a sitting room and bedroom designed for Macy's 1928 exhibition.

Americans, too … seven rooms by seven recognized American experts.[19]

It was an exciting time for the decorative arts in New York. The highly influential American Designers' Gallery was founded in the city in 1928 to promote high aesthetic standards in the modern decorative arts and to support designers' professional standing. Its headquarters were at the gallery of the interior designer and decorator Paul T. Frankl, and Donald Deskey, Ruth Reeves, Joseph Urban and Henry Varnum Poor were among its members. An inaugural show was held in the Chase National Bank building in New York in 1928, showcasing fifteen designers across ten room settings. Urban showcased boudoir style in a lady's bedroom and dressing room, while Deskey's 'Man's Room' highlighted industrial design using such materials as cork, vitrolite and aluminium. In the second exhibition, held in 1929, the American Designers' Gallery offered something not previously seen by the American public: a coherent vision of modern design, based on developments in France, Germany and Austria, but adapted so as to be characterized by affordability, simplicity and practicality to fit into both a modern city apartment and a traditional home.

Luxurious French Art Deco was too exclusive to adapt to mass production for the American home, but it was a very important influence on American commercial design. The elements of what was known as the jazz style – sharp diagonal lines, bold colours and design inspired by machinery – appeared across modern home furnishings, on rugs, curtains, armchairs, and in such items as bookends shaped like factory cogs and glass bowls from industrial moulded lenses. Designers drew on the dominant profile of the skyscraper for their home interiors products, including the 'skyscraper' bookcases deigned by Paul Frankl, while the Stehli Silks Corporation engaged contemporary designers to produce a collection of American prints that incorporated the skyscraper, jazz and other notes of energetic America.[20]

Walter Dorwin Teague, Lens Bowl.

While the Paris Exposition had been characterized by artisan-produced objects in the decorative arts tradition, when the new design styles hit New York the forces of mass production harnessed good design to produce machine-made objects to symbolize progress. The styling that was shaping the automotive industry was also reflected in such items as perfume bottles and the cocktail sets that were so fashionable in the period, with cocktail shakers, ice buckets and ashtrays taking on the streamlined shapes that were becoming apparent in cars, trains and planes. Objects that could be shown off when entertaining were particularly made in this form, such as Walter Dorwin Teague's Lens Bowl for the Steuben Company, which used the moulds that Steuben employed to produce railway signal lights. The bowl's concentric circles were designed to disperse light and made a dramatic presence on the dining table. Designers used a wider range of materials than in traditional work, including plate glass, tubular steel and wrought iron, all of which had previously been used exclusively in construction.

The emigration of a number of talented designers from Europe to the United States led to the cross-fertilization of French avant-garde artistic movements with Austro-Hungarian and German design training and the American interest in industrial design and production. This meant that modern design was not only compelling in its originality but also available at a price that many New Yorkers could afford. One of the design icons of the 1920s that continues to the present day is the martini glass, introduced at the Exposition. It was completely different from the rounded coupe glass or Paris goblet that had dominated up to that point. The aesthetic of the martini glass is angular and sleek, intrinsically modern. It had immediate cachet and has never been out of style since.

7

I Got Plenty of Nothing

A plaque at the entrance to New York's Center for Jewish History quotes a remark by Sultan Bayezid II, ruler of the Ottoman Empire from 1481 to 1512: 'You call Ferdinand a wise king, he, who by expelling the Jews has impoverished his country and enriched mine.'

That 'wise king' was Ferdinand of Aragon, who in 1492, along with his wife, Queen Isabella of Castile, issued the Edict of Expulsion that banished nearly 100,000 Jewish people from Spain. (The king and queen were known as the Catholic Monarchs.) The exodus of the people who had contributed the lifeblood to Spain's intellectual and scientific life resulted in a massive dispersal, not only throughout the Ottoman Empire, but also across Europe and even to Latin America.[1] Evidence of this near-global dispersal was borne out more than a century and a half later, when in August 1654 Jacob Barsimson, an Ashkenazi of Central European descent, became the first Jew to set foot in New Amsterdam. A month later, 23 Jewish descendants of the Spanish expulsion braved the fierce Atlantic swell, sailing north from Brazil to the Dutch colony that was to become New York. They were followed shortly thereafter by a group of refugees from Curaçao who, like their brethren, were fleeing religious persecution in their homeland.

As a gesture of affirmation of their faith in 1655, the recently landed Sephardic Jews from Brazil founded Congregation Shearith

New York City, with the Lower East Side.

Israel, New York's Spanish and Portuguese Synagogue, in what is today William Street near Battery Park at the southern tip of Manhattan. This was the first Jewish congregation to be established in North America. The neoclassical colonnaded synagogue was built in 1896–7 as the fourth home of the congregation, and stands in West 70th Street.

Most of these refugees were given a hostile reception by Peter Stuyvesant, the settlement's governor in the seventeenth century. They were offered little opportunity to eke out a living in trades other than meatpacking and retail butchery, which became a staple of Jewish employment in Manhattan's Lower East Side. This policy of job exclusion carried on well into the 1920s. Fearful of competition from better-educated, more skilled newcomers, labour organizations such as the Irish-dominated construction workers' brotherhood proscribed Jews from membership. In spite of the difficulties they faced in their new home, tens of thousands of Jewish people escaping a life of hardship and persecution in Russia and Eastern Europe chose to make the Atlantic crossing to settle in the area bounded roughly by Broadway and Pearl Street to the west, 14th Street to the north, Fulton and Franklin streets to the south, and the East River to the east.

When Stuyvesant left office in 1664, after the English takeover of the colony that was to change its name from New Amsterdam to New York, restrictions were gradually relaxed and Jewish immigrants were given rights they had been hitherto denied. They could now acquire property and take up employment in most trades, though they were still barred from holding public office.

The event that sparked the flight of hundreds of thousands of Russian Jews, as well as a number of Polish Jews, was the assassination in 1881 of Tsar Alexander II. Regardless of the fact that Alexander had followed a moderately benevolent policy towards his Jewish subjects, the Russian hierarchy immediately pointed the finger at the Jews, a traditional target of hatred in nineteenth-century Russia. It later emerged that the culprits were four agents of the revolutionary political organization Narodnaya Volya (People's Freedom), an organized group of thugs who conducted assassinations of government officials in an attempt to overthrow the country's autocratic system and sabotage Alexander's reforms. The bloody pogroms that followed prompted 150,000 Jewish people to emigrate to America in less than a decade, most of whom settled in New York.

By the 1920s New York's Jewish population far exceeded one million, making the city home to the world's largest Jewish community. Most had grown up in towns and cities, so it was unsurprising that agricultural work attracted few if any of the Jewish settlers seeking to carve out a living in their new country. Nearly 200,000 gave their occupation as tailor, shoemaker, clerk or bookkeeper, and, as the historian Alyn Brodsky explains:

> These immigrants were the dominant labour force in the garment industry, known colloquially as 'the rag trade'. Most

– the so-called sweaters – were forced to work in either the sweatshops of subcontractors or, for the most part, in their own dingy rooms on a piece-work basis. They were underpaid and exploited. Those unable to find jobs resorted to peddling, which became a big business on the Lower East Side.[2]

In the early years of the decade the Lower East Side had become home to tens of thousands of Jewish immigrants. While these people made up the district's overwhelming ethnic majority, they also shared the crowded, bustling streets with settlers from Hungary, Romania, Greece and several other European countries. As the decade progressed, Jewish men found their way into unglamorous but at least money-earning trades, from pushcart vendors

Life on the Lower East Side.

New York garment workers parading on May Day.

of cheap clothing to shop owners selling household items. Their wives would sometimes turn their dwellings into garment workshops, earning derisory wages to produce fashion ware that would find its way into stylish department stores, such as Bloomingdale's, B. Altman and Saks Fifth Avenue. It is worthy of note that some earlier Jewish immigrants of formidable entrepreneurial spirit had managed to surmount the barriers of religious prejudice and create great retail empires. In fact, all three of these landmark Manhattan retail emporiums had been founded in the nineteenth century by German Jewish émigrés.

The ramshackle tenements of the Lower East Side attested to the fact that not all New Yorkers of the Roaring Twenties were swept up in a life of jazz clubs, cocktail bars and ballroom dance halls. The word 'substandard' would be a gross understatement for describing living conditions in the cramped, insalubrious houses of the neighbourhood, often lacking indoor plumbing, with shared bathrooms and smoky coal-fired stoves and heaters. Many of these buildings were owned by earlier German Jewish immigrants, those who had made their money and settled in the genteel streets of Uptown Manhattan. Four to six storeys in height, the tenements contained four separate dwellings per floor, each measuring on average 325 square feet. The flats consisted of just three rooms: a windowless bedroom, a kitchen and a street-facing room with windows. For large families, all three rooms became bedrooms at night. Cramped, poorly lit, under-ventilated, the tenements were hotbeds of vermin and disease and were frequently swept by cholera, typhus and tuberculosis. The neighbourhood remained a prototypical big-city slum, despite attempts at mandating improvements. One proposed improvement was the introduction of 'dumbbell' tenements, a multiple-dwelling, substandard block of flats, usually three to five storeys high, containing relatively long, narrow apartments. There were windows only at the front and rear of each apartment, and shafts on one or both sides of the flat provided air and a little light to the rooms that did not face front or back. The floor plan of each dwelling resembled the outline of a dumbbell, hence the name.

The squalor and deprivation that were endemic to tenement life did not dampen these immigrants' creative spirit. In the 1920s the lower stretch of Second Avenue became home to numerous theatres performing stage classics from vaudeville to Shakespeare, as well as Yiddish productions. These playhouses represented an escape valve from the drudgery of the daily grind, and as such were

Courtyard of a Lower East Side tenement.

very popular. The Lower East Side and neighbouring areas came to be known as the Yiddish Theatre District, one of the busiest stage entertainment venues in the world, with eleven theatres showing twenty to thirty plays a night. The sumptuously crafted Moorish Revival-style Louis N. Jaffe Art Theatre, which opened in 1926, became home to the work of many of the most prominent figures of the Yiddish and English-language stage. The following year brought the opening of the Public Theatre, a building designed by H. Craig Severance, the architect of such notable New York landmarks as the Coca-Cola Building, the Nelson Tower and, most prominently, 40 Wall Street.

The profusion of Second Avenue theatres kick-started an explosion of cinemas that became an alternative to the stage and offered a more affordable evening's entertainment for those of lesser means. The early cinemas were called 'nickelodeons', as tickets cost five cents, or a 'nickel' and were basically simple rooms with camp chairs, a screen and a rudimentary projector. The Lower East Side became a byword for motion pictures, especially after the premiere in 1927 of the first 'talkie', *The Jazz Singer*, starring Al Jolson – himself raised in the neighbourhood. This vibrant New York community produced the studio moguls Marcus Loew and William Fox, along with many eminent names of the silver screen. By the late 1920s Second Avenue and its environs boasted the densest concentration of cinemas not just in New York City, but in the entire nation.

One of the most enterprising promoters of the cinema vogue was the movie mogul Adolph Zukor, who was raised – as were Jolson, Loew and others of his generation – on the Lower East Side. Entertainment-deprived people craved a night out at the cinema, an opportunity that Zukor grasped with both hands. 'The public is never wrong!' he proclaimed. Zukor, a Jewish immigrant from Hungary, rose from humble origins to become one of the most successful film producers of the 1920s. His career took off with the premiere in 1920 of *Humoresque*, the semi-autobiographical story of a Lower East Side boy from a poor Jewish family who becomes a successful violinist and brings fortune to the family. The film was partially financed by William Randolph Hearst, the right-wing press baron who nevertheless sympathized with the Jewish people and once confronted Hitler over his antisemitism. Zukor began his working life as an apprentice in an upholstery shop and later became a successful furrier, but he knew his true vocation lay elsewhere. When it became apparent that the cinema craze was spreading rapidly across Lower Manhattan, he took a gamble and invested in the first motion-picture theatre chain in America, led by the brothers Mitchel and Moe Mark. Zukor went on to launch his own film distribution company, which in 1927 became known as the renowned Paramount Pictures.

Yiddish theatre gave rise to an entire ecosystem of cafes and restaurants along Second Avenue, for the growing community of Jewish people who had managed to fight their way up the social ladder. Café Royale, on the corner of 12th Street and Second Avenue, became the forum of Jewish intelligentsia, the place to learn anything

Yiddish theatre took off in the 1920s. Actors at a Brooklyn party in 1925.

about Yiddish theatre, music, art or letters. The doyenne of Jewish theatre, Sara Adler, held court almost nightly at the Royale. Reuben Guskin, manager of the Hebrew Actors Union, interviewed people in the cafe, where many a business deal was also consummated. The nearby Romanian steakhouse Moskowitz & Lupowitz appealed to tastes high and low. The restaurant was name-dropped to impress a girl in the James Cagney film *City for Conquest* in 1940, but it also released winning Yiddish radio jingles, promising free parking at the 'most prominent and popular' Romanian restaurant on the East Side.

East Side, West Side

The Jews were not the first group of refugees to seek a life of financial security and, it cannot be overemphasized, personal survival in New York. They had been pre-dated by some four decades by tens of thousands of Irish people fleeing the ravages of the potato famine of 1845. Five years after the first émigrés had set sail on what were dubbed 'famine ships', primarily from Liverpool as well as from the Irish ports of Cork and Limerick, the United States census reported that 133,000 New Yorkers – about a quarter of the total population – had been born in Ireland. Although vastly outnumbered by the Jewish presence, by 1920 the Irish still made up a fifth of New York's population. They invariably gravitated towards the most affordable areas of Lower Manhattan. A clannish people, they gathered in wards that became replicas of their home counties. Housing in these neighbourhoods could be described only as slums, an assortment of dilapidated wooden dwellings. A run-down tenement in the predominantly Jewish Lower East Side could by contrast be considered a desirable place to live.

Unlike the Jewish workers of the rag trade and other 'soft' professions, a number of Irish men found employment as manual workers, many of them as day labourers on construction sites. By 1860 Irish-born men accounted for 38 per cent of the workforce in

Family shelling pecans in a Lower East Side tenement.

skilled manual jobs, and an even higher percentage were to be found toiling in unskilled lines of work. Irish women immigrants also became part of the workforce, most of them employed as domestic servants and seamstresses. The Irish also gained a reputation as skilled plumbers, carpenters, plasterers and bricklayers, although working generally at the low-paid end of these trades. Irish peddlers were a not uncommon sight in the teeming cobbled streets of Lower Manhattan. They hawked commodities denied to Jewish pushcart merchants, such as clams and other non-kosher varieties of seafood. Many enterprising Irish peddlers managed to turn their pushcarts into thriving enterprises. The edition of *Trow's New York Directory* from 1865 makes mention of one Hugh Torpey, whose street-seller business is given as 'pocketbooks'. Torpey had by that year had amassed an almost unheard-of balance of $2,000 in his bank account, equivalent in purchasing power to more than $37,000 today.

An even more impressive example of the Irish resolve to turn starvation at home into triumph in New York was the career of

Michael Moran. Shortly after stepping off the boat in 1850, Moran began earning his living at fifty cents a day as a mule driver on the Erie Canal. Ten years later he had accumulated sufficient funds to pay $2,700 for a tow boat used to haul cargo-laden barges from New York to Albany. By the 1920s his descendants were operating the world's largest fleet of tugboats.

Irish entrepreneurship was by no means confined to street trading, working on building sites and other manual labour. Far from it: the ranks of the police department, the fire brigade and several areas of city government were in due course dominated by Irish immigrants or their descendants. It was not by serendipity that the Irish came to prevail in those professions. For well over a century, they had enjoyed the support of what had by that time become New York City's most powerful political benefactor.

In 1789, a few weeks after George Washington's inauguration as the first American President at New York's Federal Hall, an Irish-American veteran of America's War of Independence, William Mooney, founded a political club that went by the name of the Society of St Tammany. The organization was headquartered in a large brownstone on East 14th Street, dubbed by its members 'The Wigwam' and in time to be known as Tammany Hall. At the time of Tammany's foundation – ostensibly as a humanitarian association with the aim of supporting the common citizen – the Irish of New York had become the target of the Anglo-American establishment's anti-alien and anti-Catholic prejudices.

A characteristic of the city's Irish working-class ghettos was the omnipotence of Tammany Hall. The Machine's (as it was known) formula for success lay in its ability to satisfy basic human needs, mostly in the form of municipal jobs and benevolent acts to ease the daily burdens of constituents – a bucket of coal when money was tight, bailing a son out of jail after a night of hooliganism – as well as the provision of a sense of community. All this forged a spirit of fealty between Machine and constituent, and secured generations of political loyalty. These operations also required exorbitant sums of money, easily obtained over decades of looting the city treasury.

Tammany became the single most important factor in the virtual Irish takeover of New York politics from 1880, the year in which the city elected its first Irish Catholic mayor, the Tammany-backed candidate William R. Grace. From that date onwards, the Irish began to acquire what became almost total control of the city's Democratic Party, thanks to the power of Tammany. It is not by coincidence that John Francis Hylan and Jimmy Walker, the two men who served as Mayor of New York during the Roaring Twenties, were both sons of Irish immigrants. 'The great majority of appointed government officials' under Walker, the writer Donald Miller explains,

> including most department heads, were Irish, as were six of
> the eight members of the Board of Estimate and most of Walker's
> personal staff. Under Walker, the Irish would continue to
> dominate in official circles, while the Board of Aldermen, with
> jurisdiction over such weighty matters as parades, steamboat
> whistles and circuses, was a kind of Hibernian social club.[3]

Under Tammany's vote-seeking patronage, the Irish presence in New York's political, social and business life grew to become virtually ubiquitous. Most of Tammany's enduring power and prestige lay in its ability to provide jobs and political preference for the Irish immigrants who were pouring into the city in the early 1920s. The process of filling vacancies in the police and fire departments with citizens of Irish descent gave to these branches of the municipal service an Irish complexion that has persisted to this day. In 1928 a group of Irish journalists founded the *Irish Echo*, the nation's first Irish newspaper. Irish bars and restaurants resounded with the voices of Irish tenors, and by the end of the decade nearly twenty radio stations were broadcasting Irish programmes. The Irish have also given Broadway and the cinema world some of its most notable actors, dramatists and producers. Look no further than the screen star James Cagney, a native of the Lower East Side, or the playwright and composer George M. Cohan, whose statue stands in Times Square.

If ever there were an irrefutable chalk-and-cheese clash of cultures, the Jews and the Irish would be an ideal fit – or so the popular perception might have it. On closer inspection, this is a flawed stereotype on several counts. Jewish and Irish people met informally on streets and in apartment buildings, and connected in the labour movement, through politics and schools. In these encounters, Irish Americans, who had been in New York longer and had established crucial power bases, often served as mentors, models and mediators for Jewish people. The latter received a welcome at New York's Irish-Catholic St John's University during the interwar period, and Jewish athletes became standard-bearers for the institution. Even the traditional corned beef and cabbage sandwich enjoyed by the New York Irish on St Patrick's Day is a dish of Jewish origin.

In the early days of the so-called melting pot of New York City, both these peoples shared an entrepreneurial drive, as well as a penchant for uninhibited fun when the occasion called for it, along with a talent for the arts in its various guises. The Irish took to New York their age-old love of music. One of the Irish community's outstanding musical virtuosos was Michael Coleman, an exponent of the Sligo fiddle style, who recorded for dozens of labels in New York as well as his native country. Irish music halls opened across the city, from the Star of Munster in the Bronx, to the Innisfail on the Upper East Side. Almost a dozen more of these lively venues were clustered in central Harlem.[4]

The Irish also shared with the Jews a history of victimization, at the hands of Russian and Eastern European governments in the case of the Jewish people, and of their English overlords in the case of the Irish. After the Irish Civil War of 1922–3, in which the British-backed Provisional Government defeated the pro-Republican forces, many ex-combatants on the losing side emigrated and settled in New York.

Governor Alfred E. Smith, champion of New York's Irish blue-collar workers.

Once they had become integrated in their new neighbourhoods, Irish Republican militants turned their efforts to supporting the city's working class. They became instrumental in the organized labour movement, notably the Transport Workers Union, which, by the end of the decade, counted Irish-born members as about half of its membership. The union was founded by New York subway workers belonging to the Irish nationalist organization Clan na Gael (Family of the Gaels), which had received an influx of Irish Republican Army veterans.

Alfred E. Smith was undeniably the champion of the New York Irish blue-collar worker. A native of the Lower East Side and grandson of immigrants from County Westmeath, Smith had a meteoric political career, propelled by the hand of Tammany, that took him from president of the New York City Board of Aldermen to four-time Governor of New York State and, in 1928, Democratic Party nominee for President of the United States (the first Catholic to run for that office). Given his humble origins as a newspaper hawker and fishmonger's assistant, Smith's rise to prominence has no exact parallel in American history. He brought a common touch to New York politics, with his bowler hat, Lower East Side accent and campaigning theme song, 'The Sidewalks of New York'. In his years in office Smith, a native of the overwhelmingly Irish Fourth Ward, reorganized the city's political structure. He pushed through a host of bills favouring the working class, from improved social housing to progressive education in state schools and massive public works projects. He became known as the city's 'First Citizen', but the country 'voted against his Catholicism and his New York urbanism in the presidential election of 1928'.[5]

Herbert Hoover, the Republican Party candidate and scion of the Protestant establishment, polled nearly 6.5 million more votes than Smith. But if not the presidency of the United States, Smith was destined to hold that title in an epic business enterprise shortly after his retirement from politics. He returned to New York from Washington to become the president of Empire State Inc., the corporation that built and operated the Empire State Building.

I Wanna Be Loved by You

The seemingly endless groundswell of foreigners disembarking at New York Harbor was destined to provoke a backlash, from United States officialdom as well as from those who had preceded the new arrivals and regarded them as a threat to their established way of life and livelihoods. It was decided that some form of supervision over the numbers and nationalities of entrants was required. To this end the government opened Ellis Island as an immigrant processing centre on New Year's morning in 1892. By the mid-1920s sixteen million people, the vast majority from Southern and Central Europe, had passed through the wooden building on this island, a ten-minute ferry journey from the Statue of Liberty.[6]

Antipathy towards immigrants remained a festering sore well into the twentieth century. It was first enshrined in a law of 1917, enthusiastically adopted by Congress, which set down 'medical' guidelines in language that almost beggars belief. The list of exclusions consisted of persons who are 'mentally defective', 'idiots', 'imbeciles', 'persons of constitutional psychopathic inferiority' and 'persons afflicted with a loathsome or dangerous contagious disease'. It was the sort of language that could have been lifted from a Nazi manifesto. This was a clear, albeit decidedly objectionable expression of the United States government's determination to prevent a repetition of the nineteenth-century avalanche of immigrants.

Those who were fortunate enough to be admitted to the country in the early years of the 1920s can truly be said to have slipped in under the wire. In 1924 the gates shut with a resounding clang when – with some two million foreign-born people making up nearly a third of New York City's total population – Congress enacted the

Italian
immigrants
arriving at
Ellis Island.

Immigration Act. This draconian piece of xenophobic legislation supplanted earlier statutes, its spirit justified by one of its leading proponents, U.S. Representative Albert Johnson, as a bulwark against 'a stream of alien blood'.

The congressional decision effectively slapped a ban on all immigration from Asia and set a total entry quota of 165,000 people per year for natives of countries outside the Western hemisphere. This represented an 80 per cent reduction from the average number of foreigners disembarking in New York before the First World War.

In the years immediately after the war, followers of the Italian anarchist Luigi Galleani unleashed a surge of terrorist acts across the United States. Galleani cautiously distanced himself from this campaign and managed to work behind the scenes until his eventual deportation back to Italy. On 20 September 1920 the Wall Street financial district of Manhattan became the target of the deadliest of these attacks. On that afternoon, a horse-drawn carriage drew up in front of crowds on their lunch break across the road from the J. P. Morgan headquarters. Without warning, a gigantic bomb filled, it is believed, with more than 100 pounds of dynamite and iron shrapnel was detonated, leaving 38 bystanders dead and hundreds more injured.

No group or individual ever claimed responsibility for the bombing. Based on similar attacks over the previous decade, the Bureau of Investigation (the predecessor to the FBI) initially suspected followers of Galleani of carrying out the bombing, but the case could not be proved. Over the next three years, hot leads turned cold and promising trails turned into dead ends. The bombers were never identified. The best evidence and analysis since that fateful day suggests that a small group of Italian anarchists were to blame, but more than a century later the mystery remains unsolved.

The bombing drew outraged calls for a crackdown on immigration. Add to that the fear of alien ways of life taking hold in society, mainly in the aftermath of the Bolshevik takeover in Russia, and

Anarchist bombing of Wall Street in 1920.

electoral victories in the New York Assembly by self-declared social-
ists, and it was not long before traditional moderates added their
voices to the outcry demanding a clampdown on foreigners coming
to live in New York.

Less than a month after the Wall Street bombing the *New York
Times*, the establishment newspaper whose editorial line is custom-
arily associated with restraint and moderation, ran the incendiary
headline 'Ellis Island Faces Influx of Millions'. The paper seemed to
be warning its readers: 'Since early in the summer aliens have been
entering American in unprecedented numbers. There is no sign of
a let-up and the landing agent of an Italian Line said yesterday that
thousands of families were now gathered at Italian ports awaiting a
chance to get here, whether it be in steerage or cabin.'[7] This reflected
growing resentment of a trend that, as the influential American journalist Henry Louis Mencken noted in *Diary*, his book of personal
memoirs, was turning New York into 'a bawdy freeport, without
nationality or personality'.

The fact is that the U.S. government at that time had in hand
267,000 applications for passports from Poland alone, while between
three and four million Italians were seeking domicile status and

citizenship. Among the more curious reasons offered for wishing to emigrate to the United States, many Italian farmers declared that they had been forced to quit tilling their native soil because of the danger from explosives scattered about the old wartime battlefields.

The rising flood of poverty-stricken Europeans disembarking in record numbers at the Port of New York in the early 1920s set alarm bells ringing in anti-immigration circles. One could pick almost any date at random and find a large number of ships arriving on that day alone. Take, for instance, 23 May 1922, when seventeen passenger ships docked in New York from Hamburg, Genoa, Rotterdam and other European points of departure.

The cries for tighter U.S. immigration laws did not go unheeded by the tens of thousands hoping to make the Atlantic crossing. In an astute effort to sidestep official restrictions, many Italians booked passage to Canada via the Port of New York, allegedly to continue their journey northwards to seek work as agricultural labourers on Canadian farms. There were at that point 600,000 Italians waiting to enter the United States, far in excess of the 42,000 yearly quota. Canadian immigration authorities, working with Ellis Island officials, were not amused to discover that a considerable number of these newly disembarked passengers were quietly slipping off their Canada-bound trains at Manhattan's 125th Street station, to vanish into the nooks and crannies of Harlem. Those unfortunate enough to be traced and arrested were summarily deported.

The restrictions imposed on foreign entrants did not prove as effective a deterrent as had been hoped. Manhattan was where most immigrants chose to make their home. By the end of the 1920s Jewish people accounted for almost 642,000 Manhattanites, a quarter of the island's population. Black migrants from other parts of the country or abroad numbered some 225,000, while almost 118,000 Italians comprised the second-largest foreign-born white community.

Far from having to tolerate harassment by immigration officials after the 1924 Act, Italians could claim their historic right to settle in a city that one of their countrymen was the first to explore more than 450 years ago. After all, it was the Florentine seafarer Giovanni da Verrazzano (whose name was given to the suspension bridge that opened in 1964 connecting Staten Island to Brooklyn) who sailed past these two future boroughs on his exploration of New York Bay in 1524.

The Italians found few friends in the city's political circles, despite the fact that by 1921 they comprised more than 15 per cent of New York's foreign-born population. Neglected by Tammany Hall, they were slow to infiltrate the Irish-dominated machine. On the other hand, newly landed Italians did not restrict themselves to conventional immigrant habitats, such as the Lower East Side. They instead formed cohesive ethnic groups in the Red Hook section of Brooklyn and eventually in the Bronx, south of Fordham Road. East Harlem's Little Italy was where some 50,000 people of Italian heritage built a community in an area that extended from 110th to 125th streets, along the East River waterfront. This was for many years New York's chief Italian quarter, home to a future mayor, Fiorello La Guardia, and not a few Mafia chieftains. Another Italian enclave, which in popular culture has always been known as Little Italy – though far more populous than its smaller neighbour uptown – was in Lower Manhattan. There are today about 100,000 residents of mostly second- and third-generation Italian Americans living in this neighbourhood. This is a far cry from the 100,000 who inhabited its bustling streets in the 1920s, originating at Mulberry Bend south of Canal Street, just north of what was the notoriously crime-ridden Five Points.[8]

It was never going to be an easy life for those who managed to put together sufficient money to obtain passage to New York and who evaded immigration restrictions. Pasquale D'Angelo, who hailed from the lush, mountainous Abruzzi region east of Rome, found himself toiling as a day labourer on the dusty highways north of New York City. When a job came to an end, with no prospect of another in sight, D'Angelo and his compatriots returned to Mulberry Street, the headquarters of dozens of Italian padroni, the term applied to employers who exploited immigrant workers. As time passed and still no work was on the horizon, he would dip into his meagre savings to rent a room in one of the overcrowded boarding houses of the Five Points slums. As D'Angelo once remarked,

> A man may pay a large part of his scanty savings for fare (to work in a distant region) and when he gets there he may find living conditions impossible and the foreman too overbearing. Perhaps he will be fired at the end of the week. Where will he be then?[9]

Had D'Angelo remained at home in Italy tilling his fields or tending his goats, he would never have been motivated to grab the American dream with both hands: 'Once he had a command of basic English vocabulary, D'Angelo bought a second-hand dictionary for 25 cents and began obsessively memorizing its contents.'[10]

Inspired by the possibilities New York offered a person of determination, D'Angelo embarked on a remarkable literary career. This nearly destitute Italian immigrant made the public library his second home, and there he developed a passion for such poets as Percy Bysshe Shelley and John Keats. D'Angelo gave up his waterfront job and doggedly ignored the steady stream of rejection slips from literary journals and magazines. His perseverance paid off when the critic and academic Carl Van Doren, who judged *The Nation*'s annual poetry competition, wrote a profile of D'Angelo in that journal. This was D'Angelo's big break, which opened doors for his poetry and eventually a full-length autobiography that catapulted him to literary fame. It was the classic rags-to-riches tale that interlocked with the dauntless spirit of 1920s New York.

The Italians, perhaps more than any other European immigrants, were filled with a patriotic enthusiasm for their new home, having come from a country that fought on the side of the Allies in the First World War. When U.S. Army major La Guardia returned to his native Harlem from the firing line in Europe and was nominated for president of the Board of Aldermen, it was the city's Italian Americans who secured his victory over the Tammany candidate.

In spite of the encroachment of Chinatown since 1965, when laws restricting the entry of Asian immigrants were relaxed, the Italians of Little Italy hold fast to traditions of the Old Country. For eleven days in September, more than a million visitors fill a six-block area during the feast of San Gennaro, patron saint of Naples, a street festival celebrating Italian culture. The feast was founded in 1926 as a one-day religious commemoration to celebrate the arrival of immigrants from Naples. The neighbourhood has always been clannish to its marrow. Suffice it to cite the election for New York Supreme Court judges in 1923. Votes cast in the predominantly Italian Second Assembly District, bounded by Elizabeth and Mulberry streets, returned three hundred votes for Salvatore A. Cotillo, another three hundred for John J. Freschi and a single vote (presumably cast by the candidate himself) for Aaron J. Levy.

Walk Right In

There was one group of people who remained virtually untouched by immigration restrictions and thus escaped the humiliation of a three- to five-hour interrogation and medical examination on arrival at Ellis Island. These were the black Americans, who by 1925 (the year after the Immigration Act came into force) numbered more than 200,000 in the five boroughs of New York City. This formed the largest black community in the United States.

The greatest concentration of black residents was to be found in the northern reaches of Manhattan, from 128th to 145th streets, between Seventh and Fifth avenues. During much of the city's history, the words 'Harlem' and 'black' have been very closely linked. Yet until the early twentieth century Harlem was overwhelmingly and at different periods an Anglo-Saxon, German, Jewish and Irish stronghold. This uptown neighbourhood for years stood as a retreat for those New Yorkers, native and immigrant alike, who could afford to rent the elegant brownstones built for upper-middle-class whites. Many of these town houses sit in 'Strivers' Row', on both sides of West 138th and 139th streets, in what is now the St Nicholas Historic District. With New York's economic expansion in the boom years of the 1920s, when per capita income grew by a third, many of the well-to-do began moving into even more luxurious accommodation on the Upper East Side. For years, a number of these grand Harlem brownstones stood empty, or were converted into rental flats. When the property manager Philip A. Payton, who came to be known as the 'Father of Harlem', offered to fill the vacant houses with black tenants, the neighbourhood management company relented and gave its consent. Black professionals, albeit few in number, who had amassed sufficient equity in such fields as medicine, law, dentistry and the arts soon began purchasing houses, which at the time were selling for the considerable sum of $8,000 each.

That is not to suggest that the influx of black tenants and property owners was met with indifference in the white community. There was actually an organized resistance to keep Harlem an exclusively white neighbourhood. Such groups as the Save Harlem Committee, Anglo-Saxon Realty and the Protective Association for 130th to 132nd Streets fought to preserve the ethnic status quo. Most infamous of these organizations was the Harlem Property Owners Improvement Association, led by John G. Taylor, who, as the historian Jonathan Gill explains, 'had made his money investing in black saloons in the Tenderloin'. The association raised $100,000 'to buy properties that were in danger of being sold to Negroes.'[11] Taylor, a police officer, committed bigot and Harlem resident, launched a campaign to prevent black people from using the New York Public Library branch at West 135th Street. He gave his seal of approval to mass evictions of black tenants, attempted to reinstate racial segregation of the elevated subway lines that crossed Harlem, and advocated for the installation of a high fence to stop black people from moving north of 136th Street. Needless to say, the rants by Taylor and his associates were doomed to die as thousands more black home-seekers followed their brethren into Uptown Manhattan. By 1920 black people accounted for 32 per cent of Harlem's population, and a decade later the figure had risen to 70 per cent.

The years starting with the United States' entry into the war in 1917 brought a tide of black labourers to New York, not only from the South but also from the West Indies. More than 25,000 émigrés from these island territories arrived in the five years to 1925. Many made tremendous sacrifices to invest their earnings into property. By that year, the Harlemite and real-estate operator John E. Nail estimated that housing owned by black investors exceeded an astonishing $60 million. The West Indians were the elite of the business community, and many set up as grocers, tailors and jewellers. By contrast, black Americans from within the United States were in the main employed as waiters, messengers, lift operators and janitors, and in other menial jobs.

One institution staunchly bound together black people of diverse social and economic station: the Church. The proliferation of parishes over the years made Harlem a haven of spirituality, and there was never a problem persuading church members to donate money for the expansion and improvement of their houses of worship. One September morning in 1924 the congregation of the Salem Methodist Episcopal Church assembled in the meeting rooms of a converted block of flats on Seventh Avenue. From there, they processed solemnly uptown to another Methodist church, where the pastor and his white congregation turned over the church, parish house and parsonage to their new owners. This became one of the most imposing black worshippers' churches in Harlem.

In that same year, the owners of St Mark's Protestant Episcopal Church began building a new facility on 188th Street, at what was

Harlem became a haven of spirituality in the 1920s,
with the proliferation of churches.

then the phenomenal cost of $500,000. Almost simultaneously, the
Grace Congregational Church of Harlem took over the building of a
Swedish congregation west of Eighth Avenue, while the vast Lutheran
Church on 140th Street was bought and occupied by the Calvary
Independent Methodist Church. The combined seating capacity of
the churches and missions of Harlem by the mid-1920s was estimated
at 24,000, and many of these buildings also served as gathering places
for the area's social and cultural life.

After morning church services, Harlemites would promenade
along the busy avenues between 125th and 138th streets in their Sunday
best. The fashion-conscious paraded furs and feathers, form-fitting
frocks and bright shawls, checked suits and bright parasols, white
spats, and silk handkerchiefs protruding from breast pockets, as an
affirmation of a new-found self-esteem.

'Harlem is the heart and the pulse of the coloured population
of Greater New York,' declared the writer Konrad Bercovici, an

immigrant of Jewish-Romanian descent, in 1924. 'The centre of the coloured people is in Harlem. Indeed it is the centre, the intellectual centre, of the coloured population of the United States. Nowhere in the city does one hear so much frank laughter as in Harlem.'[12] Harlem was beginning to acquire its distinctive cultural identity as the abode of the 'New Negro', so dubbed by the black writer and patron of the arts Alain LeRoy Locke. Gone were the days of the Uncle Tom stereotype, unquestioning, servile, obedient to his white overlords. 'He [the Old Negro] had long become more of a myth than a man,' Locke wrote in 1925.

> Harlem is the centre of this movement and the home of the Negro's 'Zionism'. The mind of the Negro seems suddenly to have slipped from under the tyranny of social intimidation and to be shaking off the psychology of imitation and implied inferiority. By shedding the old chrysalis of the Negro problem we are achieving something like a spiritual emancipation.[13]

This Harlem liberation movement, whose shoots began to flourish in the post-war years, brought with it a surge in literary and artistic creativity that transformed the New Negro movement into what became the celebrated Harlem Renaissance, adding lustre to the glitter of New York in the Roaring Twenties.

8

Make Believe

Just as Charles Dickens exposed the squalor of Victorian London and Miguel de Cervantes brought to light the picaresque antics of seventeenth-century Madrid, so too F. Scott Fitzgerald encapsulated in his novels the flamboyance of New York in the madcap decade of the 1920s. He even gave the period a name: the Jazz Age. Of the many new writers catapulted to stardom after the First World War, Fitzgerald shone as the most eminent chronicler of those topsy-turvy years. Short stories, novels, film scripts and stage productions flowed from his prolific pen, from the day he was crowned the philosopher of the merrymakers and social elite of New York City.

The story of Fitzgerald as the extravagant storybook idol of the decade is bound at the waist with that of his no less rambunctious wife, Zelda (née Sayre). They met at a country-club dance in Alabama, where Fitzgerald, a lieutenant in the U.S. Army, was stationed during the war to train conscripts. He fell head over heels for the Montgomery belle at first sight, although their relationship met with resistance from her parents, who refused to sanction the marriage until Fitzgerald was demobbed and gainfully employed.

It was implausible, to say the least, that a man from the monotonous prairies of Minnesota and a woman raised in the evangelical subtropics of Alabama should come to be hailed the torch-bearers of New York's Roaring Twenties. Scott and Zelda made their move to the city shortly after the publication in 1920 of his debut runaway bestseller, *This Side of Paradise*, which examines the lives and morality of carefree youth at the dawn of the Jazz Age. For the feisty Midwesterner hungry for cosmopolitan glamour, 'New York had all the iridescence of the beginning of the world. The returning troops marched up Fifth Avenue, and girls were instinctively drawn East and North toward them – this was the greatest nation and there was gala in the air.'[1]

To find inspiration for his plots, Fitzgerald often had only to fictionalize the frenzied events of his own life. When he walked out of his job as an advertising copywriter in New York, the frustrated novelist embarked on a drunken spree of despair lasting several weeks. This experience later appeared as a vivid sequence in *This Side of Paradise*. The semi-autobiographical novel set the tempo for the era of hedonism. It was an echo of the freewheeling lifestyle and relaxed morals displayed by what the novelist Gertrude Stein called the 'Lost Generation', a reference to the aimless spirit that took hold in many of those who had lived through the war. As the presumed inspiration for the character Rosalind Connage, the overwhelming Zelda, whom Fitzgerald dubbed 'the first American flapper', likewise became an instant celebrity.

Fame went to the Fitzgeralds' heads with the force of an interstellar rocket launch. The newlyweds moved into the luxurious Biltmore Hotel in Midtown Manhattan – a recently opened Renaissance Revival-style structure that became one of the most fashionable resorts in the country – and took to their palatial abode like a duck to a martini. In fact, that is precisely what Scott was imbibing one evening in the hotel's upstairs lounge when he announced his intention to throw himself out the window: 'No one objected. On the contrary, it was pointed out that [the windows] were French and ideally suited for jumping, which seemed to cool his ardour.'[2] During their time at the Biltmore, the couple became national celebrities, as much for their wild behaviour as for the success of

Fitzgerald's novel. On particularly bibulous evenings, he would be found entertaining a crowd of bemused onlookers by performing handstands in the lobby, while she, not to be outdone, would slide down the hotel banisters. Her exhibitionist feats included riding to appointments on the roof of a taxi, disrobing in Grand Central Terminal and downing prodigious quantities of cocktails. Zelda once vanished from the table at a dinner party hosted by the stage producer John D. Williams. Noticing her prolonged absence, Fitzgerald and Williams rushed out into Union Square, where they found her, stark naked, having a shower in the fountain. She was in the custody of a pair of New York's Finest, who arrested an agitated Fitzgerald as well, as an accomplice to indecent exposure. Scott and Zelda lived up to their reputation as the *enfants terribles* of the New York scene, often trying to top each other's attention-grabbing exploits. Fitzgerald took it upon himself to dance in the aisle with an usher when the band struck up 'I'm Just Wild about Harry' at the revue *Shuffle Along*, and to rip off his shirt at the premiere of *George White's Scandals*.

F. Scott Fitzgerald and his wife Zelda on honeymoon.

We'll Take Manhattan

Fitzgerald's road to stardom unfolded in fits and starts. It was anything but a smooth journey for the future messiah of the Jazz Age. He wrote advertising copy for a pittance by day, turning to fiction at night in an Upper West Side boarding house in Morningside Heights, which he described in his short story *The Sensible Thing* as 'one room in a high, horrible apartment house in the middle of nowhere'. The aspiring novelist had to swallow the bitter pill of more than a hundred rejection slips for a variety of his offerings before the highly respected journal *The Smart Set* agreed to publish 'Babes in the Woods' for a fee of $30 in September 1919. The plot was based on the author's meeting with Ginevra King, and their first kiss. The glamorous American socialite and heiress, named after a portrait by Leonardo da Vinci of the Florentine aristocrat Ginevra de' Benci, served as inspiration for many characters in Fitzgerald's novels, in particular that of Daisy Buchanan in his most feted work, *The Great Gatsby* (1925).

Fitzgerald's iconic tale of the Roaring Twenties is a work of fiction, but, in common with most of his novels, it was born out of the author's own life and a multitude of specific experiences. The story of Jay Gatsby of West Egg is told by Nick Carraway, a Midwest émigré who has moved to New York and found in Long Island a fascinating but dangerous playground. The character of Gatsby resembles Fitzgerald, the romantic with an almost obsessive admiration for the rich. Fitzgerald came from a humble background and in New York he picked up the habits and values of the rich. All his life, he longed to be a wealthy, upper-class socialite, and through Gatsby, he finds his doppelgänger.

The Smart Set – subtitled, with the utmost diffidence, *A Magazine of Cleverness* – became the 1920s showcase for Fitzgerald and many of his literati companions.[3] Fitzgerald was but one of a host of writers whose work appeared in the pages of *The Smart Set*. The list reads like a writers' hall of fame of the 1920s, and Eugene O'Neill, James Joyce

Novelist John Dos Passos wrote about New York in the 1920s.

and John Dos Passos are but a few among the titans of prose whose works were published or reviewed in the magazine.

Until the mid-1920s, the guiding spirit of this monthly journal of the intelligentsia was Henry Louis Mencken, one of the foremost intellectuals of his day. The reporter and political commentator Walter Lippmann, in an article in the *Saturday Review of Literature*, called him 'the most powerful personal influence on this whole generation of educated people'. The *New York Times* took its acclaim of Mencken a step further, albeit with a surge of hyperbole uncharacteristic of this establishment newspaper. For the *Times*, Mencken was nothing less than the most powerful private citizen in America.

In 1914 Mencken and his friend the drama critic George Jean Nathan had taken over the magazine from its retiring founder, the Civil War veteran-turned-newspaper and magazine publisher Colonel William d'Alton Mann. Nathan is almost always veiled under the shadow of his cigar-chomping colleague Mencken, a figure conspicuous in the public limelight for his vast output of newspaper articles, scholarly and satirical essays, and erudite criticism. Yet it was the lesser-known man who spotted the promise of greatness in the utterly unknown 24-year-old Fitzgerald and published his first story in *The Smart Set*. Nathan also suggested that Fitzgerald write some playlets for the magazine, as well as his only full-length play, *The Vegetable* (1923), a fantasy about the misadventures of a postman who dreams he has been elected President.

For Fitzgerald the short-story writer, *The Smart Set* was not the only game in town. The *Saturday Evening Post* grew to become the most widely circulated magazine in the United States. It was scorned by avant-gardists as a frowzy interloper among highbrow publications, yet its stable of contributors included such notables as Agatha Christie, William Faulkner and C. S. Forester. The *Post* became one of Fitzgerald's most lucrative sources of income. By early 1920 it had published six of his stories – which Mencken contemptuously dismissed as 'drivel' – for a total fee of $2,400. This compares favourably with the less than $900 he had so far earned from his writing.

A number of new rival journals were popping up, some of them showcasing Luigi Pirandello, Jean Cocteau and other European writers much in vogue in the 1920s. Noteworthy among these publications was the slick monthly *Vanity Fair*, which gained fame as essential reading for New York sophisticates. It made its appearance in 1913 as an offshoot of the men's fashion magazine *Dress*, and was founded by entrepreneur Condé Nast, who saw it as a potential rival to his four-year-old *Vogue*. Cross-breeding his two acquisitions, he rebaptized it *Dress and Vanity Fair*, which eventually morphed into the magazine that is still published today as *Vanity Fair*. In the magazine's heyday, Nast took on a host of big-name designers and illustrators, including the cartoonist Theodor Seuss Geisel, best known for his children's books published under the name Dr Seuss. The magazine was so highly revered that at an auction in 1923, a first-edition copy sold for $2,100 (nearly $36,000 today). Its name was synonymous with New York high-society events, such as the *Vanity Fair* musical revue of 1921 at the Waldorf-Astoria hotel, which featured a fashion show, a garden fete and an Apache dance.

Frank Crowninshield is a name that for New York's fashionable set of the 1920s held a unique place in the city's life, as the suave apostle of gracious living, elegant manners and true urbanity. 'Crownie', as he was known to a legion of friends and admirers, was editorial adviser to Condé Nast, serving for 22 years as editor of *Vanity Fair*, during which period he introduced to American readers many new names that are now bywords for great writers of the time. Given to wearing a boutonnière with his daytime casualwear as well as his evening dress, Crownie was himself a flower in the buttonhole of a large segment of New York socialites.

It was almost inevitable that the editor of *Vanity Fair* – a person in possession of so high a social profile – would collide with an explosive ego or two among his editors and columnists. A memorable blowup shattered the calm of the luxurious Plaza Hotel's cocktail lounge one January afternoon in 1920. Crownie was having a drink or three with Dorothy Parker, the magazine's theatre critic. Parker, a satirical, wisecracking wit, smelled a rat when Crownie ordered the waiter to bring a bouquet of roses with the next round. Then he dropped the bombshell: the English writer P. G. Wodehouse was pushing to resume his old job as *Vanity Fair*'s theatre critic. Parker had held the post for four years and was not beguiled when Crownie tried to sugar-coat the pill with the offer to carry on collaborating with her 'much-valued' freelance writing. Parker lurched to her feet and stomped out through the revolving doors into the esplanade of Fifth Avenue. 'It serves me right for putting all my eggs in one bastard' might have been the typical wisecrack heard as she burst into the street.

In a flurry of rage, Parker telephoned her friend the *Vanity Fair* humorist Robert Benchley to tell him about her dismissal. The next morning, in solidarity with his colleague, Benchley burst into

Dorothy Parker, one of the luminaries of the Algonquin Round Table.

Crownie's office to tender his resignation. That afternoon, Parker and Benchley turned up for a ritual lunch at a hotel that occupies pride of place in the annals of New York's intellectual life.

JOHN PETER TOOHEY was a publicist who in 1919 was looking for a way to plant a story about a client of his, the playwright Eugene O'Neill, with the influential *New York Times* columnist Alexander Woollcott. Toohey persuaded a mutual friend, the art critic Murdock Pemberton, to set up a lunch meeting for the three at the Algonquin Hotel on West 44th Street. The rest, as they say, is history. Thus was born the Round Table lunch, which its disciples called the Vicious Circle, a daily rendezvous of New York's leading writers and wits in the hotel's secluded Rose Room. According to Round Table members, it was Toohey who devised the title of New York's most famous

Alexander Woollcott, drama critic, commentator for the *New Yorker* magazine and regular of the Round Table.

weekly magazine. The story goes that when several of the Algonquin regulars were trying to come up with a name for the publication their confrère Harold Ross proposed to establish, Toohey asked, 'Who are the intended readers?' The answer was, New Yorkers. 'Then call it *The New Yorker*,' he proposed, and turned to his lunch.

The new weekly showed every sign of becoming a podium for lively journalism and social criticism, by enlisting several of the Round Table worthies to its editorial board, most notably Woollcott, Parker and the playwright and critic George S. Kaufman. With characteristic sardonic humour, Ross set out the magazine's guiding principles in the first issue, which appeared in 1925. 'On general principles, this magazine expects to take a firm stand against murder,' read the leading article. 'But we don't want to be bigoted. If, for instance, someone should ask you to advertise in *The New Yorker* and throw out the hint that your refusal might lead to some unwelcome publicity, you wouldn't shock us much if you poured him into the nearest drain.' There follows a description of the publication's target audience. The *New Yorker* starts with a declaration of serious purpose but with a concomitant assurance that it will not be too serious in executing it: 'It has announced that it is not edited for the old lady in Dubuque [Iowa]. By this it means that it is not of that group of publications engaged in tapping the Great Buying Power of the North American steppe region by trading mirrors and coloured beads in the form of our best brands of hokum.'[4]

Before long, the Round Table daily lunch became an informal meeting attended by friends and adversaries, including some of the city's best-known editors, journalists and social commentators. Woollcott, Benchley, Kaufman, Ross, the playwrights Russel Crouse and Robert E. Sherwood, and even the inimitable Harpo Marx eventually became adherents of the Round Table brotherhood, as did – how could it be otherwise? – Parker. Her acerbic quips were a dominant feature of the daily banter. Such remarks as 'If all the girls at Smith and Bennington [colleges] were laid end-to-end, I would not be surprised' triggered

New Yorker cover, 7 March 1925.

raucous laughter from the martini set. Speaking of which, there was even a verse attributed to Parker about one of her favourite tipples, although a whisky sour was more her style:

> I love a martini –
> But two at the most.
> Three, I'm under the table;
> Four, I'm under the host.

The Vicious Circle was a confirmed martini-loving crowd. That is what they drank before, during and, on not a few occasions, instead of lunch.

Parker's short stories capture the spirit of the Jazz Age and life among New York's smart set just as much as Fitzgerald's do. They were published in *Vanity Fair*, *The Smart Set*, the *New Yorker* and *Life*, among other magazines.

These doyens of the smart set embarked on the pilgrimage from their homelands in the deepest recesses of the American hinterland, determined to make their mark in the Big Apple. Edna Ferber, born

Members and associates of the Round Table, *c.* 1919 (standing left to right): Art Samuels and Harpo Marx (seated): Charles MacArthur, Dorothy Parker and Alexander Woollcott.

in Kalamazoo, Michigan, to a Hungarian-born Jewish shopkeeper, exploded on the New York scene to become a Pulitzer Prize-winning novelist and playwright. Her work inspired numerous Broadway plays and Hollywood films, including *Show Boat* (1927) and *Saratoga Trunk* (1945). Ferber engineered her way into the lunches by writing plaintively to Woollcott, 'Could I maybe lunch at the Round Table, once?' Woollcott agreed and later had cause to regret his decision, for he and Ferber, who became a regular at the hotel, had a bitter falling out and ended up as lifelong enemies. It did not take long for Ferber to see through the fanciful jocularity and bonhomie of her luncheon companions. 'They were actually merciless if they disapproved. I have never encountered a more hard-bitten crew,' she wrote in her book *A Peculiar Treasure*.

In spite of the occasional rancour that erupted around the table, the Round Table came to represent all that was racy, refined and romantic in the era of the smart set of Manhattan. 'The New York City they inhabited was a shadow of what it is today,' explains the writer Kevin C. Fitzpatrick, 'but even while the Round Table was in full swing, a cultural sea change was remaking the metropolis. Nothing ever stays the same in New York City, and the Vicious Circle was in the thick of it all, experiencing and observing the city's dizzying highs and crushing lows.'[5]

More than an assembly of distinguished writers, the daily Round Table gatherings bore a resemblance to a lunch break in the editorial office of a magazine or newspaper. On the odd occasion, the core group of friends was joined by others who drifted in for short periods or hung about the periphery, including such notables as Tallulah Bankhead and Noël Coward. Members of the aristocracy of letters were never expected to become regular guests. This was understandable, since they would have found that much of the natter dwelled on the worthiness of their work. It is improbable that the likes of Fitzgerald would have accepted an invitation from people whom he doubtless scorned as newsroom ruffians.

There were literary luminaries associated in the public eye with the Algonquin who never partook in the West 44th Street revelries. One such grandee was Edith Wharton, the doyenne of old-money, upper-crust New York, who in 1921 became the first woman to win the Pulitzer Novel Prize, for her novel *The Age of Innocence* (1920). Although in spirit a 1920s New Yorker to the marrow, Wharton wrote mostly about the city during the 'Gilded Age', roughly 1870–1910. She drew on her insider's knowledge of the New York 'aristocracy' to chronicle the lives and morals of the pre-war and pre-pandemic years, when the city's upper classes were revelling in prosperity.

Fitzgerald aspired to the upper crust, as we have seen, so he viewed Wharton with awe and reverence and even claimed to have once burst into her publisher's office and knelt at her feet. The two classics of New York's privileged classes bear a certain resemblance. *The Great Gatsby* is the tale of a parvenu who died because of his love for a woman of the elite. In Wharton's novel, the offspring of one of New York City's most illustrious families, Newland Archer, begins to doubt his forthcoming marriage to the well-born but simple May Welland when her exotic cousin Countess Ellen Olenska arrives on the scene. Nevertheless, the marriage goes ahead, and 26 years later, with May now dead, Newland is in Paris and arranges a visit to Ellen's apartment, only to change his mind and walk away broken-hearted.

Wharton and Fitzgerald embody two key pillars of the literary awakening of New York in the 1920s. Both were supreme portraitists of manners – or lack of, as the case may be. Their New York characters are observed with penetrating irony, but search not for the immigrant of the Lower East Side or labourers of the Garment District sweat-shops. These novels illustrate the lives of a class of people living an extravagant, devil-take-the-hindmost existence, oblivious to the impending cataclysm.

By 1932 half of New York's manufacturing plants were closed, one in every three New Yorkers was unemployed and roughly 1.6 million people were receiving some form of benefits. One spring afternoon in that year found Ferber strolling in Midtown Manhattan when, on an impulse, she decided to drop into the Algonquin Hotel for lunch. She had not been to a Round Table get-together for some time and fully expected to meet up with at least some of the old crowd. Instead, she found a family from Kansas sitting at the famous table, marking the end of an era.

THERE WAS ANOTHER SIDE to the New York literary scene, one that spoke of a reality quite distinct from the world of flapping peacock fans and popping champagne corks. There was one gigantic figure in the world of fiction who had very little in common with the chattering bright sparks of the Round Table. John Dos Passos published his first novel, *One Man's Initiation*, in 1920. The book confirmed the 24-year-old veteran of the bloody battlefields of Verdun as an outstanding member of Gertrude Stein's 'Lost Generation' of writers. The novel, which he wrote while serving as an ambulance driver during the First World War, echoes with the horrors of poison gas, devastated cathedrals, dying wagon-mules and trenches littered with human corpses. The moment his troopship raises anchor in New York to embark on the voyage that will immerse him in the carnage sweeping Europe, the reader is given a foretaste of the young author's vision of a city radically inharmonious with the cocktail-induced merriment of the beau monde. Dos Passos's impression of what he observed as his troopship sailed out of New York Harbor was no harbinger of the glitz to come in the post-war years: 'Rosy yellow and drab purple, the buildings of New York slide together into a pyramid above brown smudges of smoke standing out in the water, linked to the land by the dark curves of the bridges.'[6]

Dos Passos's seminal work on life in New York, *Manhattan Transfer* (1925), casts the city in a darker hue than could be envisaged by those whose eyes were fixed on a flapper's knees and the gin and tonic conveyed about the room by a liveried waiter. The narrative is a subway rider's view of the metropolis, shuttling back and forth among the lives of more than a dozen characters in nervous, jerky, impressionistic flashes. It would be equally out of the question to expect any bona fide member of the Round Table set to acknowledge that the author is speaking about New York when he describes daybreak in the tenements:

> Morning clatters with the first L train down Allen Street . . . The cats are leaving the garbage cans, the chinches are going back into the walls, leaving sweaty limbs, leaving the grime-tender necks of little children asleep. Men and women stir under blankets and bedquilts on mattresses in the corners of rooms, clots of kids begin to untangle to scream and kick.[7]

Dos Passos's depiction of New York in the 1920s takes the reader beyond the sparkle and fizz of the Fitzgerald clique, to reveal the lower depths of city life as he saw it:

> There's more wickedness in one block in New York City than there was in a square mile in Nineveh, and how long do you think the Lord God of Sabbaoth will take to destroy New York City and Brooklyn and the Bronx? Seven seconds. Seven seconds.[8]

Literary greats of the age were not unanimous in their adoration of New York, but there was no escaping the fact that this was the make-or-break city for any writer aspiring to greatness. Son of the Midwest Ernest Hemingway was another giant among writers who had what might charitably be termed a detached attitude to the Big Apple. He rarely visited the city. In fact, he studiously avoided staying there if he could on his trips between Europe or the Caribbean and the United States. He kept a small Midtown apartment off Fifth

Avenue, which he used on visits to museums or when meeting his publisher. In 1950 the *New Yorker* veteran staff writer Lillian Ross caught up with Hemingway on one of his rare visits to the city. During a taxi journey across Manhattan, she recorded some of his typical flair for the dramatic, a commentary that could have dropped from the pages of one of his novels. Hemingway said New York was 'a rough town, a phony town, a town that was the same in the dark as it was in the light . . . He looked out the window and pointed to a flock of birds flying across the sky. "In this town, birds fly, but they're not serious about it," he said. "New York birds don't climb."'[9]

Had Fitzgerald been sharing that cab, he would certainly have been bewildered by Hemingway's disparaging remarks about the city of his dreams. Hemingway and Fitzgerald actually happened to cross paths in Paris in 1925. Fitzgerald had just published *The Great Gatsby*, which initially met with a lukewarm reception from the critics. Hemingway was putting the finishing touches to *The Sun Also Rises* (1926), which curiously also received mixed reviews. These two novels are now generally considered their greatest works. It is unsurprising that the friendship did not prosper for long, given the chalk-and-cheese personalities of the two writers. Hemingway, the brash mouthpiece of masculinity, was by nature wary of Fitzgerald's charm and urbane manner. Fitzgerald, the embodiment of the New York martini set, would not have found Hemingway's heroics and proclivity for warfare to his taste.

You Must Take the 'A' Train

The city's literary landscape was blossoming beyond the cocktail-sodden gatherings at the smart end of Manhattan and the boisterous Round Table jamborees of West 44th Street. Less than 5 miles north of the Algonquin Hotel, a group of novelists, poets and playwrights were giving birth to the Harlem Renaissance, New York's explosive manifestation of black creativity.

Langston Hughes, author
and social activist of the
Harlem Renaissance.

The acclaimed writers and artists of Harlem would have cause
to look back on 1921 as a milestone year in the creative movement of
New York's black community. Langston Hughes arrived in the city
that summer, fresh off the steamer from Mexico, to which his father
had emigrated in order to escape racist persecution in the United
States. The nineteen-year-old's plan was to earn a degree in mining
studies at Columbia University. No sooner had he enrolled than
Hughes received an unpleasant taste of exactly what his father had
sought to run from. The young undergraduate was never made to feel
comfortable in his all-white dormitory or at ease in the community
of students. The dreamy-eyed teenager's true aspirations marked a
radical departure from a course of studies in mining. He abandoned
the university after his first year, denouncing it as a haven of racism.
He then drifted from job to job, working (among other things) as a
seaman on voyages to Europe, a cook in a Montmartre nightclub and
a busboy at a Washington hotel.

Hughes always had pencil and paper at the ready and would scribble poetry where and whenever the inspiration struck him. One afternoon in 1925, during his busboy stint at the Wardman Park Hotel in Washington, he summoned up the courage to drop three sheets of paper beside the poet Vachel Lindsay, who was lunching on his own. Obviously annoyed to be distracted from his meal, Lindsay nonetheless picked up the notes and read a poem entitled 'The Weary Blues'. As he read, his interest grew. He called the busboy to his table and said, 'Who wrote this?' Hughes replied enthusiastically that the author was none other than himself. Lindsay was impressed with the young poet's potential and decided to help him win a scholarship to Lincoln University in Pennsylvania. Hughes's first book of poetry, *The Weary Blues*, was published that same year.

Hughes, who has been portrayed as the 'O. Henry of Harlem', was renowned for his versatility and folksy humour. The urge to take up the pen had emerged early in his secondary-school days, when he was named class poet, as his obituary in the *New York Times* reported:

'I was a victim of a stereotype,' he observed wryly. 'There were only two of us Negro kids in the whole class and our English teacher was always stressing the importance of rhythm in poetry. Well, everyone knows – except us – that all Negroes have rhythm, so they elected me class poet. I felt I couldn't let my white classmates down, and I've been writing poetry ever since.'[10]

Hughes was painfully aware of the challenges he and other members of the Harlem Renaissance faced in convincing the white literary establishment, as well as the general reading public, of their credibility as poets, novelists and dramatists. He wrote in one of his essays, 'My Adventures as a Social Poet' (1947):

Poets who write mostly about love, roses and moonlight, sunsets and snow, must lead a very quiet life. Seldom, I imagine, does their poetry get them into difficulties ... Unfortunately, having been born poor – and also coloured – in Missouri, I was stuck in the mud from the beginning. Try as I might to float off into the clouds, poverty and Jim Crow would grab me by the heels, and right back on earth I would land. A third floor furnished room is the nearest thing I have ever had to an ivory tower.[11]

This experience, Hughes said, left him little choice but to write 'social' poems. Not to do so would have been to deny his own life experience. He brings to the fore this artistic and intellectual philosophy in one of his most powerful poetic works, 'Christ in Alabama'. In thirteen devastating lines, Hughes lays bare the pain of being black in the American South: 'Christ is a Nigger, Beaten and Black ...' he writes in the opening stanza.

James Weldon Johnson was an influential participant in the Harlem Renaissance, as well as being a civil-rights activist and leader of the National Association of Colored People, founded in 1909 to fight for racial equality. As well as being a literary celebrity, Johnson stood out as a powerful political figure in the movement. His views on black literature highlighted a cultural divide among Harlem writers of the 1920s. Johnson argued that to break the negative stereotypes, it was necessary to show that black writers could produce enduring artistic works – in other words, that the Harlem elite could write like Fitzgerald, Wharton and Dos Passos. Some, among them the conservative black journalist George Schuyler, echoed Johnson's words and turned their backs on the political protest movement:

He [Schuyler] expressed the hope that black poems, stories and novels would forever eliminate white portrayals of blacks 'in which it is only necessary to beat a tom-tom or wave a

rabbit's foot and he is ready to strip off his Hart, Schaffner &
Marx suit, grab a spear and ride off wild-eyed on the back of
a Harlem Renaissance crocodile'.[12]

Harlem's written legacy was not confined to poets and creators
of literary fiction. W.E.B. Du Bois was a powerful influence who spoke
with dignity about the plight of black people, including early in the
movement in the pages of his magazine *The Crisis: A Record of the
Darker Races*. Du Bois, a character of Edwardian appearance, has
been described as having a 'Brahmin hauteur' and aspired to advance
progressive race politics and art, with the emphasis on sincerity and
beauty.

Du Bois's book of essays *The Souls of Black Folk* (1903) was an
important early influence on future Harlem literary figures. It throws
light on the complexity of the problem, for it shows that the key-
note of at least some black aspiration is still the abolition of the social
colour line. It is the Jim Crow car, and the fact that a black man may
not smoke a cigar or drink a cup of tea with the white man in the
South, that most enrages Du Bois. That this social colour line must
in time vanish like the mists of the morning is the writer's firm belief,
but in the meantime he admits the 'hard fact' that the colour line is,
and for a long time must be. His message to aspiring black writers
was set forth unambiguously in *The Crisis*: 'A renaissance of American
Negro literature is due. The material about us in the strange, heart-rend-
ing race tangle is rich beyond dream and only we can tell the tale and
sing the song from the heart.'[13]

More radical personalities within the movement, such as Hughes,
were not to be restrained by a call for moderation. It would be ingen-
uous to expect the writings of the Harlem Renaissance to mirror those
of a privileged white elite that had never suffered the harassment –
and far worse – that the black community was obliged to endure. The
literary awakening presented black artists with an opportunity to
denounce the prejudices they faced and to challenge the perception

of inferior creative skills to those of establishment writers. While Johnson and other older Harlem notables embraced what might be termed a 'restrained' stance on cultural prejudice, the newer generation aimed to rub their readers' noses in the plight of black Americans.

There was ample cause for anger. Exploitation was endemic to life in Harlem, where monthly rents were $12–30 higher than in other parts of Manhattan and most people earned substantially lower salaries. Rent parties became a vehicle for helping families to cope with the inflated prices that were costing residents on average 40 per cent of their earnings. Cards announcing these galas were passed around pool halls and launderettes and handed out to passers-by along Seventh Avenue. On a Saturday night, people paid an admission charge (usually half a dollar maximum) to be admitted into a parlour lit with red lights. The radio would be blasting music from the Cotton Club until a band arrived to provide live music. In this way, tenants pocketed enough to keep the landlord at bay for another month.

Jean Toomer was a sharp-witted light of the new wave of black fiction, although he was reluctant to be openly associated with the Harlem Renaissance, preferring to maintain an independent profile. Not much was known about him in New York literary circles because he never chose to belong to any. His debut novel, *Cane* (1923), sings naturally and effortlessly of the passion and vulnerability of black life in America. The book was an immediate hit among Harlem writers, including Hughes and Zora Neale Hurston, who both praised it as a work of genius and whose own writing was influenced by it. It is innovatively structured as a series of vignettes, alternating between prose, poetry, and theatre-like passages of dialogue. This extract from the book is, if nothing else, in-your-face in a way that the advocates of restraint and decorum – Johnson for one – would not have found to their liking:

Becky was the white woman who had two Negro sons. She's dead; they've gone away. The pines whisper to Jesus. The Bible

flaps its leaves with an aimless rustle on her mound. Becky
had one Negro son. Who gave it to her? Damn buck nigger,
said the white folks' mouths. She wouldn't tell. Common,
God-forsaken, insane white shameless wench, said the white
folks' mouths. Her eyes were sunken, her neck stringy, her
breasts fallen, till then. Taking their words, they filled her,
like a bubble rising – then she broke. Mouth setting in a twist
that held her eyes, harsh, vacant, staring . . . Who gave it to
her? Low-down nigger with no self-respect, said the black
folks' mouths. She wouldn't tell. Poor Catholic poor-white
crazy woman said the black folks' mouths. White folks and
black folks built her cabin, fed her and her growing baby,
prayed secretly to God who'd put His cross upon her and cast
her out.[14]

HARLEM'S ANSWER TO the chattering classes who held court at
the Algonquin's Round Table was the Hotel Olga, on the corner of
West 145th Street and Lenox Avenue. The more obviously suitable
Hotel Theresa, despite being in the heart of Harlem twenty blocks
to the south, was blocked to them by segregation laws from allowing
black people and white to share a hotel. The initiative came from the
black businessman Edward Wilson, who acquired a hotel called the
Dolphin and in 1920 reopened it as the Olga. This three-storey building provided lodgings for an exclusively black clientele, with a library
and reading room that became the unofficial sanctuary for the crème
of Harlem's literati.

It was just as well that these writers had a place to hang their hats,
for, in common with many of their white confrères living south of
110th Street, very few of the leading figures of the Harlem Renaissance
had been born in New York. Hurston came up from Alabama in 1925,
when the movement was at its most ebullient. The only black student to conduct anthropological research at Columbia University,

she went on to produce a wealth of short stories and four acclaimed novels, mainly about racial struggle in the South. In 1926 she, Hughes and Wallace Thurman – with deliberate irony calling themselves the 'Niggerati' – produced the literary magazine *Fire!!*, which featured the work of many young artists and writers of the Harlem Renaissance. Jessie Redmon Fauset, a disciple of Du Bois, was born in New Jersey. She made the pilgrimage across the Hudson River in the late 1920s to pursue a career as a literary editor, a supporter of up-and-coming black writers and a successful novelist in her own right. Toomer was from Washington, DC, and when he moved to New York he became a close friend of the novelist Waldo Frank, who for several years served as his mentor and editor.

Black talent was not confined to writing fiction. The painter Aaron Douglas came from rural Kansas. Distinguished by his ubiquitous pipe and avuncular smile, he settled in New York in the mid-1920s, and there he produced illustrations for *The Crisis* and *Opportunity*, the two most important magazines associated with the Harlem Renaissance. Douglas painted murals that today adorn the walls of Fisk University in Tennessee, whose student body was historically black, as well as the New York Public Library. Charles S. Johnson, later the first black president of Fisk, left his native Virginia to distinguish himself in New York as a sociologist and a leading promoter of aspiring young black writers, for whom he sponsored literary prizes. Johnson was also editor of *Opportunity*, the National Urban League's monthly magazine.

In May 1925 the Harlem Renaissance reached one of its high points at an awards dinner sponsored by *Opportunity* at the Fifth Avenue Restaurant. Under Charles S. Johnson's editorship, *Opportunity* had chronicled the Great Migration of black people from south to north and advocated the writing by and about members of the new urban black society. The *Opportunity* awards symbolized the acceptance of, or at least interest in, this writing by black literary elites. Among the presiding judges was Woollcott, the unofficial leader of the Round Table lunches.

Harlem was a magnet for people from all points of the United States, artists who displayed their talents in diverse fields of creative endeavour. The Renaissance laid the groundwork for a social awakening. It brought a blossoming of black culture the likes of which had never been seen in the city or elsewhere. Thanks to the writers, the intellectuals and the social crusaders who set Harlem abuzz in the 1920s, the black community made itself heard across New York City and America more widely.

9

Ain't We Got Fun

Aloysius Anthony Kelly was the very personification of the blithe frivolity that took New York City by storm in the 1920s. Kelly was a slum child, who came into the world in 1893 in what was at that time the city's treacherous Hell's Kitchen neighbourhood.[1] His father died before his arrival, and his mother did not survive childbirth. Given his hapless start in life and the infamous surroundings into which he was born, Kelly might well have been expected to embark on an unconventional lifestyle: and he did.

Kelly was all of thirteen when he ran away to sea, changed his name to Alvin and later enlisted in the U.S. Navy to serve in the First World War. Claiming to have pulled through more than thirty disasters at sea, he earned the nickname Shipwreck Kelly, and he even maintained – although this was unsubstantiated – that he had survived the sinking of the *Titanic*. After the war he took up a series of disparate trades, from steelworker to boxer and cinema stuntman. It was his stint as church steeple repairman that planted the seed of what was to catapult this singular character to national celebrity status.

In 1924 Kelly turned his talent for working on altitudinous structures into a celebrated career. He spent 22 days sitting atop a flagpole in Madison Square Garden, to the immense delight of onlookers and passers-by. A fad had been born. Marathon dances and swallowing goldfish were fashionable antics of the 1920s, but flagpole sitting became a wildly popular caper almost overnight, and Kelly its undisputed champion.

Kelly boasted of having spent more than 20,000 hours perched on flagpoles throughout his career, during which he earned his keep by charging admission to his sessions and by making celebrity endorsements. He avoided tumbling from his perch while asleep by inserting his thumbs into holes he cut in the flagpole shaft. If he began to lose his balance while dozing, the sudden pain enabled him to right himself without, he avowed, waking up. Food was sent up on a pulley, although there is no record of how he attended to other bodily needs. His flagpole-sitting days ended abruptly at the age of 59, when he suffered two heart attacks during a performance. He collapsed and died on a New York street that same year, a short walk from Hell's Kitchen itself.

Kelly's outlandish showmanship mirrored something beyond a source of merriment for a public possessed of an insatiable appetite for fun. New York had become the economic powerhouse of American cities, and this industrial and financial behemoth needed space to grow. Manhattan's horizontal expansion was bounded by the harbour to the south, a narrow channel of the Harlem River to the north, and the Hudson and East rivers on either side, so urban development had to be boldly upwards. New York's quest for verticality was about to shift into top gear.

While merrymakers foxtrotted their way blissfully across the ballroom floor, pragmatic minds in City Hall's planning departments set about devising an infrastructure worthy of New York's new status. By the beginning of the twentieth century the city had established its credentials as headquarters for more than two-thirds of the top one hundred American corporations, and its factories turned out a vast array of industrial products that were sold across the country and abroad. New York was well ahead of any American city in the number of factories in operation and workers on the assembly line.

Pole-sitter Aloysius Anthony Kelly epitomized the frivolity of 1920s New York.

The Port of New York Authority was formed at the start of the 1920s to deal with this surge in the city's economic power. It was set up to overcome the physical and political divides between what were essentially two sovereign states: New York and New Jersey. That is why its major structures are composed of four bridges, two tunnels and two bus terminals connecting or serving New York City and New Jersey, as well as several docks and piers in both states handling seaport traffic. The plan focused on regional transportation and

New York became an industrial powerhouse whose factories
turned out a vast array of products, including teddy bears.

quickly initiated a series of massive construction projects that still
serve the city today. The 'Comprehensive Plan for the Development
of the Port District' of 1921 encompassed 105 municipalities, embrac-
ing almost six million people.[2] Over the next five years New York
steadily overtook London, its closest rival for global supremacy, in
population.

The plan encompassed the largest body of sheltered waters of any
port in the world. Its shorelines measure about 800 miles, and much
of the adjacent land was as yet undeveloped and available for industrial and commercial needs. Its natural advantages, therefore, for
expansion and for the service of the nation's commerce were almost
limitless. The port was served by twelve trunk-line railways, carrying
in total more than 75 million tons of freight per annum. The connecting roads made freight-handling cheaper than in any other harbour in
the world. An immense number of foreign and domestic steamships
– at least 8,000 each year – delivered or loaded more than 45 million
tons of freight annually. There was an almost incalculable flow of
local seaborne traffic plying the waters of Lower Manhattan, which

became the most prodigious manufacturing centre in the world compared to those of a similar area. It comprised an unprecedented variety of products and commodities, including some 4 million tons of foodstuffs annually required by the people of the Port District.

New York now accounted for one-twelfth of the country's manufacturing by value, beating second-place Chicago by 45 per cent. At the turn of the decade the city manufactured goods worth more than $5 billion a year, equivalent in purchasing power to $65 billion today. More than 800,000 workers were employed in 32,590 factories, and the clothing industry came first in importance, particularly womenswear, which was almost double that of menswear. New York was manufacturing three times as much women's fashion as the rest of the nation's factories combined.[3]

Thanks to the efforts of the planners in 1921, in that decade construction was under way or plans had been approved for some of the most ambitious transport projects in the city's history. These included the George Washington Bridge spanning the Hudson River, the Lincoln Tunnel linking New Jersey to Midtown Manhattan, the Floyd Bennett airfield (which was built by the Department of Docks) along Brooklyn's Jamaica Bay and, most notable of all, the Holland Tunnel, the first mechanically ventilated vehicular tunnel in the world, connecting New Jersey to Lower Manhattan and its bustling financial district. This last was the real turning point in New York's transit system. In early October 1927 the *New York Times*, a paper whose editorial style was not usually associated with tabloid hyperbole, ran this front-page headline: 'The Holland Tunnel Is a Modern Marvel'. The article proclaimed the project's forthcoming inauguration in equally effusive words:

On Nov. 13 Manhattan Island is to be connected with the United States. Instead of standing in line at the entrances of fifteen ferries that now serve as the physical means of communication between New Jersey and New York City, 15,000,000 automobiles and motor trucks will dive every year into the twin tubes of the Holland Tunnel under the Hudson River and speed from shore to shore in a few minutes.[4]

In the early 1920s Mayor John Hylan, whose background included a stint as a labourer on the city's elevated railway, proposed a major expansion of the underground rail network to facilitate rapid transport for the city's burgeoning army of office and factory workers. The New York City Transit Commission, inaugurated in 1921, set out to extend the New York City Subway, whose Interborough Rapid Transit Company and Brooklyn–Manhattan Transit Corporation had been in operation since 1904. In March 1925 the ground-breaking ceremony of the Eighth Avenue Independent Subway System (IND) took place at 123rd Street and St Nicholas Avenue. Within a decade, IND trains were running under Sixth and Eighth avenues, creating the nation's largest mass-transit system.

Shipping and financial services had secured New York's international standing as early as the mid-nineteenth century, while

The Holland Tunnel, connecting New Jersey to Lower Manhattan and its bustling Wall Street financial district, marked a turning point in New York's transit system.

manufacturing provided jobs for its teeming population. A multitude of small businesses had set up shop in Manhattan by the 1850s and the clothing, furniture, pianos, cigars and dozens of other products they created boosted city exports. Around that time, New York became the printing centre of the United States, with more than 1,000 establishments. The influx of skilled Jewish immigrants, many of whom had escaped the pogroms of Russia and Eastern Europe, transformed an already dominant clothing industry into a gargantuan one, employing nearly half of all city workers in the early years of the twentieth century. The interaction of capital, cheap labour and access to raw materials, as well as entrepreneurial initiative and transportation facilities, secured global eminence for the city by the 1920s. As the decade kicked off, New York was producing more than half of the U.S. output in a dozen lines of factory goods, and it was competitive in many more. In 1923 the city's manufacturing industry accounted for nearly 10 per cent of the nation's production. At the same time, New York quickly developed advertising, insurance and legal services to serve the needs of the burgeoning manufacturing sector.

This rampant wave of industrialization inevitably had an impact on the urban environment, most notably in Midtown Manhattan's leisure and entertainment centre. Conflicts of interest arose as manufacturing companies began to invade Times Square and its environs, the traditional domain of the city's theatres and hotels. The newly formed Save New York Committee, headed by prominent citizens and political figures, stepped in to persuade the planning authorities to extend a protection zone to Times Square and its surrounding streets, banning manufacturing lofts from encroaching on Manhattan's leisure district.

The problem, however, was not so much the threat of an invasion of bricks and mortar in Times Square itself as the spillage from the neighbouring shop floors. In those days Fifth Avenue and its adjoining streets of retail emporiums were overrun every weekday by thousands of factory employees, particularly during the noon lunch break. Their noisy and crammed workplaces – sweatshops, for the most part – occupied the lofts surrounding Union Square and stretched more than 1 mile north to the edge of Times Square. So great was the midday congestion, the Committee complained, that shoppers by their hundreds had taken to avoiding this important retail quarter. A new location had to be found for manufacturing, specifically the garment industry. The Columbia Trust Company property developer, a subsidiary of the Irving Bank of New York, was given the mandate to erect premises in Seventh Avenue south of 39th Street. The two new factory and office buildings that went up were 24 and 17 storeys high, respectively. They reflected a shift in thinking with regard to urban expansion, one that brought about a transformation of the New York skyline.

The Race for Verticality

In 1910 Frank Winfield Woolworth, founder of the five-and-dime chain that bore his name, quietly began buying up properties on Broadway and Barclay Street in Lower Manhattan. Having eventually acquired the entire block front along Broadway, Woolworth retained the world-famous architect Cass Gilbert and sent him to London to have a look at the Houses of Parliament. Gilbert's mission was to capture the essence of the elegant nineteenth-century Gothic Revival buildings on the banks of the River Thames and use it as a template for his employer's ambitious undertaking. On its completion in 1913, at 792 feet high and with 56 storeys, the Woolworth Building took the trophy of the world's tallest. This Gothic Revival tower, a pharaonic monument to Woolworth's business empire, was inaugurated by President Woodrow Wilson in an elaborate ceremony that involved flicking a switch in the White House to illuminate the entire building.

The Woolworth Building retained its crown for nearly two decades. Its elegant terracotta facade soared above the New York skyline until it was overtaken, albeit fleetingly, by the neo-Gothic tower known

The Woolworth Building held the title of the world's tallest building
until 1930, when it was overtaken by 40 Wall Street.

to most New Yorkers as 40 Wall Street. The Manhattan Company Building, as it was originally called, was intended to become the world supremo of skyscrapers. The limestone-clad base of the steel-framed building rises through a midsection with a series of setbacks to a tower, clad in buff brick, with continuous vertical piers and recessed spandrels. This French Gothic-style jewel is crowned by a pyramidal roof capped by a spire. Although the engineering and construction were extraordinarily complex, the 71-storey, 927-foot skyscraper was completed in one year, an unprecedented feat for such an enterprise. Its architect, H. Craig Severance, and his associate Yasuo Matsui, along with consulting architect Shreve & Lamb, were specialists in commercial buildings and skyscraper design.

The announcement for the record-shattering 40 Wall Street building was made in April 1929. Six months later this titanic endeavour, along with several bolder, even more intrepid projects set out on the drawing board that same year, were to turn almost overnight into a financial ball and chain for their backers.[5]

Anything You Can Do

So blinded was this generation by the illusion of endless prosperity that even an eminent tycoon like John J. Raskob failed to spot the proverbial writing on the wall, certainly not on the 1,250-foot colossus he was about to finance in Midtown Manhattan. In 1927 Raskob, chairman of the finance committee of General Motors Corporation, affirmed confidently that the following year would bring an all-time record surge in the country's economy. Addressing a gathering of business leaders at New York's five-star Ritz-Carlton Hotel, Raskob told his colleagues that 1928 would bring the greatest prosperity the United States had ever enjoyed:

'There is little, if any, inflation anywhere, an abundance of credit . . . and my prediction is that with the Ford Motor Co.

in production the automobile industry will produce 5,000,000 units in 1928,' he told the assembled grandees of finance and commerce. This would represent a 40 per cent increase on the previous year, he said, which would 'add tremendous impetus to an otherwise prosperous condition'.[6]

A piece of bad news for Walter Chrysler's formidable self-image surfaced only weeks after the pinnacle atop his building had been bolted into place. On 20 November 1929 the former Governor of New York State Al Smith was the guest speaker at a Fifth Avenue Association luncheon at the McAlpin Hotel in Herald Square. Smith chose this influential forum to make the startling announcement that New York City was to become home to the greatest skyscraper of all time, rising a vertiginous 102 storeys above Fifth Avenue, between 33rd and 34th streets.

This piece of intelligence was received by many with incredulity. How could a monster of such magnitude remain erect? Surely the sheer weight of 365,000 tons of steel and masonry, if not the gale-force winds of a New York winter, would send it toppling over, killing thousands and obliterating a large tract of Midtown Manhattan. Stability is of prime importance in a skyscraper, yet this is easily achievable provided the building sits on a solid foundation. New York in fact has little trouble supporting the weight of its great buildings, since Manhattan consists of large tracts of solid bedrock, known as Manhattan schist.

With this encouraging fact in mind, in August 1929 Raskob established Empire State Inc., a consortium with associates including such renowned financiers as Louis Graveraet Kaufman (chairman of Chatham National Bank of New York) and captains of industry, including the cousins T. Coleman and Pierre S. du Pont. The firm proposed to erect an eighty-storey commercial building, which could if desired be raised another five penthouse levels and topped by an observation tower. The ultimate plan would take the building to 1,250 feet, made possible by the development of fast-running lifts and improved steel technology. Raskob contracted the architects William F. Lamb and Richmond Shreve of Shreve & Lamb to produce drawings for what was to become the Empire State building. This was the defining moment in the determination to take New York to greater heights, in the most literal sense, than any city in the country: 'In New York City's history, as far as construction, the Empire State is it. More than all the other great projects – the Brooklyn Bridge, the aqueducts, the water tunnels, the other skyscrapers – the Empire State Building represents New York City to America and America to the world.'[7]

Smith had entered the presidential election on the Democratic ticket but was beaten by more than six million votes by the Republican candidate Herbert Hoover. The defeated Irish Catholic politician now turned his energies to the business world, where he took on the chairmanship of Empire State Inc. The two commanding figures of Smith and Raskob epitomized the wheeling and dealing of 1920s New York: Raskob had the deep pockets and Smith the political clout to secure the green light from every quarter.

SO THERE IT WAS, the world's tallest human-made structure, the last hurrah of the decade, conceived and launched with great bally-hoo in the waning days of the Roaring Twenties. The ground-breaking ceremony took place on 17 March 1930, St Patrick's Day, in deference to the wishes of Smith, a dyed-in-the-wool Irish New Yorker. The building was completed in thirteen breathtaking months: 10 million bricks, 60,000 tons of steel, 200,000 cubic feet of stone, 300 tons of exterior chrome-nickel steel, 450 tons of cast aluminium, 10,000 tons of plaster, nearly 7 miles of shafts for 67 lifts capable of running at a speed of 1,200 feet per minute to serve 1,239 entrances, more than 17 million cubic feet of telephone and telegraph wire, 6,400 windows, 6,700 radiators, 51 miles of plumbing, 396 openings into mail chutes, and a ventilating system delivering 725,000 cubic feet of air per minute. The Empire State Building stood majestic, resplendent – and nearly vacant.

Raskob, the building's chief promoter, sank into a protracted state of despondency. For fully five years after completion, only a quarter of the available office space had been rented, with 56 floors remaining empty. By contrast, Walter Chrysler must have looked on in muted smugness. His own Art Deco masterpiece, which opened a year ahead of its rival and before the city had suffered the full impact of the Great Depression, could boast a 70 per cent occupancy rate. To dispel the image of a white elephant in the sky, Raskob instructed the maintenance staff to go about switching on lights in unrented offices at night, to send out an appearance of activity behind the building's aluminium-panelled curtain walls.

Dancing in the Dark

Early in September 1929 the stock market embarked on a roller-coaster ride, provoking gasps and heart flutters in the brokerages of Wall Street as the index swooped downhill, only to bring smiles of relief as it soared back up to ever higher levels. Indeed, many saw this as the time to cash in according to the infallible mantra of share-dealing: buy low, sell high. Over the course of several weeks, however, it became increasingly evident that something was wrong. The lows were slipping lower and recovery was slowing painfully after each dip.

On 8 September 1929 the market index skyrocketed to unprecedented new highs. On 19 September AT&T was valued at $4 billion, up a massive $138 million on the day. Then, ten days later, Wall Street pundits gazed in disbelief as more than a hundred stocks plunged into net loss, dragging the market to new low ground for the year. By November, blue-chip AT&T's share price had dropped from $304 to $222. In quiet corners of Lower Manhattan's speak-easies, punters struggled to explain what exactly was triggering this alarming negative volatility. Why was the great speculative orgy of the past two years suddenly turning sour? When would the market recover a semblance of stability?

The warning signals were flashing red for those who bothered to take any notice. The more circumspect in the investment adviser community had been counselling caution for some time. No less a patrician of the banking world than Paul Warburg had spoken out about the dangers of an overheated stock market in an address to the Board:

> On October 7th, the Standard Trade and Securities Service of the Standard Statistics Bureau [now S&P Global Ratings] advised its clients to pursue an 'ultra-conservative policy' and ventured this prediction: 'We remain of the opinion that, over the next few months, the trend of common stock prices will be toward lower levels.'[8]

History was to show how right Warburg was. Initially, many thought the Wall Street collapse was a temporary phenomenon and that the stock market would recover in a few months or years (as, in fact, happened with the later crashes of 1987 and 2008). This did not prove to be the case. After some upward spurts, shares on the New York Stock Exchange continued to fall for the next three years and economic conditions throughout the city continued their downward spiral, so that by the end of 1932, the market closed at a hitherto unimaginable low of 41, a drop of 89 per cent from its high of 381 in 1929.

TO ALL APPEARANCES, New York's broader economic life took scant notice of this turmoil. From the start of the decade, the story of the city had been an epic one of advances in innovation and infrastructure. In 1920 the Wonder Wheel opened at Coney Island, along with the first subway line to transport day trippers to the Brooklyn resort. Eight years later crowds paraded up Fifth Avenue to celebrate the extension of the Queensborough Line to Flushing, while a few months later the Outerbridge Crossing enabled commuters to travel for the first time between Staten Island and New Jersey. New York took centre stage at home and abroad in a multitude of diverse pursuits, a metropolis overflowing with energy and self-confidence.

The intervening years brought the opening of Yankee Stadium and the Museum of the City of New York, the creation of the New York Federal Reserve and Macy's inaugural Thanksgiving Day parade. Manhattanite Gertrude Ederle became the first woman to swim the English Channel, telephone service was established between New York and London and Charles Lindbergh took off from Roosevelt Field in Long Island on his historic non-stop solo flight across the Atlantic, to be cheered on his return by a record throng in New York's most elaborate ever ticker-tape parade.

The pace failed to slacken in the year of the final meltdown. In 1929 commercial flights began at Glenn Curtiss Field in Queens, the city's original transcontinental airport. Ten years later it was renamed in honour of Fiorello La Guardia, New York's hugely admired mayor of the 1930s. New York State Governor Franklin Delano Roosevelt inaugurated Long Island's Jones Beach, which welcomed 1.5 million sun-seekers in that season. The Italian Baroque-style 4,000-seat Loew's Paradise cinema opened in the Bronx, followed shortly afterwards by the almost equally grand Loew's Kings movie house in Brooklyn. In October Mayor Jimmy Walker presided at the ground-breaking ceremony of the $60 million Triborough Bridge (now the Robert F. Kennedy Bridge), while a month later the Museum of Modern Art opened its doors on Fifth Avenue. Sherman Billingsley started up the Stork Club as a speakeasy in West 58th Street, garnering the description 'New York's *New Yorkiest* place' from the gossip columnist Walter Winchell. Lastly, work was completed on Brooklyn's Williamsburg Bank, capped by the world's largest four-sided clock, an appropriate omen for time running out on the Roaring Twenties.[9]

Down Hearted Blues

The game was well and truly up on 29 October. The Dow Jones index had peaked at 381.17 in early September, a point that was not to be reached again for sixteen years. On that fateful trading day, the stock market took a dive of 11.73 per cent, setting the scene for what was to become known as the Great Depression. Only days before the Dow fell into the abyss, indications of foresight, even in what were regarded as the best-informed circles, were conspicuous by their absence. The prestigious Harvard Economic Society shrugged off the market's shakiness as simply a 'period of readjustment'. Its soothsayers gave assurances that even in the event of a prolonged downturn, the Federal Reserve would step in to carry out what is today known as quantitative easing, an injection of liquidity into the market to increase economic activity.

On 16 October, less than a fortnight before the collapse, the esteemed Yale University economist Irving Fisher announced at the Purchasing Agents Association's monthly dinner meeting that stock prices had reached 'what looks like a permanently high plateau'.[10] He told his audience that in a few months stock prices were certain to be much higher.

For sure, shareholders recalled with a sense of foreboding past instances of unexpected market slippage, most notably during the summer of the previous year and a repeat fall in prices in the days leading up to Christmas. But savvy speculators who had kept their heads managed to cash in on the sudden slide and saw their unshakeable belief in the Dow rewarded in the turnaround that followed. Trouble was afoot, however, and

> the decline began once more. The wiseacres of Wall Street, looking about for causes, fixed upon the collapse of the Hatry financial group in England . . . and upon the bold refusal of the Massachusetts Department of Public Utilities to allow

the Edison Company of Boston to split up its stock. They pointed, too, to the fact that the steel industry was undoubtedly slipping, and to the accumulation of 'undigested' securities.[11]

'FAILED TO SEE' is an expression that appears almost invariably in commentary by historians, economists and market forecasters concerning the days preceding the stock market crash. This throws up two overarching questions. Why were the alarm bells ignored or, perhaps more generously, almost universally misinterpreted by investors? Second, why did the calamity happen? A possible explanation is that if the idea of an everlasting bull market was too good to be true, the alternative was too awful to contemplate. The catchphrase of today that best encapsulates the prevailing state of mind in Wall Street in the closing weeks of 1929 would be 'living in denial'.

On 30 October the Empire State Building's principal sponsor, John Raskob, declared to the world at large that stocks were trading at bargain prices. Now, he proclaimed, was the time to pile into the market. The all-but-crowned head of Wall Street, John D. Rockefeller, sublimely oblivious to the stampede, assured his nervous colleagues that there was nothing to worry about. Rockefeller boasted that he and his son had spent the past few days on a buying spree. Earlier in the week the chairmen of New York's largest banks – Chase National Bank, Guaranty Trust Company, Bankers Trust and First National Bank – had gathered for a meeting at the offices of J. P. Morgan. They agreed to inject $40 million each into stocks, a strategy that was intended to stabilize trading activity. It brings to mind the man spotted in the streets of Lisbon after the devastating earthquake of 1755, hawking anti-earthquake pills.

How the crash came about is a well-documented chronicle of day-by-day events. The build-up to the ultimate debacle followed a cycle of buying and selling binges in the closing months of 1929: the downturns ever lower, the rallies inexorably failing to reboot the Dow

Jones Index to its previous bullish levels, until that 'Black Tuesday' in October when the market slipped irretrievably over the edge.

The day after catastrophe struck Wall Street, Mayor Walker spoke to 75 film-industry moguls attending a lunch at the Hotel Astor, located suitably enough in Times Square, the heart of the city's entertainment district. 'Beau James', as Walker was informally dubbed by New Yorkers, beseeched his audience to refrain from showing movies that put a pessimistic outlook on conditions in the market:

> Show pictures that will reinstate courage and hope in the hearts of the people. Give them a chance to forget their financial losses on the stock market and look with hope to the future. Industry and basic financial organizations are sound. It is only the abnormal inflation of the market that has sagged. There is no panic and no likelihood of there being one. Just the same, the morale of the people must be maintained and you can do it.[12]

'Only the abnormal inflation of the market'? 'There is no panic'? The cinema industry bigwigs attending the lunch had undoubtedly caught a glimpse of a less light-hearted account of events in that morning's *New York Times*. The front page screamed of the virtual collapse of stock prices, swept downwards with gigantic losses and wiping out billions in open market values, in the most disastrous trading day in the nearly 140-year history of the New York Stock Exchange.

There was no reason to expect disaster. It was not until the bottom fell out that people began to contemplate the possibility of things becoming a lot worse for a long while. As the early years of the 1930s were to make evident, such fears were justified in spades. The Dow Jones Industrial Average for November 1929 closed at 224. By July 1932 it had sunk to 58. The Rockefellers' market champion, Standard Oil, tumbled from 50 to below 20 in the same 32-month period.

General Motors, another blue-chip giant, went from 73 to 8, while AT&T plummeted from 304 to 72. And so on.

This did not respond to any sudden awareness that the market was about to go belly up. Speculators took fright at the steady drop in the indexes, which in turn led them to unload their portfolios. The consequence was a burst bubble, which economic history shows will one day inevitably repeat itself. It is taken for granted that the Great Crash was the result of a culture of rampant speculation and easy credit available to all who sought to try their hand at investing on margin, exposing the buyer to debt by borrowing from a broker. There is no more persuasive debunker of this fallacy than John Kenneth Galbraith, whose classic account of the market meltdown pins the blame on a single word: 'mood'. 'Far more important than rate of interest and the supply of credit is the mood,' Galbraith explains in

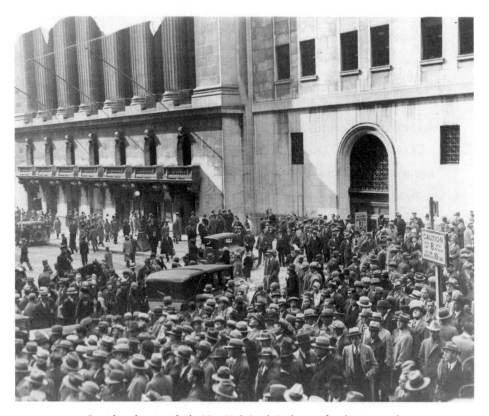

Crowds gather outside the New York Stock Exchange after the 1929 crash.

his succinct study of the crash and the events that brought it on, *The Great Crash 1929* (1954):

> A speculative outbreak has a greater or less immunizing effect. The ensuing collapse automatically destroys the very mood speculation requires. It follows that an outbreak of speculation provides a reasonable assurance that another outbreak will not immediately occur. With time and the dimming of memory, the immunity wears off.[13]

Brother, Can You Spare a Dime?

As New York slipped into a decade marked by anxiety and uncertainty, the change of 'mood' Galbraith had spotlighted as the principal factor behind the crash began to take hold across the city. A single episode speaks volumes of the passing of an age of unshakeable belief in frivolity as a way of life. Early in 1930 a crestfallen Shipwreck Kelly descended from his pole at the summit of the 33-storey Paramount Building in Times Square when it became apparent that passers-by were taking little interest in his antics.

Lois 'Lipstick' Long, once hailed as the playgirl of the Roaring Twenties, portrayed with acerbic wit an altogether more sombre frame of mind. In a six-part series in 1931, suitably titled 'Doldrums', Long sceptically assessed the flavour of the new decade. She saw the modern party scene as merely a setting for people to exhibit and discuss their newly discovered psychological problems:

> It is all so discouraging; so very, very, sad. Six million people in New York, and apparently no one in the white-collar class who can lose himself for a moment in the ecstasy of a roller-coaster. Six million people in New York, and every one of them a curious little study in maladjustment. Thousands of young men who own dinner jackets, and I am always drawing

someone who makes scenes in public because he once had a little cat that died and he has never got over it . . . I won't go out any more on parties. No, dear, I'm awfully sorry, but I have a previous engagement with a good book. I don't want to meet Shipwreck Kelly. I want to sit at home and think idle thoughts at myself.[14]

Long was understandably downhearted when the magazine decided to axe her nightlife column, 'Tables for Two', a few months after the crash.

The lights of New York may have dimmed, but they did not go out. Far from it. Even as the New Year 1930 celebrations faded into memories of happier times, the construction of skyscrapers contin-ued its inexorable march upwards, as builders of a 3,400-strong workforce began digging the foundations for the Empire State Building. A few months later the Chrysler Building formally opened its doors to admirers of its spectacular Art Deco lobby. Academic life was given a boost with the creation of Brooklyn College and the New School for Social Research. In the same spirit, the first bookmobile, dubbed the Pioneer Book Bus, took off on its run around the neigh-bourhoods of Queens. Trolleybuses started operating in Brooklyn, the restaurateur Louis Morino opened his iconic Sloppy Joe's in Lower Manhattan, and an overflowing crowd of worshippers attended the inaugural service at Riverside Cathedral, a project funded by Rockefeller.

It all looked more or less like life as usual, even as an ominous reality began to take hold in the first year of the Great Depression. Far more harrowing times lay ahead, bringing nearly a decade of massive unemployment, gnawing poverty, destitution and, in thou-sands of cases, outright hunger. Ultimately, millions of downtrodden New Yorkers were to find themselves thrust into a state of despair.

With the onset of harder times, breadlines became a common sight in some of the city's most deprived neighbourhoods. In the notoriously down-and-out Bowery, for instance, every morning some 2,000 of the city's 200,000 jobless stood shivering in the cold, waiting for a meagre handout of food. This mile-long street in Lower Manhattan became the squalid abode of the homeless and the hungry. Many spent their nights dossing in doorways and on park benches while others – the more fortunate – set up living quarters in shanties in Bryant Park. The comedian Groucho Marx was quoted as commenting that things were so bad 'the pigeons started feeding the people in Central Park'. Less amusing was the grim fact that for the first time, New York's hospitals were recording deaths from starvation.

As the money dried up, work came to a standstill on a number of major construction projects, among them the Triborough Bridge. Such was also the fate of the Hampshire House, a 37-storey apartment house and hotel in Central Park South, which went into receivership, was boarded up and left to the mercy of the elements.

Victims of the Great Depression in a New York City breadline.

On with the Show!

To be sure, with the murky dawn of a new decade, New York appeared to be well and truly on the skids. But was it? Shoppers out for a stroll along Fifth Avenue would have found brightly lit department stores – Saks, Lord & Taylor, Bergdorf Goodman and others – displaying the season's latest fashions behind glowing neon adverts. The avenue was jammed with honking southbound traffic, which reached a frenzied pitch at 51st Street, where traffic came nearly to a standstill at the sprawling Rockefeller Center. The flowing Art Deco lines of this $350 million complex were taking shape oblivious to the human devastation in dilapidated, unheated tenements only a few blocks away. When completed, it would cover nearly 12 acres with more than ten skyscrapers, including the 850-foot Radio Corporation of America Building, then the largest office tower in the world in terms of floor area.

The new decade created a culture rich in fantasy escapism to quench the ubiquitous thirst for escapism. This ushered in something akin to an era of split personality: the struggle to come to terms with unprecedented economic ruin, combined with the frantic pursuit of art and entertainment as a distraction from the mood of despair. It marked a turning point in general culture, one in which radio, the revolutionary mode of communication introduced in the 1920s, came of age. The most popular programmes of the day faithfully reflected what the listeners gathered around their mahogany-encased radios were seeking. All the rage of the day were the zany slapstick frolics of Bud Abbott and Lou Costello, *Amos 'n' Andy* and, the one that truly lifted spirits, Raymond Knight's high satire *The Cuckoo Hour*. Melancholy evenings were enlivened by the action-packed mystery shows of Ellery Queen, Sherlock Holmes and Sam Spade. In the theatre world, a number of George Gershwin's most unforgettable musicals – among them *Of Thee I Sing, Girl Crazy* and the opera *Porgy and Bess* – premiered on the Broadway stage during the Depression.

Irving Berlin produced some of his most memorable music in those painful years, notably for the film *Top Hat* (1935) and the stirring patriotic song 'God Bless America'.

In 1924 movie fans had to dig into their pockets for forty cents to see Buster Keaton's masterpiece *Sherlock Jr*. Six years later cinema owners began introducing Great Depression prices to draw cash-strapped fans into their theatres. In 1930 an affordable 25 cents bought a ticket to watch Greta Garbo burst on to the screen as an Italian opera star in the love story *Romance*. Cheap cinema tickets enabled the masses to indulge their fantasies in screwball comedies, horror films and gangster pictures. The last genre is significant, for organized crime was spreading its tentacles across almost all sectors of life. The introduction of Prohibition in 1920 had fuelled a vicious rise of gangsterism, with mobsters growing rich on the profits from bootleg liquor. The repeal of the Volstead Act in 1933 deprived the Mafia of these lucrative operations, forcing the criminals to fall back on gambling and prostitution, as well as new opportunities in loan-sharking, labour racketeering and drug-trafficking. The battle between Mafia families to control these sources of illicit income brought an unprecedented spike in violence, and during the final four years of Prohibition more than two hundred New York City gang members were shot, garrotted or stabbed to death with ice picks. Some simply vanished, never to be seen again.

Crushed under the heel of the Great Depression, millions of New Yorkers were forced to endure a wretched slide into financial and social ruin. Yet for the privileged, at least at the outset, the pulse of the city remained tempestuous. Hopping to the Charleston at the Parody Club in Downtown Manhattan morphed into swaying to big-band swing at Harlem's Savoy Ballroom and at the stylish Midtown venue Roseland. From slurping platters of Oysters Rockefeller washed down with an Old-Fashioned at the 21 Club or another swanky speakeasy, the smart set now moved on to downing champagne cock-tails and rubbing shoulders with film stars, celebrities and showgirls at the Stork Club. It was not to last. Over the years, the bright sparks who had romped blithely through the Roaring Twenties took to reminiscing over James Laver's reverie of those madcap, bygone days:

> We've boyish busts and Eton crops,
> We quiver to the saxophone
> Come, dance before the music stops
> for who can bear to be alone?[15]

Oh well, they might have shrugged, giving a swirl to the slice of lime in their Gin Rickeys, in the meantime, in between time, *ain't we got fun?*

REFERENCES

1 Down Hearted Blues

1 To maintain morale in the closing months of the First World War, censors of the belligerent countries minimized early reports of the influenza and its high mortality rate. Spain did not take part in the war, so its newspapers became the only source of information about the disease. Such stories created a false impression that Spain was the source of the pandemic, hence the nickname 'Spanish flu'. In May 1918 King Alfonso of Spain was reported to be stricken by the flu. This was a headline-grabbing story that drew even more attention to the country. The monarch was quickly isolated and did not infect anyone else in the Spanish royal family, and later made a full recovery. The hospital camp in Étaples, northern France, has been identified by researchers as a probable centre of the outbreak. The overcrowded camp, through which more than 100,000 soldiers passed every day, was ideal for the spread of a respiratory virus.

2 *New York Times*, 28 September 1918, p. 1.

3 Although newspapers reported that the first cases of influenza in New York came via the port on 14 August 1918, the cases from the Norwegian steamship were not the first to reach the city's shores. Roughly 180 cases of 'active' influenza arrived on vessels bound for New York City between 1 July and mid-September 1918. Approximately 305 cases of suspected influenza were reported throughout the voyages of 32 ships that port health officers examined during that period, including victims who died while at sea and those who recovered from the illness. Health officials simply did not report any secondary outbreaks of influenza from the index cases that arrived through the harbour before the arrival of the *Bergensfjord*. *New York Evening Post*, 19 September 1918, p. 3.

4 Francesco Aimone, 'The 1918 Influenza Epidemic in New York City: A Review of the Public Health Response', *Public Health Reports*, 125 (supplement 3) (2010), pp. 71–9.

5 Coney Island received its name from the Dutch settlers for the colonies of wild rabbits (*konijn*) that abounded there in the seventeenth century.

6 *New York Times*, 6 February 1921, p. 16.

7 Kenneth, T. Jackson, ed., *The Encyclopedia of New York City* (New Haven, CT, 1995), p. 1105.

8 'The Master Builder', *Newsday*, 11 December 2006, p. 16.

9 *Readers' Guide to Periodical Literature*, headquartered in the Bronx, was founded in 1898 by H. W. Wilson, and is still being published. See www.hwwilsoninprint.com/periodicals.php.

10 Crystal radios were among the first to be manufactured. These devices used a piece of lead galena crystal and a cat's whisker to find the radio signal. They allowed many people to join the radio craze in the 1920s because they were easy to make from home. Many boys' magazines encouraged readers to make their own sets and included step-by-step assembly instructions. All necessary supplies could be purchased for as little as $6 (equivalent of $107 today). However, the sound in the earphones was very weak and often interrupted by static. Armstrong devised the De Forest Audion tube, also known as a vacuum tube, which eventually replaced the crystal. His first model of a radio using vacuum tubes in 1924 was called the Radiola Superheterodyne.

11 Jordan Simon, 'The History of "Radio Row", NYC's First Electronics District', *Gothamist Daily*, www.gothamist.com, 25 July 2016.

12 *New York Times*, 25 May 1930, p. 144.

13 Frederick Lewis Allen, *Only Yesterday: An Informal History of the 1920s* [1931] (New York, 1997), p. 62.

14 Edward Robb Ellis, *The Epic of New York City* (New York, 1997), p. 234.

15 Tammany societies were founded in several American cities after the American War of Independence. Tammany Hall of New York, as it became known, was the only society to have a long life. Tammany took its name from Tamanend, a leader of the indigenous Lenape people.

16 George J. Lankevich, *American Metropolis: A History of New York City* (New York, 1998), p. 157.

17 Michelle Nevius and James Nevius, *Inside the Apple: A Streetwise History of New York City* (New York, 2009), p. 230.

2 Ain't (Much) Misbehavin'

1 Daniel Okrent, *Last Call: The Rise and Fall of Prohibition* (New York, 2010), p. 8.

2 Anthony Young, *New York Café Society: The Elite Meet to See and Be Seen, 1920s–1940s* (Jefferson, NC, 2015), p. 26.

3 Okrent, *Last Call*, p. 26.

4 Michael A. Lerner, *Dry Manhattan: Prohibition in New York City* (Cambridge, MA, 2008), p. 12.

5 Young, *New York Café Society*, p. 27.

6 Lerner, *Dry Manhattan*, p. 46.

7 Young, *New York Café Society*, p. 30.

8 Matthew B. Rowley, *Moonshine! Recipes, Tall Tales, Drinking Songs, Historical Stuff, Knee-Slappers, How to Drink It, Pleasin' the Law, Recoverin' the Next Day* (Asheville, NC, 2007), p. 141.

9 The Mob Museum, 'Alcohol as Medicine and Poison', https://prohibition. themobmuseum.org (accessed 19 May 2022).

10 Amanda Schuster, *New York Cocktails* (Kennebunkport, ME, 2017), p. 78.

11 The Mob Museum, 'Queens of the Speakeasies', https://prohibition. themobmuseum.org (accessed 17 July 2022).

12 Jef Klein, *The History and Stories of the Best Bars of New York* (Nashville, TN, 2006), p. 49.

13 *New Yorker*, 29 August 1925.

14 Lerner, *Dry Manhattan*, p. 148.

15 *Brooklyn Daily Eagle*, 18 December 1927.

16 Louise Berliner, *Texas Guinan: Queen of the Nightclubs* (Austin, TX, 1993), p. 7.

17 Ron Chepesiuk, *American Gangster: The History of the Gangs of Harlem* (Lytham, Lancashire, 2007), p. 55.

18 Young, *New York Café Society*, p. 31.

19 Chepesiuk, *American Gangster*, p. 7.

20 Carl Sifakis, *The Mafia Encyclopedia* (New York, 1987), p. 248.

21 Claudia Roth Pierpont, 'Black, Brown, and Beige: Duke Ellington's Music and Race in America', *New Yorker*, www.newyorker.com, 10 May 2010.

22 Jimmy Breslin, *Damon Runyon: A Life* (New York, 1991), p. 187.

23 Sifakis, *Mafia Encyclopedia*, p. 321.

24 Greg Young, 'Mayor Jimmy Walker: A Finer Class of Corruption', www. boweryboyshistory.com, 27 May 2009.

3 Broadway Melody

1 Ken Bloom, *Broadway: An Encyclopedia* (New York, 2004), p. xvi.

2 *New York Times*, 19 January 1919, p. 24.

3 Bloom, *Broadway*, p. 109.

4 David H. Lewis, *Broadway Musicals: A Hundred Year History* (Jefferson, NC, 2002), pp. 7–8.

5 *New York World*, 11 November 1925.

6 Bloom, *Broadway*, p. 445.

7 *New York Tribune*, 28 July 1920, *New York Globe*, 28 July 1920.

8 Lewis, *Broadway Musicals*, p. 22.

9 Oscar Hammerstein II, *Lyrics* (New York, 1949), p. 19.

10 The New Amsterdam Theatre was used as a cinema from 1937 onwards. It closed its doors in 1985 and was renovated in 1995 as the venue for Disney Productions on Broadway. The Beaux Arts exterior and Art Deco interior have been designated New York City landmarks, and the building is one of the oldest surviving Broadway venues.

11 Billie Burke, *With a Feather on My Nose* (New York, 1949), p. 9.

12 Randolph Carter, *The World of Flo Ziegfeld* (New York, 1974), p. 84.

13 Herbert G. Goldman, *Fanny Brice: The Original Funny Girl* (New York, 1992), p. 56.

14 Richard Ziegfeld and Paulette Ziegfeld, *The Ziegfeld Touch: The Life and Times of Florenz Ziegfeld, Jr* (New York, 1993), p. 292.

15 Nimisha Bhat, 'The Ziegfeld Midnight Frolic', Museum of the City of New York, https://blog.mcny.org, 1 July 2014.
16 *New York Times*, 6 August 1924.
17 *Miami News*, 17 June 1921, p. 10.
18 Anita Loos, *Gentlemen Prefer Blondes* (New York, 1925), p. 104.
19 J. Brooks Atkinson in the *New York Times*, 25 August 1926.
20 *New Yorker*, 5 June 1926, p. 34.
21 Phyllis Rose, *Jazz Cleopatra: Josephine Baker in Her Time* (New York, 1989), p. 57.
22 Barbara Glass, *When the Spirit Moves: African American Dance in History and Art* (New York, 1999), p. 76.
23 Allen L. Woll, *Black Musical Theatre: From Coontown to Dreamgirls* (Baton Rouge, LA, 1989), p. 78.
24 Siduri Beckman, '1920s Broadway: The Women behind the Scenes', Penn Libraries blog, www.uniqueatpenn.wordpress.com, 20 July 2016.
25 Jordan Schildcrout, *In the Long Run: A Cultural History of Broadway's Hit Plays* (New York, 2020), p. 24.
26 Ibid., p. 7.
27 Ibid., p. 26.

4 Crazy Rhythm

1 Stuart Nicholson, *Jazz and Culture in a Global Age* (Boston, MA, 2014), p. 163.
2 Contrary to popular belief, the original Dixieland Jazz Band was composed of five white New Orleans musicians. It also happened to be the first jazz group whose music was recorded. This took place in 1917, when it gave a concert at Riesenweber's Cafe on Columbus Circle, Manhattan.
3 Scott DeVeaux and Gary Giddins, *Jazz: Essential Listening* (New York, 2010), p. 114.
4 The term 'stride piano' refers to a style of New York ragtime, in which the pianist's left hand leaped or went striding across the keyboard. It is highly rhythmic because of the alternating bass note and chord action of the left hand.
5 Ted Gioia, *The History of Jazz* (New York, 1997), p. 55.
6 Charles-Édouard Jeanneret-Gris (Le Corbusier), *When the Cathedrals Were White: A Journey to the Country of Timid People* (New York, 1947), p. 159.
7 Gioia, *History of Jazz*, p. 56.
8 Satchmo's home is now the Louis Armstrong House Museum. See www.louisarmstronghouse.org.
9 *Downbeat* magazine (Chicago), September 1971, p. 168.
10 Robert Nippoldt and Hans-Jürgen Schaal, *Jazz: New York in the Roaring Twenties* (Cologne, 2021), p. 6.
11 Quoted ibid., p. 16.
12 Quoted in the *New York Times*, 12 March 2006, p. 37.
13 Blue laws are rules in force in some parts of the United States that restrict or ban certain activities, such as public sports competitions, or place restrictions on shopping on specified days, usually Sundays.
14 *New York Times*, 12 December 1922, p. 16.

5 Oh! Lady Be Good

1 *The Times,* London, 20 May 1910.
2 Alison Maloney, *Bright Young Things: A Modern Guide to the Roaring Twenties* (London, 2012), p. 11.
3 Anonymous reader ('C.E.L.'), poem on letters page of *Brooklyn Daily Eagle*, 27 March 1922, p. 21.
4 Zelda Fitzgerald, 'Eulogy on the Flapper', *Metropolitan Magazine*, June 1922.
5 'Slim and Stylish: How Tobacco Companies Hooked Women by "Feminizing" Cigarettes', Truth Initiative, www.truthinitiative.org, 4 April 2017.
6 Joshua Zeitz, *Flapper: A Madcap Story of Sex, Style, Celebrity, and the Women Who Made America Modern* (New York, 2006), p. 89.
7 Lipstick, 'Tables for Two', *New Yorker*, 17 October 1925.
8 Ibid., 21 November 1925.
9 Stephen Duncombe and Andrew Mattson, *The Bobbed Haired Bandit: A True Story of Crime and Celebrity in 1920s New York* (New York, 2006), p. 35.
10 Ibid., p. 122.
11 *New York Telegram and Evening Mail*, 6 May 1924.
12 Lettie Gavin, *American Women in World War I: They Also Served* (Boulder, CO, 2006), p. 54.
13 Marion May Dilts, *The Telephone in a Changing World* (London, 1941), p. 98.
14 Ellen Dewitt, 'Fifty Most Common Jobs Held by Women 100 Years Ago', *Stacker*, www.stacker.com, 12 January 2021.
15 Kate Simon, *A Wider World: Portraits in an Adolescence* (New York, 1986), p. 19.
16 Paula S. Fass, *The Damned and the Beautiful: American Youth in the 1920s* (New York, 1977), pp. 275–7.
17 Zeitz, *Flapper*, p. 122.
18 Carolyn Hall, *The Twenties in Vogue* (London, 1983), p. 13.
19 Simon, *A Wider World*, p. 177.
20 Paulina Bren, *The Barbizon: The New York Hotel That Set Women Free* (London, 2021), p. 18.
21 Ibid., p. 30.
22 Charlotte Fiell, *1920s Fashion: The Definitive Sourcebook* (London, 2021), p. 15.
23 Catalogue excerpts, B. Altman & Company, *1920s Fashions from B. Altman & Company* (New York, 1999), p. 102.
24 Ibid., p. 79.
25 Antony Penrose, *The Lives of Lee Miller* (New York, 1985), p. 16.
26 Thomas Bleitner, *Women of the 1920s: Style, Glamour and the Avant-Garde* (New York, 2019), p.72.
27 F. Scott Fitzgerald, *Bernice Bobs Her Hair* (New York, 1920), p. 54.
28 1 Corinthians 11:15 (King James Version): 'But if a woman have long hair, it is a glory to her: for her hair is given her for a covering.'
29 Quoted in Maloney, *Bright Young Things*, p. 51.
30 Mary Garden, 'Why I Bobbed My Hair', *Pictorial Review*, April 1927, p. 8.

31 Mary Pickford, 'Why I Have Not Bobbed Mine', *Pictorial Review*, April 1927, p. 9.
32 Dorothy Parker, *The Diary of a Lady* (New York, 1933), p. 328.

6 The Sidewalks of New York

1 R. L. Duffus, 'The Vertical City', *New Republic*, 3 July 1929, p. 24.
2 Jeffrey A. Kroessler, *New York Year by Year: A Chronology of the Great Metropolis* (New York, 2002), p. 208.
3 Ibid., p. 196.
4 *New York Times*, 16 July 1922, p. 4.
5 Arthur Tarshis, 'Thirty-One Commercial Buildings Erected by A. E. Lefcourt in Two Decades', *New York Times*, 18 May 1930, p. 2.
6 'Black Brick Building for New York City: Daring Departure from the Conventional in American Radiator Company's New Structure', *New York Times*, 20 January 1924, p. 1.
7 Anthony W. Robins, *New York Art Deco: A Guide to Gotham's Jazz Age Architecture* (New York, 2017), p. 4.
8 Ibid., p. 85.
9 Edna Ferber, *So Big* (Mineola, NY, 2020), p. 195.
10 Ibid., p. 203.
11 Lance Hosey, 'The Fountainhead: Everything That's Wrong with Architecture', *ArchDaily*, www.archdaily.com, 14 November 2013.
12 Robins, *New York Art Deco*, pp. 35–6.
13 Quoted in Catherine Coleman Brawer and Kathleen Murphy Skolnik, *The Art Deco Murals of Hildreth Meière* (New York, 2014), p. 19.
14 Francis Morrone, *The Architectural Guidebook to New York City* (Salt Lake City, UT, 1994), p. 158.
15 Robins, *New York Art Deco*, p. 81.
16 Vincent Curcio, *Chrysler: The Life and Times of an Automotive Genius* (New York, 2000), p. 428.
17 Donald L. Miller, *Supreme City: How Jazz Age Manhattan Gave Birth to Modern America* (New York, 2014), p. 249.
18 Ibid., p. 250.
19 *House & Garden*, November 1928, p. 44.
20 'Artists Localize Our Silk Designs', *New York Times*, 1 November 1925, p. 16.

7 I Got Plenty of Nothing

1 In 1924 the regime of General Miguel Primo de Rivera granted Spanish citizenship to the entire Sephardic diaspora. The ruling was designed to entice Ottoman Sephardic entrepreneurs to move back to Spain. The so-called Alhambra decree was revoked 24 years later when, in 1968, the Second Vatican Council rejected the charge of deicide traditionally laid at the Jews' door. In 2015 the Spanish Minister of Justice Alberto Ruiz-Gallardón enacted a bill to allow Sephardic Jews dual citizenship, calling it a measure laden with 'deep historic meaning', intended to compensate them for 'shameful events'

in the country's past. It is estimated that about 20 per cent of the Spanish population today has Sephardic ancestry.

2 Alyn Brodsky, *The Great Mayor: Fiorello La Guardia and the Making of the City of New York* (New York, 2003), p. 25.

3 Donald L. Miller, *Supreme City: How Jazz Age Manhattan Gave Birth to Modern America* (New York, 2014), pp. 48–9.

4 New York City is conventionally referred to as the great 'melting pot' of America, a symbol of how people of diverse ethnic backgrounds have coexisted to share their unshakeable belief in the American dream, which in itself amounts to a vague concept often defined by such sound bites as 'land of opportunity'. Perhaps the term 'stew pot' would offer a more accurate description of this hotchpotch of ingredients, a diversity of cultures and ethnicities cohabiting in physical proximity, frequently knocking into one another, but never fusing into a homogeneous whole.

5 Kenneth T. Jackson and David S. Dunbar, *Empire City: New York Through the Centuries* (New York, 2002), p. 553.

6 The original building was destroyed by fire five years after its inauguration. A French Renaissance-style brick and limestone replacement was built in 1900. It was designed to accommodate half a million immigrants a year, a capacity that was soon rendered inadequate to process the massive influx of people seeking to settle in the United States.

7 *New York Times*, 8 October 1920, p. 21.

8 Lower Manhattan's Little Italy was the locale of the fictional Corleone crime family depicted in Mario Puzo's novel *The Godfather* (1969) and the three films based on it. It is also the setting for the Martin Scorsese film *Mean Streets* (1973), starring Robert De Niro, who grew up in the area.

9 Tyler Anbinder, *City of Dreams: The 400-Year Epic History of Immigrant New York* (New York, 2017), p. 384.

10 Ibid., p. 385.

11 Jonathan Gill, *Harlem: The Four Hundred Year History from Dutch Village to Capital of Black America* (New York, 2011), p. 182.

12 Konrad Bercovici, *Around the World in New York* (New York, 1924), p. 214.

13 Alain LeRoy Locke, 'Enter the New Negro', *The Survey Graphic*, LIII/11 (March 1925), pp. 631–4. Locke, 'The New Negro', 1925, available at https://scalar.lehigh.edu (accessed 11 October 2023).

8 Make Believe

1 Andrew Turnbull, *Scott Fitzgerald* (New York, 1962), p. 99.

2 Ibid., p. 109. On another occasion Fitzgerald again threatened to leap from a window, overcome with emotion at having shared a table with James Joyce at a dinner party hosted by the publisher Sylvia Beach.

3 *The Smart Set* gained such notoriety that in 1928 Metro-Goldwyn-Mayer released a silent film bearing the magazine's title. The movie was directed by Jack Conway and starred such big-name screen personalities as William Haines, Jack Holt and Alice Day. The plot revolves around Tommy (Haines),

an egotistical polo player who struggles to redeem himself after being expelled from the national team.

4 *New Yorker*, February 1925, pp. 1–3.

5 Kevin C. Fitzpatrick, *The Algonquin Round Table: A Historical Guide* (New York, 2014), p. 4.

6 John Dos Passos, *One Man's Initiation 1917* (New York, 1920), p. 1.

7 John Dos Passos, *Manhattan Transfer* (New York, 1925), p. 129.

8 Ibid., p. 381.

9 Lillian Ross, 'How Do You Like It Now, Gentlemen?', *New Yorker*, 6 May 1950, p. 34.

10 'Langston Hughes, Writer, 65, Dead', *New York Times*, 23 May 1967, p. 1.

11 Langston Hughes, 'My Adventures as a Social Poet', *Phylon*, VIII/3 (1947), p. 205.

12 Kevin Hillstrom, *Defining Moments: The Harlem Renaissance* (Chicago, IL, 2011), p. 42. Hart Schaffner Marx is an American manufacturer of luxury tailored menswear, founded in 1887.

13 W.E.B. Du Bois, *The Crisis: A Record of the Darker Races*, XXIX/1 (November 1924), p. 11.

14 Jean Toomer, *Cane* (New York, 1923), p. 3.

9 Ain't We Got Fun

1 'Hell's Kitchen, on the west side of Midtown Manhattan, began to develop in earnest around the mid-nineteenth century, with the arrival of Irish refugees escaping the Great Famine. They were the dock workers, tanners and other industrial labourers, desperate fugitives from a struggle for survival in the home country. The neighbourhood housed the Hudson River Railroad, slaughterhouses, warehouses and factories of all sorts, as well as the tenements that housed those who worked in them. They were joined over time by other immigrants who gravitated to the area and used whatever means they could muster to beg, borrow, steal and often murder to get ahead. Fast-forward to Prohibition, and well-organized Mafia-controlled gangs ruled the bootlegging movement of contraband through a massive system of under-building tunnels. These are still evidenced in the cellars of buildings. There were frequent axe-handle arguments over clotheslines strung between buildings. Streets and individual buildings were variously dubbed "Death Avenue", "House of Blazes" and "Battle Row". Hell's Kitchen was a ramshackle slum until gentrification efforts began in the 1950s.' Rita Jakubowski, board member of the West 44th Street Better Block Association, in conversation with the authors, February 2021.

2 'The Comprehensive Plan for the Development of the Port District', 1921, Beinecke Rare Book and Manuscript Library, Yale University, digital collections, https://collections.library.yale.edu (accessed July 2023).

3 'New York Leads in Factory Output', *New York Times*, 5 June 1922, p. 25.

4 *New York Times*, 9 October 1927, p. 1.

5 The building was known variously as the Bank of Manhattan Trust Building and the Manhattan Company Building, until its founding tenant merged

to form the Chase Manhattan Bank. It is sometimes referred to today as the Trump Building, the property developer and former U.S. President Donald Trump having acquired the lease in 1995.

6 'Business: Instalment Selling', *Time*, 28 November 1927.
7 Thomas Kelly, *Empire Rising* (New York, 2005), p. 197.
8 Frederick Lewis Allen, *Only Yesterday: An Informal History of the 1920s* [1931] (New York, 1997), p. 244.
9 An exhaustive chronicle of nearly five hundred years of events can be found in Jeffrey A. Kroessler's *New York Year by Year: A Chronology of the Great Metropolis* (New York, 2002).
10 The Purchasing Agents Association, founded in 1915, was a not-for-profit educational association providing supply management, education, training, qualifications, publications, information and research.
11 Allen, *Only Yesterday*, pp. 243–4. The British entrepreneur Clarence Hatry believed he could rationalize the British steel industry by merging a number of steel and iron companies into the United Steel Companies, which he acquired in what was to be a leveraged buyout. At the last moment the bankers withdrew their financing. Hatry began borrowing money against his companies and eventually committed petty fraud. Rumours about his overextension began to circulate and the value of his companies collapsed. This led to a wave of panic selling among foreign investors. Undigested securities are those not purchased because of lack of demand during the initial public offering.
12 *New York Times*, 30 October 1929, p. 3.
13 John Kenneth Galbraith, *The Great Crash 1929* (London, 1954), pp. 188–9.
14 *New Yorker*, 10 January 1931.
15 James Laver, 'The Women of 1926', in *Cocktails with Elvira* (New York, 1932), p. 24. See also https://elvirabarney.wordpress.com/tag/james-laver (accessed 31 July 2023).

SELECT BIBLIOGRAPHY

Allen, Frederick Lewis, *Only Yesterday: An Informal History of the 1920s* [1931] (New York, 1997)

Altman, B. & Company, *1920s Fashions from B. Altman & Company* (New York, 1999)

Anbinder, Tyler, *City of Dreams: The 400-Year Epic History of Immigrant New York* (New York, 2017)

Bascom, Lionel C., *A Renaissance in Harlem: The Lost Voices of an American Community* (New York, 1999)

Bayer, Patricia, *Art Deco Architecture: Design, Decoration and Detail from the Twenties and Thirties* (London, 1992)

Bercovici, Konrad, *Around the World in New York* (New York, 1924)

Berliner, Louise, *Texas Guinan, Queen of the Nightclubs* (Austin, TX, 1993)

Berrol, Selma, *The Empire City: New York and Its People, 1624–1996* (Westport, CT, 1997)

Bleitner, Thomas, *Women of the 1920s: Style, Glamour and the Avant-Garde* (New York, 2019)

Bloom, Ken, *Broadway: An Encyclopedia* (New York, 2004)

Bossom, Alfred Charles, *Building to the Skies: The Romance of the Skyscraper* (London, 1934)

Bren, Paulina, *The Barbizon: The New York Hotel That Set Women Free* (London, 2021)

Breslin, Jimmy, *Damon Runyon: A Life* (New York, 1991)

Brodsky, Alyn, *The Great Mayor: Fiorello La Guardia and the Making of the City of New York* (New York, 2003)

Brooks, John, *Once in Golconda: A True Drama of Wall Street, 1920–1938* (New York, 1969)

Brown, Lois, *Encyclopedia of the Harlem Literary Renaissance* (New York, 2006)

Bryson, Bill, *One Summer: America, 1927* (London, 2013)

Burke, Billie, *With a Feather on My Nose* (New York, 1949)

Carter, Randolph, *The World of Flo Ziegfeld* (New York, 1974)

Charters, Samuel B., and Leonard Kunstadt, *Jazz: A History of the New York Scene* (New York, 1962)

Chepesiuk, Ron, *American Gangster: The History of the Gangs of Harlem*
    (Lytham, Lancashire, 2007)

Chilton, John, *Jazz* (London, 1979)

Clark, William C., and John L. Kingston, *The Skyscraper: A Study in the Economic
    Height of Modern Office Buildings* (New York, 1930)

Coleman Brawer, Catherine, and Kathleen Murphy Skolnik, *The Art Deco Murals
    of Hildreth Meière* (New York, 2014)

Curcio, Vincent, *Chrysler: The Life and Times of an Automotive Genius*
    (New York, 2000)

DeVeaux, Scott, and Gary Giddins, *Jazz: Essential Listening* (New York, 2010)

Dickstein, Morris, *Dancing in the Dark: A Cultural History of the Great Depression*
    (New York, 2009)

Dilts, Marion May, *The Telephone in a Changing World* (London, 1941)

Dos Passos, John, *One Man's Initiation 1917* (New York, 1920)

——, *Manhattan Transfer* (New York, 1925)

Douglas, Ann, *Terrible Honesty: Mongrel Manhattan in the 1920s*
    (New York, 1995)

Duncombe, Stephen, and Andrew Mattson, *The Bobbed Haired Bandit: A True
    Story of Crime and Celebrity in 1920s New York* (New York, 2006)

Ellis, Edward Robb, *The Epic of New York City* (New York, 1997)

Fass, Paula S., *The Damned and the Beautiful: American Youth in the 1920s*
    (New York, 1977)

Ferber, Edna, *So Big* (New York, 1924)

Ferriss, Hugh, *The Metropolis of Tomorrow* [1929] (Philadelphia, PA, 1929)

Fiell, Charlotte, *1920s Fashion: The Definitive Sourcebook* (London, 2021)

Fitzgerald, F. Scott, *Bernice Bobs Her Hair* (New York, 1920)

Fitzpatrick, Kevin C., *The Algonquin Round Table: A Historical Guide* (New York,
    2014)

Flowers, Benjamin, *Skyscraper: The Politics and Power of Building New York City
    in the Twentieth Century* (Philadelphia, PA, 2009)

Galbraith, John Kenneth, *The Great Crash 1929* (London, 1954)

Gavin, Lettie, *American Women in World War I: They Also Served*
    (Boulder, CO, 2006)

Gill, Jonathan, *Harlem: The Four Hundred Year History from Dutch Village to
    Capital of Black America* (New York, 2011)

Gioia, Ted, *The History of Jazz* (New York, 1997)

Glass, Barbara, *When the Spirit Moves: African American Dance in History and Art*
    (New York, 1999)

Glazer, Nathan, and Daniel Patrick Moynihan, *Beyond the Melting Pot:
    The Negroes, Puerto Ricans, Jews, Italians, and Irish of New York City*
    (Cambridge, MA, 1963)

Goldman, Herbert G., *Fanny Brice: The Original Funny Girl* (New York, 1992)

Hadlock, Richard, *Jazz Masters of the Twenties* (New York, 1965)

Hall, Carolyn, *The Twenties in Vogue* (London, 1983)

Hammerstein II, Oscar, *Lyrics* (New York, 1949)

Hentoff, Nat, *At the Jazz Band Ball: Sixty Years on the Jazz Scene*
    (Berkeley, CA, 2010)

——, and Albert J. McCarthy, *Jazz: New Perspectives on the History of Jazz* (New York, 1959)

Hillier, Bevis, and Stephen Escritt, *Art Deco Style* (London, 1997)

Hillstrom, Kevin, *Defining Moments: The Harlem Renaissance* (Chicago, IL, 2011)

Hortis, C. Alexander, *The Mob and the City: The Hidden History of How the Mafia Captured New York* (New York, 2014)

Jackson, Kenneth T., ed., *The Encyclopedia of New York City* (New Haven, CT, 1995)

——, and David S. Dunbar *Empire City: New York Through the Centuries* (New York, 2002)

Jeanneret-Gris, Charles-Édouard (Le Corbusier), *When the Cathedrals Were White: A Journey to the Country of Timid People* (New York, 1947)

Kelly, Thomas, *Empire Rising* (New York, 2005)

Klein, Jef, *The History and Stories of the Best Bars of New York* (Nashville, TN, 2006)

Kroessler, Jeffrey A., *New York Year by Year: A Chronology of the Great Metropolis* (New York, 2002)

Landau, Sarah Bradford, and Carl W. Condit, *Rise of the New York Skyscraper, 1865–1913* (New Haven, CT, 1996)

Lankevich, George J., *American Metropolis: A History of New York City* (New York, 1998)

Lerner, Michael A., *Dry Manhattan: Prohibition in New York City* (Cambridge, MA, 2008)

Lewis, David H., *Broadway Musicals A Hundred Year History* (Jefferson, NC, 2002)

Locke, Alain LeRoy, 'Enter the New Negro', *The Survey Graphic*, LIII/11 (March 1925), pp. 631–4

Loos, Anita, *Gentlemen Prefer Blondes* (New York, 1925)

Lowe, David Garrard, *Art Deco New York* (New York, 2004)

Lyttelton, Humphrey, *The Best of Jazz* (New York, 1980)

Maloney, Alison, *Bright Young Things: A Modern Guide to the Roaring Twenties* (London, 2012)

Mendelsohn, Joyce, *The Lower East Side Remembered and Revisited: A History and Guide to a Legendary New York Neighbourhood* (New York, 2009)

Messler, Norbert, *The Art Deco Skyscraper in New York* (Frankfurt, 1983)

Miller, Donald L., *Supreme City: How Jazz Age Manhattan Gave Birth to Modern America* (New York, 2014)

Moore, Lucy, *Anything Goes: A Biography of the Roaring Twenties* (London, 2008)

Morley, Sheridan, *Gertrude Lawrence* (New York, 1981)

Morrone, Francis, *The Architectural Guidebook to New York City* (Salt Lake City, 1994)

Nasaw, David, *Children of the City: At Work and at Play* (New York, 1985)

Nash, Eric P., *Manhattan Skyscrapers* (New York, 1999)

Nevius, Michelle, and James Nevius, *Inside the Apple: A Streetwise History of New York City* (New York, 2009)

Nicholson, Stuart, *Jazz and Culture in a Global Age* (Boston, MA, 2014)

Nippoldt, Robert, and Hans-Jürgen Schaal, *Jazz: New York in the Roaring Twenties* (Cologne, 2021)

Okrent, Daniel, *Last Call: The Rise and Fall of Prohibition* (New York, 2010)

Oliver, Paul, Max Harrison and William Bolcom, *The New Grove Gospel, Blues, and Jazz* (London, 1986)

Parker, Dorothy, *Diary of a Lady* (New York, 1933)

—, *The Penguin Dorothy Parker* (Harmondsworth, 1977)

Parker, Selwyn, *The Great Crash: How the Stock Market Crash of 1929 Plunged the World into Depression* (London, 2008)

Penrose, Antony, *The Lives of Lee Miller* (New York, 1985)

Roberts, Sam, *A History of New York in 27 Buildings: The 400-Year Untold Story of an American Metropolis* (New York, 2019)

Robins, Anthony W., *New York Art Deco: A Guide to Gotham's Jazz Age Architecture* (New York, 2017)

Robinson, Michael, and Rosalind Ormiston, *Art Deco: The Golden Age of Graphic Art and Illustration* (London, 2013)

Rose, Phyllis, *Jazz Cleopatra: Josephine Baker in Her Time* (New York, 1989)

Rowley, Matthew B., *Moonshine! Recipes, Tall Tales, Drinking Songs, Historical Stuff, Knee-Slappers, How to Drink It, Pleasin' the Law, Recoverin' the Next Day* (Asheville, NC, 2007)

Sabbagh, Karl, *Skyscraper: The Making of a Building* (New York, 1990)

Schildcrout, Jordan, *In the Long Run: A Cultural History of Broadway's Hit Plays* (New York, 2020)

Schuster, Amanda, *New York Cocktails* (Kennebunkport, ME, 2017)

Shaw, Arnold, *The Jazz Age: Popular Music in the 1920s* (New York, 1987)

Sifakis, Carl, *The Mafia Encyclopedia* (New York, 1987)

Simon, Kate, *A Wider World: Portraits in an Adolescence* (New York, 1986)

Starrett, Paul, and Webb Waldron, *Changing the Skyline: An Autobiography* (New York, 1938)

Stern, Robert A. M., Gregory Gilmartin and Thomas Mellins, *New York 1930: Architecture and Urbanism between the Two World Wars* (New York, 1987)

Stravitz, David, *New York, Empire City 1920–1945* (New York, 2004)

Tauranac, John, *New York from the Air* (New York, 1998)

—, *The Empire State Building: The Making of a Landmark* (Ithaca, NY, 2014)

Tirro, Frank, *Jazz: A History* (New York, 1993)

Toomer, Jean, *Cane* (New York, 1923)

Turnbull, Andrew, *Scott Fitzgerald* (New York, 1962)

Valentine, David T., *History of the City of New York* (New York, 1853)

Wallace, Mike, *Greater Gotham: A History of New York City from 1898 to 1919* (New York, 2017)

Ward, David, and Olivier Zunz, eds, *The Landscape of Modernity: New York City, 1900–1940* (New York, 1992)

Watson, Steven, *The Harlem Renaissance: Hub of African-American Culture, 1920–1930* (New York, 1995)

West, Aberjhani, and Sandra L. West, *Encyclopedia of the Harlem Renaissance* (New York, 2003)

Whitcomb, Ian, *Irving Berlin and Ragtime America* (London, 1987)

Willis, Carol, ed., *Building the Empire State* (New York, 1998)

Wintz, Cary D., ed., *Remembering the Harlem Renaissance* (New York, 1996)

Woll, Allen L., *Black Musical Theatre: From Coontown to Dreamgirls* (Baton Rouge, LA, 1989)

Young, Anthony, *New York Café Society: The Elite Meet to See and Be Seen, 1920s–1940s* (Jefferson, NC, 2015)

Zaczek, Iain, *Art Deco* (Bath, 2001)

Zeitz, Joshua, *Flapper: A Madcap Story of Sex, Style, Celebrity, and the Women Who Made America Modern* (New York, 2006)

Ziegfeld, Richard, and Paulette Ziegfeld, *The Ziegfeld Touch: The Life and Times of Florenz Ziegfeld, Jr* (New York, 1993)

ACKNOWLEDGEMENTS

Thanks to the team at Reaktion Books for their steadfast support of this book from commissioning through the production process. First and foremost, commissioning editor Vivian Constantinopoulos, who took on the project, along with the invaluable assistance of managing editor Martha Jay, project manager Emma Devlin and picture researcher Susannah Jayes. Zoe Ross has once again provided her excellent indexing skills.

We are most grateful to our New York friends and local fonts of wisdom. Rita Jakubowski, an expert on all things New York, shared her vast knowledge of the city's history. Anthony Robins, the undisputed top authority on New York's Art Deco architecture, was an invaluable source of illumination, while Gregory Peterson kindly agreed to enrich the tale with his enlightening foreword. We are grateful to the Queensboro Restaurant, one of the great New York eateries, for hosting our launch party. Thanks are due to the Art Deco Society of New York, whose webinars through lockdown and beyond provided fascinating insights on so many facets of design and architecture. We were drawn back time and again to the Museum of the City of New York and the New York Historical Society, two key sources of information on the city's history and purveyors of ever-changing exhibitions on aspects of art, culture and social history. Last but certainly not least, we wish to express our gratitude to friend and literary agent Duncan McAra, now retired, who fought our corner for nearly two decades.

PHOTO ACKNOWLEDGEMENTS

The authors and publishers wish to thank the organizations and individuals listed below for authorizing reproduction of their work:

Alamy: pp. 46 (Vintage Space), 49 (Everett Collection Historical), 51 (Everett Collection Inc), 69 (The Protected Art Archive), 75 (RBM Vintage Images), 111 (Pictorial Press Ltd), 114 (Lebrecht Music & Arts), 131 (History and Art Collection), 140 (Pictorial Press Ltd), 145 (Granger Historical Picture Archive), 175 (Felix Lipov), 197 (Image Bank); Flickr: p. 158; Getty Images: pp. 151 (Bettmann), 220 (Mondadori Portfolio), 246 (Library of Congress); Library of Congress, Washington, DC: pp. 19, 25, 27, 28, 31, 34, 41, 53, 61, 79, 92, 100, 106, 110, 119, 185, 190, 192, 193, 195, 199, 203, 205, 207, 224, 233, 244, 249, 259; National Museum of American History, Smithsonian Institution: p. 12; New York Public Library: pp. 82, 86, 95, 109, 223; Public Domain: pp. 85, 130, 226, 243; Shutterstock: p. 163 (Ryan Fletcher); Collection of the Skyscraper Museum: p. 166 (*Architectural Forum*, June 1930); Wikimedia Commons: pp. 15 (National Archives and Records Administration/Public Domain), 76 (Bettmann Archive/Public Domain), 89 (Ira D. Schwarz/Public Domain), 120 (National Archives and Records Administration/Public Domain), 127 (F. Scott Fitzgerald Archives/Public Domain), 146 (Jack A. Kleiman/Public Domain), 169 (Jean-Christophe Benoist/CC BY 3.0 Unported), 179 (Bryan Ledgard/CC BY 2.0), 187 (Tim Evanson/CC BY 2.0), 214 (National Archives and Records Administration/Public Domain), 218 (*Motor* magazine, Spring 1924), 227 (Public Domain), 262 (National Archives and Records Administration/Public Domain).

INDEX

Page numbers in *italics* refer to illustrations

Index